A
Graded
Reader
OF
Biblical
Greek

A
Graded
Reader
OF
Biblical
Greek

Companion to
Basics of Biblical Greek
and
Greek Grammar Beyond the Basics

William D. Mounce

ZondervanPublishingHouse
Grand Rapids, Michigan

A Division of HarperCollinsPublishers

A Graded Reader of Biblical Greek
Copyright © 1996 by William D. Mounce

Requests for information should be addressed to:
Zondervan Publishing House
Grand Rapids, Michigan 49530

Library of Congress Cataloging-in-Publication Data

Mounce, William D.
      A graded reader of biblical Greek / William D. Mounce
         p.   cm.
      Includes bibliographical references (p.) and index.
      ISBN 0 -310 - 20582-4 (softcover)
      1. Greek language, Biblical--Readers.   2. Bible. N.T.--Language,
style.   I. Title.
PA817.M65   1995
487' . 4–dc20   95-37597
                                               CIP

The Greek New Testament, edited by Kurt Aland, Matthew Black, Carlo M. Martini, Bruce M. Metzger, and Allen Wikgren. Fourth Revised Edition. © 1966, 1968, 1975, 1983, 1993 by the United Bible Societies. Used by permission. Punctuation and capitalization may vary from the published text.

Definitions are drawn from *A Greek-English Lexicon of the New Testament and Other Early Christian Literature,* second edition, edited by Walter Bauer, William F. Arndt, F. Wilbur Gingrich, Frederick W. Danker. © 1957, 1979 by The University of Chicago. All rights reserved. Published 1979. Used with permission.

Edited by Verlyn D. Verbrugge
Typeset by Teknia Software

Printed in the United States of America

96 97 98 99 /ML / 10 9 8 7 6 5 4 3 2 1

This text is dedicated to

Dr. Walter W. Wessel.

My uncle, teacher, and friend,
who has always played an important role in my family,
who nurtured my love for Greek and God's Word,
who always put students ahead of professional advancement,
and whose knowledge of Greek continues to be a source of amazement.

Table of Contents

Preface

Most teachers agree that second-year Greek should include both a wide exposure to many texts and an introduction–and sometimes an in-depth exposure–to intermediate grammar. We want our students to make the transition from the building blocks of the language learned in the first year, to exegesis, application, and a fuller understanding of grammar.

One problem that faces second-year students is the frustration of a somewhat uncontrolled environment. Instead of a beginning grammar that sheltered them from the hard realities of the biblical text, they are having to look up words that occur only once and work with strange constructions they have never met, both of which sap their enthusiasm. As teachers we experienced these frustrations ourselves when learning the language, and now the same thing occurs for our students.

When I started teaching second-year Greek, it struck me as rather odd that almost every language could be learned through a graded reader approach except New Testament Greek. I enjoyed learning German by this method and wanted to apply the same approach to Greek, and hence developed this text throughout my years of teaching.

The book has several goals. (1) To take some of the frustration out of reading large portions of the biblical text. (2) To introduce students slowly to intermediate grammar, inductively. (3) To start the process of learning exegesis, to do word studies, and to become comfortable using a large lexicon and technical commentaries. (4) To help students become so accustomed to studying the biblical text in Greek that they will continue doing so long after they have left their formal schooling environment. To put it another way, I wanted to take some of the nuts and bolts time out of the classroom, helping students prepare beforehand, so that class time could be spent on the really important matters of exegesis, grammar, and application.

But the primary goal for this text has to do with the greatest commandment–to love God–and the second–to love your neighbor. If, when you are done with the *Graded Reader*, you can parse and exegete better, I am glad because that is important. But what I really hope to see is that, as a result of knowing the text better and of having the tools with which to study it, you will know God better, and that you will not have lost sight of the fact that what is really important in this world is not things, but God and your neighbor.

Each page is divided into three sections. (1) The Greek text. (2) Footnotes defining words that occur less than twenty times, and hints for difficult constructions. (3) Exegetical discussions, where students can learn intermediate grammar inductively and read comments that challenge them to move beyond the basics of biblical Greek to the meaning of God's Word. If a word is underlined in the text, it is discussed in this third section. The footnotes are essential to read; the exegetical discussions are optional.

Many of the students mentioned in the preface to my *Basics of Biblical Greek* should be thanked here as well. Their enjoyment of, and appreciation for, the *Graded Reader* was encouraging. I am also glad to thank my editor, Verlyn Verbrugge, and the rest of the people at Zondervan for their support–Ed van der Maas, Stan Gundry, and Jack Kragt. Thanks also are due to Dr. Walter W. Wessel for his input into the *Graded Reader* at its early stages and to my proofreaders, Kathleen Lopez and Ed Keazirian.

My father, Robert H. Mounce, worked through the twenty passages with me, pointing out grammatical issues that I had overlooked and seeing notes of interest that should be emphasized. As I was expressing my frustration that I had somehow stopped short of helping students use their Greek properly, he suggested including a few sample sermon outlines that illustrate how a knowledge of Greek is instrumental in the full and proper proclamation of the good news. We agreed that this was the final stage, and Dad gladly wrote the sermon outlines at the end of the first chapters.

All along my goal has been to create a series of Greek textbooks that would provide a unified approach to learning Greek. I knew that Daniel Wallace's grammar would be a great intermediate/advanced grammar for the series. I appreciate his willingness to allow me to use his grammar summary in *Appendix A*. It is not meant as a substitute for his grammar; the second-year student should get his full grammar.

I have truly enjoyed working with this text in my years of teaching second- and third-year Greek classes. I hope you enjoy working with the *Reader* as well.

Bill Mounce
January, 1996

Preface for Students

It's time to have fun! I trust that you enjoyed first-year Greek, but try as one might the beginning stages of language study tend to be the most difficult and the least fulfilling. Another way to look at this textbook is to tell yourself that this represents why you labored through, perhaps suffered through, first-year Greek.

Please read the "Preface" and the discussion of "Two Tracks" on the following page. They should give you a feel for what the *Reader* is all about. At this stage in the game, there is no better discipline than simply reading the biblical text, reinforcing what you learned in your first year, learning intermediate grammar, and most importantly seeing how a working knowledge of Greek can help you better learn the message of Scripture. The habits you learn now can stay with you throughout your life. Now is the time to decide that Greek will play an on-going role in your Bible study.

While first-year Greek tended to be somewhat rigid–it is either a noun or a verb, unless it is a participle– you will find that grammar and phrasing are more flexible. That may be confusing at first, but that is why you are learning Greek. Rarely will a knowledge of Greek tell you what something means, absolutely. Normally it gives you the range of possibilities, and then it takes other factors such as theology to help you decide what a form means. For example, in Gal 1:13 Paul says that he "was destroying" (ἐδίωκον) the church, using the imperfect. What does Paul mean? Grammatically Paul could be saying that he was *thinking* about destroying the church, *trying* to destroy the church, or *beginning* to destroy the church, or that he *was destroying* the church. This is the scope, the range of possibilities, that the Greek gives. But Greek will not tell you the answer. You have to use the Galatian context and what you know of Paul to make the final determination, just as the original Galatians had to do. This is what I mean by "flexible." Do not let it discourage you. Be glad that you have the tools necessary to know the true range of possible meanings and the tools for making your own determination.

At first the phrasing will look strange to you. I wish I could show you the letters I have received from past students. They typically say something like, "I have forgotten most of my Greek–sorry!–but to this day I use phrasing in all my Bible study and sermon preparation." My preference, of course, is that they would use both Greek and phrasing, but it is amazing how much help phrasing has been. Personally, I do not write a sermon or discuss in a commentary any passage without first going through phrasing. Like grammar, it is flexible. There is not always a "right" and a "wrong" way to do it. But it makes you ask the difficult questions and forces you to see the structure of the passage and hence the author's flow of thought. It is not grammatical diagramming. Give it a shot. I think it will become one of the most significant tools you ever develop.

It was often hard to decide what to point out in the *Exegetical Discussion* section. Sometimes the choice was obvious, but other times there were many factors that went into my decision. How hard is the passage? How much has already been pointed out on this page/chapter? What did my students find interesting? What helps to illustrate intermediate Greek grammar? If you do not see the significance for why I point something out, do not worry about it. If you want to discuss something else, great!

But have fun. Greek should be enjoyable. You have worked hard to get to this point, and now you can start using your tools and learn more, tools that can become a pillar in your ministry. But remember, the greatest commandment is not parsing perfection. It is to love your Lord. As you work through these pages do not stop at the technical level, but please go through it to the weightier matters of understanding, application, and proclamation.

Two Tracks:

How to use the *Graded Reader*

Because almost every second- and third-year Greek teacher uses somewhat different methods and has somewhat different goals for a class, it is important that the *Graded Reader* be flexible. We therefore designed two different tracks, or methods, that you can use. (If you choose track two, you will also do track one). Our assumption is that teachers will pick the one that best suits their preferences. We would appreciate hearing which track you find most helpful, and why. Correspondence can be sent to the address on page xiii.

Track One: Maximum Exposure to the Biblical Text

The most important thing you can do is to read the biblical text. The bulk of the *Graded Reader* is designed to help you do this. Following are the goals we hope you achieve by reading the text.

1. To bridge the gap between learning the basics of Greek and using it effectively in sermons, Bible study, lecture preparation, and research.

2. To gain exposure to a large amount of Greek.

    *   All words that occur less than twenty times in the New Testament are given in the footnotes. (Definitions are drawn basically from *BAGD*. We generally did not include proper names.) They are listed only the first time they occur in a passage. Students are required to look up words occurring twenty times or more. Frequencies are given at the end of the entry, and are based on the software program *acCordance*. Here is a sample footnote:

        ψηλαφάω, *I feel (about for), touch* (4).

        We choose twenty because few teachers require students to learn words that occur less than twenty times. Many teachers want students to learn words that occur thirty times or more. (*Basics of Biblical Greek* takes the vocabulary down to fifty occurrences.) Learning to use the lexicon is a necessary ability, so we did not want to define all the words. Twenty occurrences, therefore, seemed to be the most helpful. If a word occurs less than twenty times, it is listed only once per chapter.

    *   Difficult constructions are explained so that time will not be wasted or enthusiasm lost.

    *   Difficult inflected forms are keyed into *The Morphology of Biblical Greek*. If you do not understand the form of a word, we would encourage you to look it up and learn why it is the way it is.

    *   Intermediate grammar that is necessary to translate the passage is given in these footnotes.

    It is therefore crucial that every footnote be studied.

3. To read not only the easier biblical passages but also the more difficult, to read passages from different authors, and to read both theology and narrative (including the Septuagint and Didache).

    The passages chosen are in order of difficulty, starting with relatively easy passages. This encourages students and gets several chapters "under their belt." In a few places, after there was a difficult passage, we included an easier passage to help students not to become discouraged.

4.   To learn intermediate Greek grammar inductively.

The first time a student encounters a specific grammatical construction it is explained, sometimes in the footnote section, sometimes in the *Exegetical Discussion* section (see below). After that the student should recognize the construction. The grammar is summarized in *Appendix A* (referred to as *Gram Sum*). When we ask for the "type" or "kind" of construction, we are asking for the categories listed in the *Gram Sum*. This is inductive methodology, learning grammar as you see it, in context.

While intermediate grammar that is necessary to know in order to translate is given in the footnotes, grammar and other information that helps to bring the passage "alive" are given in a section at the bottom of each page. We call this the "Exegetical Discussion" section. When grammar is introduced here, its name will be in bold type. Especially significant discussions will have their reference numbers in bold type followed by an asterisk. Here is a sample discussion:

(2)   **1:1** *   ὀφθαλμοῖς is an **instrumental dative**. It describes the
                  instrument by which an action is accomplished. You can
                  use the key words "by" or "with."

Our recommendation is to translate the passage, answering the questions in the footnotes, and then translate the passage again without the aid of the footnotes, answering at least the significant questions in the *Exegetical Discussion* section.

The *Graded Reader* is tied in with Daniel B. Wallace's intermediate grammar, *Greek Grammar Beyond the Basics*. Refer to it as you have need, but eventually you should read it through carefully. Following the discussion on phrasing (below) is the *Cheat Sheet*. Be sure to read it as well as peruse the grammar summary in *Appendix A*, which is drawn from Wallace's grammar.

5.   Along with grammar, other interesting pieces of information are pointed out in the *Exegetical Discussion* section, encouraging students to experiment and think through the grammar of the passage.

6.   The *Graded Reader* encourages students to learn how to determine the meaning of words. This will be done through reference to lexical aids and commentaries.

7.   We included some discussion of textual problems but for the most part left this up to the teacher.

Two final suggestions. Students: when you are reading the passage in class or doing your final preparation for class, be sure to read the passage from an unmarked text, not from the *Graded Reader*. Teachers: we numbered the discussions in the *Exegetical Discussion* section so you can assign only those that you feel are significant.

Track Two: Phrasing

In my personal study, I developed a method of laying out a passage in a way that would help me see its meaning. I broke the passage down into phrases, individual units of thought, and then lined them up so I could see the relationship among the phrases. For example, here is Romans 3:22a.

δικαιοσύνη δὲ θεοῦ

    | διὰ πίστεως

    | Ἰησοῦ Χριστοῦ

    | εἰς πάντας τοὺς πιστεύοντας.

> But the righteousness of God (is)
> | through faith
> | in Jesus Christ
> | for all who are believing.

In my own work I have found that phrasing, as I came to call it, was the single most helpful discipline to enable me see the flow of what the biblical author is saying. When I phrase, my exegesis is much more personally rewarding because I am discovering for myself what the text says. Of course, you always follow your study by seeing what others say, but the rewards of private study more than compensate for the time spent.

Of all the tools I taught, phrasing "stuck" with my students the longest and appeared to be the most helpful tool I taught them. As I looked around at the literature, I saw other people doing the same kind of thing, such as Gordon Fee in his text, *New Testament Exegesis* (Westminster/John Knox Press, 1983, 1993) 65-80.

I recommend that once you have finished Track One, i.e., translating the passage, you move into phrasing. It does not tell you what the relationships are among phrases, but it forces you to ask the questions and is a natural lead into exegesis. The next major section of this book gives a detailed discussion of what phrasing is and suggestions on how to do it.[1]

Correspondence

In one sense, this *Graded Reader* does not offer a lot of new ideas. Many teachers are doing precisely what I am doing. But I would appreciate any comments on how to modify, improve, or alter the *Graded Reader*. I am especially interested in how helpful you find either *phrasing* or *diagramming*. I can be contacted through Zondervan (Academic Editorial, 5300 Patterson Ave., Grand Rapids, Michigan 49530) or at the following addresses. Internet is preferred. I am not able to handle phone calls. *www.iov.com/teknia/*

Bill Mounce	Internet mail:	billm@teknia.com
Teknia Software	World Wide Web:	http://www.teknia.com/teknia
1306 W. Bellwood Drive	America Online:	billm@teknia.com (or Mounce)
Spokane, WA 99218-2911	CompuServe:	INTERNET:billm@teknia.com
		(or 71540,2140)

Software

We are currently working on a computer program to help you translate the New Testament. Unlike commercial Bible search programs, the metaphor of the program is built around the needs of a translator. See the world wide web site listed above for our progress.

---

[1] There actually is a third track, and that is to enlarge on the phrasing until it becomes semantic diagramming. This process is much slower but it deals with the text in much finer detail. Some friends have been working on this technique, but we were not able to include their work in this text. They should be able to make it available at some future date.

Bibliography

We picked a commentary for each chapter of the *Graded Reader*. The bibliography for each commentary is listed in the introductory section of the chapter. Following are other books and tools that we reference.

acCordance   Roy Brown, *The Gramcord Institute.* A Macintosh Bible search program.

ALGNT   *The Analytical Lexicon to the Greek New Testament*, ed. William D. Mounce (Zondervan, 1993).

BAGD   *A Greek-English Lexicon of the New Testament and Other Early Christian Literature*, eds. W. Bauer, W.F. Arndt, F.W. Gingrich, F.E. Danker, second edition (University of Chicago Press, 1979).

BBG   *Basics of Biblical Greek,* William D. Mounce (Zondervan, 1993).

BDF   *A Greek Grammar of the New Testament and Other Early Christian Literature*, eds. F. Blass, A. Debrunner, trans. R. Funk (University of Chicago Press, 1961).

Chamberlain   *An Exegetical Grammar of the Greek New Testament,* William D. Chamberlain (Macmillan, 1941).

EDNT   *Exegetical Dictionary of the New Testament*, eds. Horst Balz, Gerhard Schneider (Eerdmans, 1990 - 93).

Fanning   *Verbal Aspect in New Testament Greek*, Buist M. Fanning (Clarendon Press, 1990).

GGBB   See "Wallace" below.

Gramcord   Paul Miller, *The Gramcord Institute.* A DOS Bible search program.

Gram Sum   The grammatical summary in *Appendix A.*

LSJ   *A Greek-English Lexicon,* Henry George Liddell, Robert Scott, Henry Stuart Jones (Oxford, 1977).

MBG   *The Morphology of Biblical Greek*, William D. Mounce (Zondervan, 1994).

McKay   *A New Syntax of the Verb in New Testament Greek: An Aspectual Approach*, K.L. McKay (Peter Lang, 1994).

Metzger   *A Textual Commentary on the Greek New Testament*, Bruce M. Metzger, second edition (United Bible Societies, 1994).

Moule   *An Idiom-Book of New Testament Greek*, C.F.D. Moule (Cambridge Univ. Press, 1971).

Robertson   *A Grammar of the Greek New Testament*, A.T. Robertson (Broadman, 1934).

Smyth   *Greek Grammar*, Herbert Weir Smyth (Harvard University Press, 1980).

UBS   *The Greek New Testament*, eds. Kurt Aland, Matthew Black, Carlo M. Martini, Bruce M. Metzger, Allen Wikgren. Fourth Revised Edition (United Bible Societies, 1966, 1968, 1975, 1983, 1993).

Wallace   *Greek Grammar Beyond the Basics. An Exegetical Syntax of the New Testament*, Daniel B. Wallace (Zondervan, 1996).

Williams   *Grammar Notes on the Noun and the Verb and Certain Other Items,* rev ed. P.R. Williams (Northwest Baptist Seminary, 1988).

Zerwick   *A Grammatical Analysis of the Greek New Testament*, Max Zerwick, Mary Grosvenor (Biblical Institute Press, 1974).

Phrasing

Introduction

Phrasing is a hermeneutical technique that is designed to help you see the structure of an author's writing, the relationship between phrases and clauses, and the basic flow of thought through a passage. It separates the main ideas from the secondary and highlights parallel thoughts. It forces you to identify the relationships between thoughts. In my experience of teaching intermediate Greek, next to developing a facility in the language, phrasing is the most significant tool my students learned.

Phrasing is not grammatical diagramming. Because we are trying to discover the meaning of the passage, and because the phrase is often the smallest unit that can be analyzed for meaning in a specific context, it is not helpful for our purposes to break the verses down into even smaller units, except in specific circumstances such as a list. Phrasing makes use of grammatical relationships, but they are usually at the phrase level, not the word level. This also makes phrasing less frightening to students, whose exposure to high school grammatical diagramming may have left a bad taste in their mouth.[1]

Phrasing's basic approach is to separate a passage into its phrases (main clause, relative clauses, prepositional phrases, etc.). It looks somewhat like an outline. It has only three basic principles.

1. *The more dominant phrases are further to the left on the page.*

2. *Subordinate ideas are indented, placed under (or over) the concept to which they are related.*

3. *Parallel ideas are indented the same distance from the left.*

> 3:22   δικαιοσύνη δὲ θεοῦ
>   διὰ πίστεως
>   Ἰησοῦ Χριστοῦ
>   εἰς πάντας τοὺς πιστεύοντας.

> 3:22   But the righteousness of God (is)
>   through faith
>   in Jesus Christ
>   for all who are believing.

The basic thought in Romans 3:22 is the righteousness of God (δικαιοσύνη δὲ θεοῦ). It is placed furthest to the left. We are told two things about God's righteousness: it is through faith (διὰ πίστεως); it is for all who have faith (εἰς πάντας τοὺς πιστεύοντας). Notice how they are subordinated under "righteousness" (δικαιοσύνη) since they modify that concept. Notice too that they are indented the same amount, meaning that they are parallel to each other. In this case the phrasing highlights the parallelism of the two prepositions, διά and εἰς. Paul further specifies that the faith is in Jesus Christ (Ἰησοῦ Χριστοῦ).

Phrasing has a minimum number of rules because it is a personal exercise. What helps one student see the structure of a passage may not help another. What is important is that you adopt the basic approach and then modify it to suit your own tastes and needs. Be consistent.

---

[1]   We use the word "phrase" in a non-technical manner. Often a "clause" or an individual word will constitute a "phrase" in our terminology.

Basic Procedures of Phrasing

1. **Break the passage into its basic phrases.** At this point, do not indent the phrases (Colossians 1:3-5).

> Εὐχαριστοῦμεν τῷ θεῷ πατρὶ τοῦ κυρίου ἡμῶν Ἰησοῦ Χριστοῦ
> πάντοτε περὶ ὑμῶν προσευχόμενοι,
> ἀκούσαντες τὴν πίστιν ὑμῶν ἐν Χριστῷ Ἰησοῦ
> καὶ τὴν ἀγάπην ἣν ἔχετε εἰς πάντας τοὺς ἁγίους
> διὰ τὴν ἐλπίδα τὴν ἀποκειμένην ὑμῖν ἐν τοῖς οὐρανοῖς,
> ἣν προηκούσατε ἐν τῷ λόγῳ τῆς ἀληθείας τοῦ εὐαγγελίου

> We give thanks to God the Father of our Lord Jesus Christ
> Always concerning you praying
> Hearing your faith in Christ Jesus
> And the love which you have among all the saints
> Through the hope which has been laid up for you in heaven
> Which you formerly heard in the word of the truth of the gospel

Notice that already we are doing exegesis, since we decided that "always" (πάντοτε) goes with the following, not the preceding phrase. Sometimes such decisions are necessary; you can always change your mind later.

Look for the following: Main clause
    Prepositional phrases
    Adverbial phrases
    Participial phrases
    Compound sentences (καί)
    Relative clauses
    Conjunctions like ὅτι, ἵνα, etc.

2. **Identify the main thought and keep it furthest to the left.**

By "main thought" we are thinking in terms of semantics, the meaning of the passage. Often the main thought will be in the main clause, but sometimes it is in a grammatically subordinate clause.

It is helpful to keep the chapter and verse reference to the left.

1:3   Εὐχαριστοῦμεν τῷ θεῷ πατρὶ τοῦ κυρίου ἡμῶν Ἰησοῦ Χριστοῦ

3. **Find those phrases that directly modify a word or concept in the main thought and indent them under it.**

1:3   Εὐχαριστοῦμεν τῷ θεῷ πατρὶ τοῦ κυρίου ἡμῶν Ἰησοῦ Χριστοῦ
           πάντοτε περὶ ὑμῶν προσευχόμενοι,

Paul gives thanks (Εὐχαριστοῦμεν) always (πάντοτε) in his prayers (προσευχόμενοι). This verse illustrates the type of question that phrasing was designed to help answer: "What is the relationship among 'always' (πάντοτε), 'give thanks' (Εὐχαριστοῦμεν), and 'praying' (προσευχόμενοι)?" Does he always pray (as above), or does he always give thanks (as below).

1:3   Εὐχαριστοῦμεν τῷ θεῷ πατρὶ τοῦ κυρίου ἡμῶν Ἰησοῦ Χριστοῦ

        πάντοτε

        περὶ ὑμῶν προσευχόμενοι,

Phrasing, of course, does not give you the answer; only context can. But phrasing does force you to ask the question, and this is its primary value.

In an "if … then" sentence you may prefer to think of the "if" clause as semantically subordinate to the "then" clause, as it would be if you changed it into a nonconditional sentence (John 15:10).

15:10   ἐὰν τὰς ἐντολάς μου τηρήσητε,

        μενεῖτε ἐν τῇ ἀγάπῃ μου

The ἐάν clause comes first, so it is written higher to maintain word order, but it is subordinate to the μενεῖτε phrase and is therefore indented. This situation explains why we added "or over" in our second principle: *Subordinate ideas are indented, placed under (or over) the concept to which they are related.*

Problem of Extent

To what extent do you subdivide a phrase? The first line in Colossians 1:3 above could be divided into many further levels.

1:3   Εὐχαριστοῦμεν

        τῷ   θεῷ [2]

        πατρὶ

            τοῦ   κυρίου

                ἡμῶν

            Ἰησοῦ Χριστοῦ

The question you must answer is, "What do I gain by further subdividing the phrase? Does it help me see the structure more clearly? Does it demonstrate parallel thoughts?" If the phrase is one thought, leave it on the same line. However, if it is a list or series, then put each item on a separate line, as in Colossians 1:16.

1:16   ὅτι   ἐν αὐτῷ ἐκτίσθη τὰ πάντα

                    ἐν τοῖς οὐρανοῖς καὶ

                    ἐπὶ τῆς γῆς,

                    τὰ ὁρατὰ καὶ τὰ ἀόρατα,

                        εἴτε θρόνοι

                        εἴτε κυριότητες

                        εἴτε ἀρχαὶ

                        εἴτε ἐξουσίαι·

            τὰ πάντα δι᾽ αὐτοῦ καὶ εἰς αὐτὸν ἔκτισται

---

[2] Notice that θεῷ and πατρί are in apposition. The increased space between τῷ and θεῷ, along with the parallelism of θεῷ and πατρί, show they are parallel in thought. See below, *Specific Problems #10.*

Difference Between Phrasing and Grammatical Diagramming

Herein lies the basic difference between phrasing and grammatical diagramming. Phrasing is not primarily concerned with the grammatical relationship of every word. It is concerned with the relationship of ideas. If nothing is gained by further subdividing, then do not.

This also illustrates the subjective, personal element of phrasing. What is significant to one person will not necessarily be helpful to another. That is okay.

4. **Locate the phrases that relate to subordinate ideas.**

   Place them under the word on which they are grammatically dependent. If multiple phrases depend on the same word, be sure to indent them the same distance.

   1:3   Εὐχαριστοῦμεν τῷ θεῷ πατρὶ τοῦ κυρίου ἡμῶν Ἰησοῦ Χριστοῦ

   πάντοτε περὶ ὑμῶν προσευχόμενοι,

   1:4   ἀκούσαντες

   τὴν πίστιν ὑμῶν ἐν Χριστῷ Ἰησοῦ καὶ

   τὴν ἀγάπην

   ἣν ἔχετε εἰς πάντας τοὺς ἁγίους

   1:5   διὰ τὴν ἐλπίδα

   τὴν ἀποκειμένην ὑμῖν ἐν τοῖς οὐρανοῖς,

   ἣν προηκούσατε

   ἐν   τῷ λόγῳ τῆς ἀληθείας

   τοῦ εὐαγγελίου

Paul tells us two basic facts about what he heard regarding the Colossian Christians. The first is that they have faith (πίστιν), and the second is that they have love (ἀγάπην). "Love" is explained with a relative clause (ἥν …). They have this love for all the saints (ἔχετε εἰς πάντας τοὺς ἁγίους), and the love comes through their hope (ἐλπίδα).

But then once again Paul branches off to tell us two things about their hope. First, it is a hope that has been laid up (ἀποκειμένην) for them in heaven. Second, it is a hope that they heard before (προηκούσατε) in the word of truth.

Finally, he adds by way of apposition that this word of truth is in fact the gospel (εὐαγγελίου).

Problem of Word Order

Sometimes the subject can be separated from the main verb. You may want to connect them with a dotted line (Romans 8:3).

8:3   ὁ θεὸς

   τὸν ἑαυτοῦ υἱὸν

   πέμψας

   ἐν ὁμοιώματι σαρκὸς ἁμαρτίας καὶ

   περὶ ἁμαρτίας

   κατέκρινεν   τὴν ἁμαρτίαν

   ἐν τῇ σαρκί,

You may also want to use a dotted line when drawing lines through text (Romans 8:6-7).

8:6   γὰρ

      τὸ ... φρόνημα τῆς σαρκὸς θάνατος,

       δὲ

      τὸ ... φρόνημα τοῦ πνεύματος ζωὴ καὶ εἰρήνη·

8:7   διότι

          τὸ φρόνημα τῆς σαρκὸς ἔχθρα εἰς θεόν,

                γὰρ

          τῷ ... νόμῳ τοῦ θεοῦ οὐχ ὑποτάσσεται.

Examples of Specific Phrasing Problems

1. As a writer's argument progresses, it will be natural to **move the bulk of the text further to the right** until it is physically no longer possible to phrase the writing on paper. In the following example, the second phrase is so close to the right side of the paper that it has wrapped around onto another line, thus making it appear that there are two phrases modifying ἐλπίδα (Colossians 1:5).

                  διὰ τὴν ἐλπίδα

                      τὴν ἀποκειμένην ὑμῖν ἐν τοῖς
οὐρανοῖς,

There are several solutions. (1) One is always to double-space between different phrases. When you see two single-spaced lines, you will know it is just one phrase.

(2) Another solution is to move the subordinate phrases farther to the left, and draw a line connecting them to what they modify.

                  διὰ τὴν ἐλπίδα

       τὴν ἀποκειμένην ὑμῖν ἐν τοῖς οὐρανοῖς,

You could use a simple line if the subordinate phrase is not a relative clause, and an arrow if it is a relative clause (see below).

(3) A third solution is to indent the second line slightly, enough to show it is not a second phrase but not so much that the second line appears to modify the first word in the first line.

                  διὰ τὴν ἐλπίδα

                     τὴν ἀποκειμένην
                     ὑμῖν ἐν τοῖς

2. **Indicate the antecedent of a relative pronoun**. If you cannot place the relative pronoun directly under the antecedent, use an arrow to connect the pronoun to its antecedent. (An arrow can distinguish it from a simple connection, as above, although this is not necessary.)

> 1:4   ἀκούσαντες
>
>   τὴν πίστιν ὑμῶν ἐν Χριστῷ Ἰησοῦ καὶ
>
>   τὴν ἀγάπην
>
>
>   ἣν ἔχετε εἰς πάντας τοὺς ἁγίους

Often a relative clause will have to be moved to the left because of space problems on the page, so the arrow will help that situation as well. In the same way, connect clauses beginning with οὖν and γάρ to the preceding phrase. If it is referring to the entire preceding verse, draw the line to the verse reference.

3. Sometimes the **main subject and verb do not appear at the beginning of the verse**. In this case, indent the subordinate phrases, even though they are prior to the main thought (Romans 3:21).

> 3:21   Νυνὶ δὲ
>
>   χωρὶς νόμου
>
>   δικαιοσύνη θεοῦ πεφανέρωται
>
>   μαρτυρουμένη ὑπὸ   τοῦ νόμου καὶ
>
>   τῶν προφητῶν

Especially in this situation you might choose to underline (or double underline) the basic thought of the verse.

> 3:21   Νυνὶ δὲ
>
>   χωρὶς νόμου
>
>   <u>δικαιοσύνη θεοῦ πεφανέρωται</u>
>
>   μαρτυρουμένη ὑπὸ   τοῦ νόμου καὶ
>
>   τῶν προφητῶν

The last two phrases are a good illustration of how to handle the situation where two phrases depend on the same word, such as two objects of the same preposition. They could both be listed under the preposition, but that unnecessarily increases the number of lines.

> μαρτυρουμένη ὑπὸ
>
>   τοῦ νόμου καὶ
>
>   τῶν προφητῶν

We recommend putting an extra space between the preposition and its first object, and then lining up the second object with the first.

> μαρτυρουμένη ὑπὸ   τοῦ νόμου καὶ
>
>   τῶν προφητῶν

4. **To emphasize the parallel nature of phrases, even though they may not appear consecutively, you can use vertical lines to identify them.**

    3:21 | Νυνὶ δὲ
          | χωρὶς νόμου
          δικαιοσύνη θεοῦ πεφανέρωται
          | μαρτυρουμένη ὑπὸ   τοῦ νόμου καὶ
                              τῶν προφητῶν

5. The vertical lines will also help indicate when several phrases are indented the same amount for grammatical reasons but are **not parallel in thought**, as in Colossians 1:16.

    1:16 ὅτι ἐν αὐτῷ ἐκτίσθη   τὰ πάντα
          | ἐν τοῖς οὐρανοῖς καὶ
          | ἐπὶ τῆς γῆς,
          τὰ ὁρατὰ καὶ τὰ ἀόρατα,

6. To help see the flow of thought through a discussion you can **underline the key words**, especially if synonyms or cognates are being used (John 15:12-13, 20). Do not overdo this or you will loose the basic flow of the passage.

    15:12 αὕτη ἐστὶν ἡ ἐντολὴ ἡ ἐμή,
                   ἵνα <u>ἀγαπᾶτε</u> ἀλλήλους καθὼς <u>ἠγάπησα</u> ὑμᾶς.
    15:13 μείζονα ταύτης <u>ἀγάπην</u> οὐδεὶς ἔχει,
                   ἵνα τις τὴν ψυχὴν αὐτοῦ θῇ ὑπὲρ τῶν φίλων αὐτοῦ.
           …
    15:20b   εἰ ἐμὲ <u>ἐδίωξαν</u>,
           καὶ ὑμᾶς <u>διώξουσιν·</u>
              εἰ τὸν λόγον μου <u>ἐτήρησαν</u>,
           καὶ τὸν ὑμέτερον <u>τηρήσουσιν.</u>

7. **The placement of connectives** (e.g., καί) between parallel phrases is a personal decision. They can be placed (1) at the end of the first phrase or (2) the beginning of the second (John 15:11).

    15:11 Ταῦτα λελάληκα ὑμῖν
              ἵνα   ἡ χαρὰ ἡ ἐμὴ ἐν ὑμῖν ᾖ καὶ
                     ἡ χαρὰ ὑμῶν πληρωθῇ.

    15:11 Ταῦτα λελάληκα ὑμῖν
              ἵνα   ἡ χαρὰ ἡ ἐμὴ ἐν ὑμῖν ᾖ
                     καὶ ἡ χαρὰ ὑμῶν πληρωθῇ.

    (3) Fee wants each connective to be placed on its own line. We have found it helpful to indent them half an inch in from the left side of the phrase (John 15:20b).

15:20b   εἰ ἐμὲ ἐδίωξαν,
                       καὶ
           ὑμᾶς διώξουσιν·
                 εἰ τὸν λόγον μου ἐτήρησαν,
                       καὶ
           τὸν ὑμέτερον τηρήσουσιν.

The advantage is that you can look down the column of connectives and clearly see the flow of the discussion. We follow this procedure except for lists, and then we usually place the connectives on the same line as the first phrase.

When a connective introduces not a parallel idea but a subordinate idea, we also keep the connective on the same line as the phrase.

8. It is best to **maintain the Greek order of words**. Sometimes this will not be possible, so you can repeat a word but place it in parentheses and perhaps mark its original place with an ellipsis (Colossians 1:16).

    1:16   τὰ πάντα (ἔκτισται)
                  δι᾽ αὐτοῦ καὶ
                  εἰς αὐτὸν …

This will happen frequently with postpositives (Mark 8:35).

8:35   γὰρ
       ὃς … ἐὰν θέλῃ τὴν ψυχὴν αὐτοῦ σῶσαι   ἀπολέσει αὐτήν·
              δ᾽
       ὃς … ἂν ἀπολέσει τὴν ψυχὴν αὐτοῦ
                   ἕνεκεν   ἐμοῦ καὶ
                        τοῦ εὐαγγελίου
                                      σώσει αὐτήν.

9. Use a **single space** to separate similar but different ideas, double spaces to separate major sections. You could also use headings to show major divisions.

10. Words in **apposition** should be indented the same amount from the left. Some indicator should show they are not both modifying the same word, but that the second is in apposition to the first. Perhaps a double vertical line would work for you (Colossians 1:14).

             ἐν ᾧ ἔχομεν ||| τὴν ἀπολύτρωσιν,
                         ||| τὴν ἄφεσιν τῶν ἁμαρτιῶν·

11. One of the few times you should break a phrase down into smaller units is when they are a **list** (Colossians 1:16).

> 1:16 ὅτι ἐν αὐτῷ ἐκτίσθη τὰ πάντα
>
> | ἐν τοῖς οὐρανοῖς καὶ
> | ἐπὶ τῆς γῆς,
> τὰ ὁρατὰ καὶ τὰ ἀόρατα,
>
> | εἴτε θρόνοι
> | εἴτε κυριότητες
> | εἴτε ἀρχαὶ
> | εἴτε ἐξουσίαι·
>
> τὰ πάντα δι᾽ αὐτοῦ καὶ εἰς αὐτὸν ἔκτισται

Sometimes the vertical lines are unnecessary, as in the second part of this example.

12. If parallel ideas are separated by several subordinate clauses, you could use **colored pens** to show the parallel thoughts, or perhaps number them down the left margin. Colored pens are also good for marking key words/phrases/thoughts throughout a passage (cf. Fee, *New Testament Exegesis*, pp. 72f.).

Limitations of phrasing

1. Phrasing is not very effective with narrative material, where the flow is more obvious. It works best with theological passages.

2. Phrasing helps show immediate relationships, but not the larger relationships. If you want to take phrasing one step further, read *Tracing the Argument* and use their method for indicating semantic relationships. It works well with phrasing too.

If you try phrasing and become frustrated because there are not enough rules, you may be missing the point. Lay out the phrases in a way that makes sense to you and shows you their structure, and do not worry if you are doing it "right." The point is to help you ask the important exegetical question of the relationships among the phrases. Do not become preoccupied with the minutia of the method.

Cheat Sheet

The following two-sided sheet, affectionately known as the "Cheat Sheet," is an inductive method of introducing you to intermediate Greek grammar. As you are reading a passage and, for example, come across a genitive you do not understand, you are encouraged to use the cheat sheet. Look at the different types of genitives, noting especially the key words/phrases and seeing which best fits the context.

After translating about the first eight passages, we encourage you to read through an intermediate grammar such as Wallace's. You will find that you already know almost half the grammatical categories. The cheat sheet is derived from the grammar summary in *Appendix A*, which in turn is drawn from Wallace's grammar. The left column lists Wallace's categories, and the glosses (i.e., "key words") are in the right column.

One good idea is to xerox the "Cheat Sheet" onto mylar or some such non-rippable material, so it can easily be used as a reference tool. You are free to make copies of the two pages for your classes or for private study.

CASES

NOMINATIVE

Primary uses
    Subject
    Predicate Nominative
    Nominative in Simple Apposition
Independent Uses
    Nominative Absolute
    Nominativus Pendens
    Parenthetic Nominative
    For the Vocative
    Exclamation
In Place of Oblique Cases
    Appellation

VOCATIVE

Simple Address
Emphatic Address

GENITIVE

Adjectival Uses	
Descriptive	*characterized by*
Possessive	*belonging to*
Relationship	
Partitive	*which is part of*
Attributive	
Attributed	
Material	*made out of*
Content	*full of*
Simple Apposition	
Apposition	*which is*
Subordination	*over*
Ablatival Uses	
Separation	*out of*
Comparison	*than*
Verbal Uses	
Subjective	
Objective	
Plenary	
Adverbial Uses	
Time	
Association	*in association with*
After Certain Words	
After certain verbs	
After certain adjectives	

DATIVE

Pure Dative Uses	
Indirect Object	*to*
Interest	*for, against*
Reference/Respect	*with reference to*
Simple Apposition	
Local Dative Uses	
Sphere	*in the sphere of*
Time	
Instrumental Dative Uses	
Association	*in association with*
Manner	*with*
Means/Instrument	*by means of*
Measure	*by*
Cause	*because of*

After Certain Words
    Direct Object
    After certain nouns
    After certain adjectives

ACCUSATIVE

Substantival Uses	
Direct Object	
Double Accusative	
Predicate	
Subject of the Infinitive	
Simple Apposition	
Adverbial Uses	
Adverbial	
Measure	*for the extent of*
Respect	*with reference to*

ARTICLE

As a Pronoun	
Personal	*he, she, it*
Relative	*who, which*
Possessive	*his, her*
With Substantives	
Simple identification	
Anaphoric	
Deitic	
Par Excellence	
Monadic	
Well-known	
Abstract	
Generic	

As a Substantiver
As a Function Marker
    Adjectival position
    Possessive pronouns
    Genitive phrases
    Indeclinable nouns
    Participles
    Demonstratives
    Nominative nouns
    Distinguish subject from pred./obj.
Absence of the article
    Indefinite
    Qualitative
    Definite

VOICE

ACTIVE	MIDDLE
Simple	Direct
Causative	Indirect
Stative	Causative
Reflexive	Permissive
	Deponent

PASSIVE	
Simple	Deponent

MOOD

INDICATIVE

Declarative
Interrogative
Conditional
Potential
Cohortative

SUBJUNCTIVE

Hortatory   *let us*
Deliberative
Emphatic Negation
Prohibitive
Conditional Sentences
Ἵνα
    Purpose
    Result
    Substantival
    Epexegetical
    Complementary
Verbs of fearing, etc.
Indirect Questions
Indefinite Relative clauses
Indefinite Temporal clauses

OPTATIVE

Voluntative
Potential

IMPERATIVE

Command
Prohibition
Request
Permissive
Stereotyped greeting

TENSES

PRESENT

Instantaneous
Progressive
Extending-from-past
Iterative
Customary
Gnomic
Historical
Futuristic
Indirect Discourse

IMPERFECT

Progressive   *continually*
Ingressive   *began doing*
Iterative   *kept on*
Customary   *used to*
Conative   *wanted to*
Indirect Discourse

FUTURE

Predictive
Imperatival
Deliberative
Gnomic

AORIST

Constative
Ingressive   *began to*
Consummative
Gnomic
Epistolary
Proleptic
Immediate

PERFECT

Intensive
Extensive
With present force

PLUPERFECT

Intensive
Extensive

INFINITIVE

Adverbial Uses
    Purpose   *in order to*
    Result   *so that*
    Time
        antecedent   *after*
        contemporaneous   *while*
        subsequent   *before*
    Cause
    Means   *by … doing*
    Complementary
Substantival Uses
    Subject
    Direct Object
    Indirect Discourse
    Appositional   *namely*
    Epexegetical

PARTICIPLE

Adjectival
Substantival
Adverbial Uses
    Temporal   *after, when*
    Manner
    Means   *by means of*
    Cause   *because*
    Condition   *if*
    Concession   *although*
    Purpose   *in order to*
    Result   *with the result of*
Attendant Circumstance
Periphrastic
Redundant
As an imperative
Genitive Absolute

Chapter 1

ΙΩΑΝΝΟΥ Α΄ 1:1-2:2; 2:28-3:10

If you have not yet learned conditional sentences, be sure you do so before working through this passage. See BBG, *p. 330, and* Wallace. *Commentary references are to I. H. Marshall,* The Epistles of John, *in The New International Commentary on the New Testament (Eerdmans, 1978).*

These two passages are a powerful discussion of the place of sin in the believer's life as well as the believer's assurance. It is a helpful exercise to count all the ways in which John shows us our assurance. In these two passages John also holds in tension the fact of our assurance and the fact of our need for vigilance, lest we fall into complacency and allow sin to have an ongoing role in our lives.

Prologue (1:1-4)

<u>1:1</u> Ὃ ἦν ἀπ' ἀρχῆς, ὃ ἀκηκόαμεν, ὃ ἑωράκαμεν τοῖς <u>ὀφθαλμοῖς</u> ἡμῶν, ὃ

<u>ἐθεασάμεθα</u> καὶ αἱ χεῖρες ἡμῶν ἐψηλάφησαν[1] περὶ τοῦ λόγου τῆς ζωῆς - **1:2** καὶ

---

[1] ψηλαφάω, *I feel (about for), touch* (4).

Exegetical Discussion

(1)   1:1   V 1. Note carefully the theological significance of the verb tenses in this verse. Marshall (107-8) summarizes the two basic concerns being addressed in this prologue.

Note also the word order. We don't meet the main verb until v 3. A grammatical diagram of vv 1-3 is helpful.

When Greek wants to emphasize a word, it puts it in an unusual place in the sentence, such as putting a direct object at the beginning. What is the significance of word order in vv 1-2?

(2)   **1:1** *   ὀφθαλμοῖς is an **instrumental dative**. It describes the instrument by which an action is accomplished. You can use the key words "by" or "with." There are many nuances to this use of the dative. See *Gram Sum*.

(3)   1:1   ἐθεασάμεθα. What is the difference in nuance between ὁράω and θεάομαι? Is the difference intended here? See Marshall, 101n8.

ἡ ζωὴ ἐφανερώθη, καὶ ἑωράκαμεν καὶ <u>μαρτυροῦμεν</u> καὶ ἀπαγγέλλομεν ὑμῖν τὴν

ζωὴν τὴν αἰώνιον ἥτις[1] ἦν <u>πρὸς</u> τὸν πατέρα καὶ ἐφανερώθη ἡμῖν - **1:3** ὃ

<u>ἑωράκαμεν καὶ ἀκηκόαμεν, ἀπαγγέλλομεν</u> καὶ ὑμῖν, ἵνα καὶ ὑμεῖς <u>κοινωνίαν</u>[2]

<u>ἔχητε</u> μεθ᾽ ἡμῶν. [3]καὶ ἡ κοινωνία <u>δὲ</u> ἡ ἡμετέρα[4] μετὰ τοῦ πατρὸς καὶ μετὰ τοῦ

---

[1] You probably learned this word as an indefinite relative pronoun. As you can see from this context, it can lose the indefiniteness and simply be translated as the relative pronoun "which," and not the indefinite relative "whichever." See *BAGD*.

[2] κοινωνία, ας, ἡ, *communion, fellowship; generosity; participation* (19).

[3] Assume the verb "is" in this part of this verse.

[4] ἡμέτερος, α, ον, *our* (7).

---

(4) 1:2 μαρτυροῦμεν. Why do you think John shifts his tenses with μαρτυροῦμεν?

(5) 1:2 πρός has a basic meaning of "toward" (*BBG*, 62). Here it may picture the pre-incarnate Christ facing the Father in eternal fellowship.

(6) 1:3 ἑωράκαμεν καὶ ἀκηκόαμεν. The first two and one-half verses have been emphasizing the historical reality of the gospel, that it actually occurred and the apostles are witnesses to the facts. What is the significance of this? How does it relate to Paul's understanding of the resurrection? How does it compare with other religions?

(7) 1:3 ἀπαγγέλλομεν. To see and to hear is to tell–the irresistible necessity of Christian witness.

(8) 1:3 κοινωνίαν. This word makes an interesting word study (Marshall, 104).

(9) 1:3 ἔχητε. What is the significance of the tense of ἔχητε? How would it be different if John wrote σχῆτε?

(10) 1:3 δέ here is the fourth word from the beginning of the sentence. It is unusual to find a postpositive (*BBG*, 42n14) so far from the beginning of the sentence.

υἱοῦ αὐτοῦ Ἰησοῦ Χριστοῦ. <u>**1:4**</u> καὶ ταῦτα γράφομεν ἡμεῖς, ἵνα ἡ <u>χαρὰ</u> <u>ἡμῶν</u> <u>ᾖ</u>

<u>πεπληρωμένη</u>.

Walk in the Light (1:5-2:2)

1:5 Καὶ ἔστιν αὕτη ἡ ἀγγελία[1] ἣν ἀκηκόαμεν ἀπ' αὐτοῦ καὶ

ἀναγγέλλομεν[2] ὑμῖν, ὅτι ὁ θεὸς <u>φῶς</u> ἐστιν καὶ σκοτία[3] ἐν αὐτῷ οὐκ ἔστιν

<u>οὐδεμία</u>. **1:6** Ἐὰν <u>εἴπωμεν</u> ὅτι <u>κοινωνίαν</u> ἔχομεν μετ' αὐτοῦ καὶ ἐν τῷ σκότει

---

[1] ἀγγελία, ας, ἡ, *message* (2).

[2] ἀναγγέλλω, *I report; announce, proclaim* (14).

[3] σκοτία, ας, ἡ, *darkness, gloom* (16).

---

(11) 1:4   V 4. In 1 John 5:13 John states his main reason for writing the epistle. This verse gives us another reason indicated by the ἵνα clause.

(12) 1:4   χαρά. Cf. the opening of the Westminster Shorter Catechism –"The chief end of man is to glorify God and enjoy him forever." Do you think of Scripture as the source of constant joy?

(13) 1:4   ἡμῶν. There is a weak textual variant ὑμῶν (cf. John 16:24).

(14) **1:4** *   ᾖ πεπληρωμένη. Does context support giving this **periphrastic construction** its historical force? What is the force of a periphrastic construction? (*BBG*, §30.10) Cf. Mark 1:6 for an explanation.

(15) 1:5   φῶς. Qumran scrolls have provided abundant evidence that contrasts such as light/darkness do not reflect a gnostic influence on the NT but were part of Semitic thought (e.g., 1QS 1:5, 9-10).

(16) **1:5** *   οὐδεμία. Contrary to English grammar, double negations in Greek do not negate each other. The second strengthens the first (*BBG*, §31.16).

(17) 1:6   εἴπωμεν. On this use of the subjunctive see *Gram. Sum.*, "Subjunctive in Conditional Sentences." It occurs four more times in the paragraph.

(18) 1:6   κοινωνίαν. Since God is light, there is no possible way for us to have fellowship with him if we are walking in darkness. It is a logical impossibility. For John issues of spiritual importance are all black and white. Not to walk the talk is to lie.

περιπατῶμεν, ψευδόμεθα[1] καὶ οὐ ποιοῦμεν τὴν ἀλήθειαν· **1:7** ἐὰν δὲ ἐν τῷ φωτὶ

περιπατῶμεν ὡς αὐτός ἐστιν ἐν τῷ φωτί, κοινωνίαν ἔχομεν μετ᾽ ἀλλήλων καὶ τὸ

αἷμα Ἰησοῦ τοῦ υἱοῦ αὐτοῦ καθαρίζει ἡμᾶς ἀπὸ πάσης ἁμαρτίας. **1:8** ἐὰν

εἴπωμεν ὅτι ἁμαρτίαν οὐκ ἔχομεν, ἑαυτοὺς πλανῶμεν καὶ ἡ ἀλήθεια οὐκ ἔστιν

ἐν ἡμῖν. **1:9** ἐὰν ὁμολογῶμεν τὰς ἁμαρτίας ἡμῶν, πιστός ἐστιν καὶ δίκαιος, ἵνα

ἀφῇ[2] ἡμῖν τὰς ἁμαρτίας καὶ καθαρίσῃ ἡμᾶς ἀπὸ πάσης ἀδικίας. **1:10** ἐὰν

εἴπωμεν ὅτι οὐχ ἡμαρτήκαμεν, ψεύστην[3] ποιοῦμεν αὐτὸν καὶ ὁ λόγος αὐτοῦ

οὐκ ἔστιν ἐν ἡμῖν.

---

[1]   ψεύδομαι, *I lie* (12).
[2]   This is a compound μι verb (*MBG*, §52.4, p. 133).
[3]   ψεύστης, ου, ὁ, *liar* (10).

---

(19)   1:6   περιπατῶμεν. How does the aspect of περιπατῶμεν, and the meaning of the word, add to your understanding of the verse?

(20)   1:6   ποιοῦμεν τὴν ἀλήθειαν. Does the idiom ποιοῦμεν τὴν ἀλήθειαν help you understand how John thinks of the truth?

(21)   1:7   μετ᾽ ἀλλήλων. To be in fellowship with the Father places us in fellowship with one another. To be at odds with other believers indicates we are not in fellowship with God.

(22)   1:7   καθαρίζει. In what sense does the blood of Christ keep on cleansing (present tense) us from every sin? Were we not completely forgiven when we first turned to him in faith?

(23)   1:8   ἁμαρτίαν οὐκ ἔχομεν. ἁμαρτίαν ἔχειν means "to possess a sinful nature" (*BAGD*, 2, on ἁμαρτία). If this is correct, how does it affect your exegesis? Had John intended here to refer to individual sinful acts, what verb would he probably have used?

(24)   1:9   ὁμολογῶμεν. The verb tenses in v 9 (ὁμολογῶμεν, present; ἀφῇ and καθαρίσῃ, aorist) suggest that confessing sin is an ongoing responsibility of the believer and that every time we confess God forgives and cleanses.

(25)   **1:9** *   ἀδικίας. When Greek wants to negate a word, it adds an alpha to the beginning of the word, much like English prefixes "ir-"or "un-." In Greek, this is called an **alpha privative**.

2:1 <u>Τεκνία</u>[1] μου, ταῦτα γράφω ὑμῖν ἵνα μὴ ἁμάρτητε. καὶ ἐάν τις

ἁμάρτῃ, <u>παράκλητον</u>[2] ἔχομεν πρὸς τὸν πατέρα Ἰησοῦν Χριστὸν <u>δίκαιον</u>· **2:2** καὶ

αὐτὸς <u>ἱλασμός</u>[3] ἐστιν περὶ τῶν ἁμαρτιῶν ἡμῶν, οὐ περὶ τῶν ἡμετέρων δὲ μόνον

ἀλλὰ καὶ περὶ <u>ὅλου</u> τοῦ κόσμου.

* * * * *

---

[1] τεκνίον, ου, τό, *little child* (8).

[2] παράκλητος, ου, ὁ, *advocate* (5).

[3] ἱλασμός, οῦ, ὁ, *atoning sacrifice, propitiation, expiation* (2).

---

(26) **2:1** *   Τεκνία is the **diminutive** form of the more common τέκνον. A diminutive is a form indicating something smaller. For example, in German "Frau" is a "woman" while the diminutive "Fraülein" ("-lein" forms a diminutive in German) is a "young woman."

(27) 2:1   παράκλητον. Be sure to do a word study on παράκλητος (see Marshall, 116-17).

(28) **2:1** *   δίκαιον. When Greek wants to use a noun to explain another noun, it places the second noun in **apposition** to the first. It is the same as placing "i.e." or "namely" before the second noun. There are two ways to place a noun in apposition. The way we see here is to put it in the same case as the main word. One interpretation of δίκαιον is as a title, "Jesus Christ the Just," in which case δίκαιον is in apposition. However, if δίκαιον merely qualifying Ἰησοῦν Χριστὸν, then it is used adjectivally.

(29) **2:2** *   ἱλασμός. Be sure you also do a word study on ἱλασμός. What is the difference between "expiation" and "propitiation"? What are the limitations of the imagery? See Marshall, 117-19.

(30) 2:2   ὅλου. Cf. the discussion of Marshall (119) with Grudem, *Systematic Theology*, 594-600. How do you feel about "limited atonement" ("particular atonement")?

The Children of God (2:28-3:3)

2:28 Καὶ νῦν, τεκνία, μένετε ἐν αὐτῷ, ἵνα ἐὰν φανερωθῇ σχῶμεν[1]

<u>παρρησίαν</u> καὶ μὴ αἰσχυνθῶμεν[2] <u>ἀπ'</u> αὐτοῦ ἐν τῇ παρουσίᾳ αὐτοῦ. **2:29** ἐὰν

εἰδῆτε ὅτι δίκαιός ἐστιν, γινώσκετε ὅτι καὶ πᾶς ὁ ποιῶν τὴν δικαιοσύνην ἐξ

<u>αὐτοῦ</u> γεγέννηται **3:1** ἴδετε[3] ποταπὴν[4] ἀγάπην <u>δέδωκεν</u> ἡμῖν ὁ πατήρ, ἵνα

τέκνα θεοῦ κληθῶμεν, καὶ ἐσμέν. διὰ τοῦτο ὁ κόσμος οὐ γινώσκει ἡμᾶς, <u>ὅτι</u> οὐκ

---

[1] What are the two hints as to the mood of this verb?

[2] αἰσχύνω, *I am ashamed; put to shame, disgraced* (5). In our literature it is always middle/passive.

[3] This verb has lost its augment and therefore must be a nonindicative form (*MBG*, §72.1).

[4] ποταπός, ή, όν, *what sort/manner* (7).

---

(31) 2:28 παρρησίαν. Be sure to do a word study on παρρησία (Marshall, 165-66). How does knowing its secular usage help to understand what John is saying here?

(32) 2:28 ἀπ' can mean either "before" or "by" (Marshall, 166n9). What is the difference here and which best fits the context?

(33) 2:29 V 29 has a close association with v 28. What is it? How does v 29 help you understand v 28?

(34) 2:29 αὐτοῦ. What is the antecedent of αὐτοῦ, God or Christ?

(35) 3:1 δέδωκεν. What does the tense of δέδωκεν suggest about the continuing influence of God's love in adopting us into his family?

(36) 3:1 ὅτι is causal. The reason the world does not know us is that it did not know him, i.e., God, or perhaps God incarnate. Cf. John 15:18-19. If you can't recognize the father, you certainly can't recognize his children.

ἔγνω αὐτόν. **3:2** Ἀγαπητοί, νῦν <u>τέκνα</u> θεοῦ ἐσμεν, καὶ οὔπω <u>ἐφανερώθη</u> <u>τί</u>

<u>ἐσόμεθα</u>. οἴδαμεν ὅτι ἐὰν φανερωθῇ, ὅμοιοι αὐτῷ ἐσόμεθα, ὅτι ὀψόμεθα αὐτὸν

καθώς ἐστιν. **3:3** καὶ πᾶς ὁ ἔχων τὴν ἐλπίδα ταύτην ἐπ'[1] <u>αὐτῷ</u> <u>ἁγνίζει</u>[2] ἑαυτὸν,

καθὼς ἐκεῖνος ἁγνός[3] ἐστιν.

The Sinlessness of God's Children (3:4-10)

3:4 Πᾶς ὁ ποιῶν τὴν ἁμαρτίαν καὶ τὴν ἀνομίαν[4] ποιεῖ, καὶ ἡ ἁμαρτία

ἐστὶν ἡ ἀνομία. **3:5** καὶ οἴδατε ὅτι ἐκεῖνος ἐφανερώθη, ἵνα τὰς ἁμαρτίας ἄρῃ,

καὶ ἁμαρτία ἐν αὐτῷ οὐκ ἔστιν. **3:6** πᾶς ὁ ἐν αὐτῷ μένων οὐχ <u>ἁμαρτάνει·</u> πᾶς

---

[1] One of the meanings of ἐπί is to state "that upon which a state of being, an action, or a result is based," whether it be an emotion, a fear, etc. (*BAGD*, 287).

[2] ἁγνίζω, *I purify;* middle: *purify oneself* (7).

[3] ἁγνός, ή, όν, *pure, holy* (8).

[4] ἀνομία, ας, ἡ, *lawlessness* (15).

---

(37) 3:2   τέκνα. In his first epistle John uses τέκνον at 3:1, 2, 10 and 5:2. He uses the diminutive τεκνίον at 2:1, 12, 28; 3:7, 18; 4:4 and 5:21. Study all the occurrences and determine whether he intends a difference in the two terms.

(38) 3:2   ἐφανερώθη. What is the subject of ἐφανερώθη? Jesus, or the following phrase? See Marshall, 172n29.

(39) **3:2 ***   τί ἐσόμεθα is an **indirect question** (see "indirect discourse" in *BBG*, §32.14-15; Wallace).

(40) 3:3   αὐτῷ. What is the antecedent of αὐτῷ ?

(41) 3:3   ἁγνίζει. Note the important relationship between 3:2 and 3:3. It is the hope of seeing God and becoming like him that provides the incentive for living a holy life until he comes. Eschatology is not pointless speculation about the future but a powerful impetus for godly living.

(42) **3:6 ***   ἁμαρτάνει. Be sure to struggle with the meaning and implications of this word. For a discussion of the possible interpretations see Marshall, 178-83, and compare it with Grudem, *Systematic Theology,* 750-53.

ὁ ἁμαρτάνων οὐχ ἑώρακεν αὐτὸν οὐδὲ ἔγνωκεν αὐτόν. **3:7** Τεκνία, μηδεὶς

πλανάτω ὑμᾶς· ὁ ποιῶν τὴν δικαιοσύνην δίκαιός ἐστιν, καθὼς ἐκεῖνος δίκαιός

ἐστιν· **3:8** <u>ὁ ποιῶν τὴν ἁμαρτίαν</u> <u>ἐκ τοῦ διαβόλου</u> ἐστίν, ὅτι ἀπ᾽ ἀρχῆς ὁ

διάβολος ἁμαρτάνει. <u>εἰς τοῦτο</u> ἐφανερώθη ὁ υἱὸς τοῦ θεοῦ, ἵνα λύσῃ τὰ ἔργα

τοῦ διαβόλου. <u>**3:9**</u> Πᾶς ὁ γεγεννημένος ἐκ τοῦ θεοῦ ἁμαρτίαν οὐ ποιεῖ, ὅτι

σπέρμα αὐτοῦ ἐν αὐτῷ μένει, καὶ οὐ δύναται ἁμαρτάνειν, ὅτι ἐκ τοῦ θεοῦ

γεγέννηται. **3:10** ἐν τούτῳ φανερά[1] ἐστιν τὰ τέκνα τοῦ θεοῦ καὶ τὰ τέκνα τοῦ

διαβόλου· πᾶς ὁ μὴ ποιῶν δικαιοσύνην οὐκ ἔστιν ἐκ τοῦ θεοῦ, καὶ ὁ μὴ ἀγαπῶν

τὸν ἀδελφὸν αὐτοῦ.

---

[1] φανερός, ά, όν, *visible, clear, plain, evident* (18).

---

(43) **3:8** *   ὁ ποιῶν τὴν ἁμαρτίαν. Note the emphasis John places on doing: τὴν
            ἀλήθειαν (1:6), τὸ θέλημα τοῦ θεοῦ (2:17), τὴν δικαιοσύνην (2:29), τὴν
            ἁμαρτίαν (3:4). Theology, for John, inevitably leads to action. How you
            move yourself and those around you from theology to practice is cru-
            cial in your life and ministry. How do you plan to do this?

(44) 3:8   ἐκ τοῦ διαβόλου. The ἐκ of origin indicates the satanic origin of all who
            continue to sin. Cf. ἐκ τοῦ θεοῦ in 3:9-10. Our allegiance is either to God
            or to the devil. There is no room for compromise.

(45) **3:8** *   εἰς τοῦτο is an idiom meaning *for this reason*. The author can have just
            stated the reason and the idiom refers back to it, or the author can be
            preparing to state the reason and the idiom points forward to it.

(46) **3:9** *   V 9. Very important! Be able to explain the tenses of all the verbal
            forms in 3:9!

Grammar Summary

1. An *instrumental dative* describes the instrument by which an action is accomplished. You can use the key words "by" or "with."

2. A *periphrastic construction* uses a form of εἰμί and the participle of the verb. Originally it stressed the linear aspect of the verb.

3. *Double negations* in Greek do not negate each other. The second strengthens the first.

4. The *alpha privative* is an alpha added to the beginning of the word that negates the word, much like English prefixes "ir-"or "un-."

5. A *diminutive* is a form indicating something smaller.

6. When Greek wants to use a noun to further explain another noun, it places the second noun in apposition to the first. Greek often puts the second word in the same case as the first word.

7. One of the meanings of ἐπί with the dative is to state "that upon which a state of being, an action, or a result is based," whether it be an emotion, a fear, etc.

8. *Indirect question* is the repeating of a question but not claiming to use the exact words of the speaker. Like *indirect discourse,* Greek retains the verbal tense of the direct question/discourse.

9. εἰς τοῦτο is an idiom meaning *for this reason.*

Phrasing

If you are going to be phrasing, be sure to have read the discussion of phrasing in the *Introduction*. At the end of the first several chapters, we will discuss phrasing as it relates directly to the passage. In *Appendix B* we have included phrasing for six of the the first seven passages. Please do yourself a favor and do not look at them, except to check your work. Do not miss the enjoyment of first-hand Bible study. After the seventh passage, you are on your own.

Remember too that phrasing is personal and is based on your exegesis. Yours may differ from our phrasing, and that is fine.

1 John 1 is a good passage for you to start phrasing. For example, here is verse 3.

1:3   ὃ   ἑωράκαμεν
                      καὶ
                  ἀκηκόαμεν,
          ἀπαγγέλλομεν καὶ ὑμῖν,
              ἵνα καὶ ὑμεῖς κοινωνίαν ἔχητε
                          μεθ᾽ ἡμῶν.

              καὶ ... δὲ
          ἡ κοινωνία ... ἡ ἡμετέρα
              μετὰ   τοῦ πατρὸς
                  καὶ
              μετὰ   τοῦ υἱοῦ αὐτοῦ
                  Ἰησοῦ Χριστοῦ.

John's main statement is that he is announcing something (ἀπαγγέλλομεν καὶ ὑμῖν). His announcement is based on two facts (ὃ ἑωράκαμεν; ἀκηκόαμεν) and has a desired result (ἵνα καὶ ὑμεῖς κοινωνίαν ἔχητε). We also learn that his fellowship is with two persons (πατρὸς; υἱοῦ), the second receiving a further description (Ἰησοῦ Χριστοῦ).

It is best to start with relatively simple verses. Try phrasing 1:9 and 3:6. If you are comfortable with those, try 1:5 and 3:9. Of course, you can phrase the entire passage if you would like to.

The answers are given in *Appendix B,* but please do not cheat yourself. Try the exercise and then check your work.

I had a suggestion from a colleague. His students did not quite grasp what phrasing was all about, so he printed out the text and had the students cut the text into phrases. Then they arranged the pieces in a way that made sense to them. If this would help you get started, then by all means do it.

Reflections on the Text

Introduction

The outline for this sermon grows out of the structure of 1:9-10. Look at the phrasing diagram and you will see that the unit consists of two basic conditional sentences, each of which includes a twofold response in the apodosis. Analysis also shows the interrelatedness between the two verses. They each deal with how a person reacts when faced with the responsibility of owning up to sin. V 9 adds the clause about God's being faithful and just–a point that is equally applicable to v 10.

Sermon introductions are not simply ways to gain the attention of the audience. They should lead the listener into the major theme of the sermon by way of an analogous relationship between introduction and sermon.

Make sure you understand exactly what the Greek text is saying. You will also want to do word studies on ὁμολογέω, ἁμαρτία, δίκαιος, and ἀδικία in order to provide a larger and more accurate contextual background for the message you want to communicate.

Before preaching the sermon, come to grips with whether or not you yourself have submitted to the specific terms of your message. To communicate truth you must have allowed that truth free access to your own personal life.

Caught In The Act

(1 John 1:9-10)

Introduction

Down deep it is a "John Wayne" world: there is right and there is wrong.

Good writers know that clarity is a number one concern.

The Apostle John was a black-and-white person, without shades of gray.

One place you see it is in his attitude about sin.

A. Two possibilities when facing the fact of sin in your life

1. Deny that you have sinned (v. 10a).

2. Confess that you have sinned (v. 9a).

B. The results of your decision about sin

1. If you deny that you have sinned (10b).
   a. You are guilty of making God a liar.
   b. You show that God's word is not in you.

2. If you confess your sin (9b).
   a. You are forgiven of your sin.
   b. You are cleansed from all unrighteousness.

C. The twofold basis for God's action

1. He is absolutely faithful.
   a. He will hold the one who denies responsible.
   b. He will forgive and cleanse the one who confesses.

2. He is absolutely just: He will always do what is right.
   a. Withhold his favor from the proud.
   b. Shower his favor upon the humble.

Conclusion

1. Denial obstructs spiritual growth.

2. Confession nourishes spiritual growth.

If God is black and white about sin, should that not be our response as well?

How do you maintain absolute standards in a relativistic world?

Chapter 2

ΚΑΤΑ ΙΩΑΝΝΗΝ 15:1-27

In this passage you will see the value of watching shifts in tenses very carefully. It also illustrates the importance of recognizing that even in the indicative, the primary significance of a tense is its aspect, not its time. You will need to understand the force of the subjunctive in conditional statements, especially when the subjunctive indicates a general (axiomatic) truth. Be careful that your translation does not make the truth of the statement conditional. What is conditional is whether or not you will do the action described in the "if" clause. Typically in John, the vocabulary is simple and repetitive.

Theologically, note carefully the necessity of abiding and the implications if you do not, especially in terms of one's fruit. What does this passage teach about "Carnal Christians"?

Much of this passage is enjoyable to phrase. You may want to look especially at 15:7-8 and 15:15-16.

Commentary references are to Leon Morris, *The Gospel According to John,* in The New International Commentary on the New Testament (Eerdmans, 1971).

Jesus, the True Vine; God the Father, the Vine-Dresser (15:1-4)

15:1 Ἐγώ εἰμι ἡ ἄμπελος[1] ἡ ἀληθινὴ καὶ ὁ πατήρ μου ὁ γεωργός[2] ἐστιν.

---

[1] ἄμπελος, ου, ἡ, *vine* (9).

[2] γεωργός, οῦ, ὁ, *farmer; vine-dresser, tenant farmer* (19).

Exegetical Discussion

(1)   15:1   ἄμπελος. What is the Old Testament imagery behind this word? See Morris, 668.

15:2 πᾶν κλῆμα[1] ἐν ἐμοὶ <u>μὴ φέρον</u> καρπὸν <u>αἴρει</u> αὐτό, καὶ πᾶν[2] τὸ καρπὸν φέρον

<u>καθαίρει</u>[3] αὐτὸ ἵνα <u>καρπὸν</u> πλείονα[4] φέρῃ. **15:3** ἤδη ὑμεῖς καθαροί ἐστε διὰ τὸν

λόγον ὃν <u>λελάληκα</u> ὑμῖν· **15:4** μείνατε[5] ἐν ἐμοί, <u>κἀγὼ</u> ἐν ὑμῖν. καθὼς τὸ κλῆμα

οὐ δύναται καρπὸν φέρειν ἀφ᾽[6] ἑαυτοῦ ἐὰν μὴ μένῃ[7] ἐν τῇ ἀμπέλῳ, οὕτως οὐδὲ

ὑμεῖς ἐὰν μὴ ἐν ἐμοὶ μένητε.

---

[1] κλῆμα, ατος, τό, *branch* (4). Used especially of vine branches. There are three words/phrases modifying this word. What are they?

[2] The trick to translating the phrase πᾶν τὸ καρπὸν φέρον is to correctly parse φέρον, and then to see why πᾶν and καρπόν are in the case they are.

[3] καθαίρω, *I make clean*; when used of a vine: *I clean, prune* (1).

[4] πλείονα is the comparative of πολύς (*MBG*, p. 221).

[5] Before parsing this form, pay close attention to the stem vowels and compare them to the lexical form of the word (*MBG*, §72.3).

[6] The following word begins with a vowel and rough breathing (*MBG*, §14.7; §6.5).

[7] The key to translating μένῃ is the preceding expression ἐὰν μή and knowing what you can expect to follow it.

---

(2) 15:2 μὴ φέρον. What are the implications, if any, of this concept on the doctrine of the perseverance of the saints? See Morris, 669.

(3) **15:2** * αἴρει could be an **iterative present**, which describes an ongoing action as a series of events, much like waves lapping against the side of a boat. It could also be a **gnomic present**, which describes something that is always true.

(4) **15:2** * καθαίρει occurs only once in the New Testament. We call this a **hapax legomenon** (ἅπαξ λεγόμενον), meaning "spoken only once." It can be abbreviated "hapax."

(5) 15:2 καρπόν. To what does καρπόν refer? See Morris, 670.

(6) **15:3** * λελάληκα. The perfect tense can place its emphasis on the beginning of the action or on its ongoing results. When it is the latter we call it an **intensive perfect**, which is the case here.

(7) 15:4 κἀγώ. Is the verbal idea linked with this word an imperative or a promise? What is the difference? See Morris, 670.

Jesus Is the Vine; We Are the Branches (15:5-11)

15:5 ἐγώ εἰμι ἡ ἄμπελος, ὑμεῖς τὰ κλήματα. ὁ μένων ἐν ἐμοὶ κἀγὼ ἐν

αὐτῷ <u>οὗτος</u> φέρει καρπὸν πολύν, ὅτι χωρὶς ἐμοῦ οὐ δύνασθε ποιεῖν οὐδέν.

15:6 ἐὰν μή τις μένῃ ἐν ἐμοί, <u>ἐβλήθη</u> ἔξω ὡς τὸ κλῆμα καὶ ἐξηράνθη[1] καὶ

<u>συνάγουσιν</u> αὐτὰ καὶ εἰς τὸ πῦρ βάλλουσιν καὶ <u>καίεται</u>.[2] **15:7** ἐὰν μείνητε ἐν

ἐμοὶ καὶ τὰ ῥήματά μου ἐν ὑμῖν μείνῃ, ὃ ἐὰν θέλητε <u>αἰτήσασθε</u>, καὶ γενήσεται

---

[1] ξηραίνω, *I wither, dry up* (15).

[2] καίω, *I burn* (12). What is the subject of this verb? It explains why the verb is singular.

---

(8) 15:5   οὗτος. It is typical for John to use a phrase as the subject of the sentence and then to repeat the subject as a pronoun.

(9) **15:6** * ἐβλήθη. Did you notice that although ἐβλήθη is a past tense form, it does not describe a past action? The same is true of the following ἐξηράνθη. The problem of interpreting this tense is compounded by the fact that it occurs in the apodosis of a third class condition, stating a present general truth, and this fact governs much of the verb's meaning.

It may be an **immediate past (dramatic) aorist**, which is the use of the aorist to describe an event that has just occurred. You can use the key phrase "just now." However, it just occurred in reference to the three final verbs in the verse that are present. The branches must be cast outside and wither before they can be gathered together, thrown into the fire, and burned.

(10) **15:6** * συνάγουσιν is a **customary present**, describing an event that regularly occurs or an ongoing state.

(11) **15:6** * καίεται can be **transitive** or **intransitive**. A "transitive" verb is one that takes a direct object. An "intransitive" verb does not take a direct object. Sometimes Greek verbs can have subtle differences in meaning depending on whether they are transitive or intransitive. For example, καίω can mean "burn (up)" as an active transitive or "be burned" as a passive intransitive.

(12) 15:7   αἰτήσασθε. Is αἰτήσασθε middle or passive? What is the significance of its voice? What is the relationship between remaining in Christ and prayer? How does "my words" affect your understanding of this verse and prayer in general?

ὑμῖν. **15:8** ἐν τούτῳ <u>ἐδοξάσθη</u> ὁ πατήρ μου, ἵνα καρπὸν πολὺν φέρητε καὶ

<u>γένησθε</u> ἐμοὶ μαθηταί. **15:9** καθὼς ἠγάπησέν με ὁ πατήρ, κἀγὼ ὑμᾶς ἠγάπησα·

μείνατε ἐν τῇ ἀγάπῃ τῇ ἐμῇ. **15:10** ἐὰν τὰς ἐντολάς μου τηρήσητε, μενεῖτε[1] ἐν

τῇ ἀγάπῃ μου, καθὼς ἐγὼ τὰς ἐντολὰς τοῦ πατρός μου <u>τετήρηκα</u> καὶ μένω

αὐτοῦ ἐν τῇ ἀγάπῃ. **15:11** Ταῦτα λελάληκα ὑμῖν ἵνα ἡ <u>χαρὰ</u> ἡ ἐμὴ ἐν ὑμῖν ᾖ καὶ

ἡ χαρὰ ὑμῶν πληρωθῇ.

---

[1] Did you notice that this is a liquid verb? Does that help you determine the
tense? (*MBG*, §43.3)

---

(13) **15:7 *** ὑμῖν is called the **dative of advantage**. It means that the action of the
word, which the dative form modifies, is done for the advantage of the
word in the dative. When the same construction specifies that an
action is done for the disadvantage of something, the dative is called
the dative of disadvantage. It is exactly the same construction; context
determines whether it is *advantage* or *disadvantage*. You can use the key
phrase "for the advantage of" or "for the disadvantage of," depending
upon the context. If you can find a smoother way of translating that
carries the same force, such as "for," then do it. It is listed under *dative
of interest* in the *Gram Sum.*

(14) **15:8 *** ἐδοξάσθη. Somewhat like the *dramatic aorist*, ἐδοξάσθη is called the **gnomic aorist**. It describes something that is eternally true, and the undefined nature of the aorist lends itself to this meaning. As you can see,
this aorist has lost all time significance.

(15) 15:8   γένησθε. What exactly does this phrase mean? See Morris, 672-73.

(16) 15:10   τετήρηκα. Note the emphatic use of the personal pronoun ἐγώ (*BBG*,
§11.8) and the perfect tense of τετήρηκα. What is the point Jesus is
emphasizing?

(17) 15:11   χαρά. See Morris (674) for an encouraging discussion of the believer's
joyous life.

Love One Another (15:12-25)

15:12 αὕτη ἐστὶν ἡ ἐντολὴ ἡ ἐμή, ἵνα[1] ἀγαπᾶτε ἀλλήλους καθὼς

ἠγάπησα ὑμᾶς. **15:13** μείζονα[2] ταύτης ἀγάπην οὐδεὶς ἔχει, ἵνα τις τὴν ψυχὴν

αὐτοῦ θῇ[3] ὑπὲρ τῶν φίλων αὐτοῦ. **15:14** ὑμεῖς φίλοι μού ἐστε ἐὰν ποιῆτε ἃ ἐγὼ

ἐντέλλομαι[4] ὑμῖν. **15:15** οὐκέτι λέγω ὑμᾶς δούλους, ὅτι ὁ δοῦλος οὐκ οἶδεν τί

ποιεῖ αὐτοῦ ὁ κύριος· ὑμᾶς δὲ εἴρηκα φίλους, ὅτι πάντα ἃ ἤκουσα παρὰ τοῦ

---

[1] Remember that ἵνα can mean both "that" and "in order that." The two meanings are definitely different, and be sure to choose between the two.

[2] μείζων is always followed by what is called the **genitive of comparison**. The word following μείζων will be in the genitive and you use the key word *than* after you translate μείζων. (If you have learned the eight-case system, it is an *ablative*, and it is listed as such on the *Cheat Sheet*.) There are several other words that will also be followed by the genitive of comparison.

[3] The stem of this word is *θε, and it is in a ἵνα clause (*MBG*, §52.4).

[4] ἐντέλλω occurs only as a middle deponent, meaning *I command, order* (15).

---

(18) 15:12 ἠγάπησα. What is the significance of the tense shift from ἀγαπᾶτε to ἠγάπησα? See Morris, 674.

(19) 15:14 ἐὰν. What are the implications of this type of conditional friendship in today's cultural environment?

(20) **15:15** * λέγω. In this context λέγω requires two direct objects to make complete sense, and hence the two objects are called a **double accusative**. Usually, one of the words in the accusative refers to a person and the second to a thing, although both can refer to things.

As you can see, λέγω is flexible in its meaning.

(21) 15:15 φίλους. What is the essential difference between a δοῦλος and a φίλος in this context? See Morris, 675.

πατρός μου ἐγνώρισα[1] ὑμῖν. **15:16** <u>οὐχ</u> ὑμεῖς με ἐξελέξασθε,[2] ἀλλ᾽ ἐγὼ

ἐξελεξάμην ὑμᾶς καὶ ἔθηκα ὑμᾶς ἵνα ὑμεῖς ὑπάγητε καὶ καρπὸν φέρητε καὶ ὁ

καρπὸς ὑμῶν μένῃ, ἵνα ὅ τι ἂν αἰτήσητε τὸν πατέρα ἐν τῷ ὀνόματί μου δῷ[3] ὑμῖν.

15:17 <u>ταῦτα</u> ἐντέλλομαι ὑμῖν, ἵνα ἀγαπᾶτε ἀλλήλους.

15:18 <u>Εἰ</u> ὁ κόσμος ὑμᾶς μισεῖ, γινώσκετε ὅτι ἐμὲ πρῶτον[4] ὑμῶν

<u>μεμίσηκεν</u>. **15:19** εἰ ἐκ τοῦ κόσμου ἦτε, ὁ κόσμος ἂν τὸ ἴδιον ἐφίλει· ὅτι δὲ ἐκ

---

[1]   This is not from γινώσκω.

[2]   If a compound verb is formed with ἐκ, when it augments, the κ turns into a ξ
       (*MBG*, §19.3). This is common, so be aware of it.

[3]   There is a word earlier in the sentence that tells you what mood to expect. As
       far as the word itself, the root of the verb is *δο. If you know your μι verb rules,
       the rest should be easy (*MBG*, §52.4).

[4]   πρῶτον is an adverb acting as a preposition and requires the genitive for its
       object.

---

(22)   15:16   V 16. Here is one for you Calvinists/Arminians. What is the scope of
               v 16? Who is the "you"? If it is the disciples, do any of the implications
               of this verse affect anyone who is not one of the twelve apostles?

               Also, be sure to note the tense of the verbs. How are they significant?

(23)   15:16   οὐχ. Note the emphatic form of the negation as well as its emphatic
               placement in word order. What is the point?

(24)   15:17   V 17 can go with vv 1-16 or with vv 18-21. Which option makes the
               best sense to you, and why?

(25)   15:17   ταῦτα. Why is ταῦτα plural? See Morris, 678-9.

(26)   15:18   Εἰ. Does the occurrence of εἰ indicate that there is some question as to
               whether or not the world might hate the disciples? Cf. first class con-
               ditional statements (*BBG*, p. 330).

(27)   15:18   μεμίσηκεν. Did you notice the tense shift from μισεῖ to μεμίσηκεν? "It is
               not without its significance that the disciples are to be known by their
               love, the world by its hatred" (Morris, 678).

(28)   15:19   V 19 contains all the parts of a contrary-to-fact conditional sentence.
               There are two more in this passage but they are missing parts.

τοῦ κόσμου οὐκ ἐστέ, ἀλλ' ἐγὼ <u>ἐξελεξάμην</u> ὑμᾶς ἐκ τοῦ κόσμου, διὰ τοῦτο μισεῖ

ὑμᾶς ὁ κόσμος. **15:20** μνημονεύετε[1] τοῦ λόγου <u>οὗ</u> ἐγὼ εἶπον ὑμῖν, Οὐκ ἔστιν

δοῦλος μείζων τοῦ κυρίου αὐτοῦ. εἰ ἐμὲ ἐδίωξαν, καὶ ὑμᾶς διώξουσιν· εἰ τὸν

λόγον μου ἐτήρησαν, καὶ τὸν ὑμέτερον[2] τηρήσουσιν. **15:21** ἀλλὰ ταῦτα πάντα

ποιήσουσιν εἰς ὑμᾶς διὰ τὸ ὄνομά μου, ὅτι οὐκ οἴδασιν τὸν πέμψαντά με.

<u>**15:22**</u> εἰ <u>μὴ</u> ἦλθον καὶ ἐλάλησα αὐτοῖς, ἁμαρτίαν οὐκ εἴχοσαν.[3] νῦν δὲ

πρόφασιν[4] οὐκ ἔχουσιν περὶ τῆς ἁμαρτίας αὐτῶν. **15:23** ὁ ἐμὲ μισῶν καὶ τὸν

πατέρα μου μισεῖ. **15:24** εἰ τὰ ἔργα μὴ ἐποίησα ἐν αὐτοῖς ἃ οὐδεὶς ἄλλος

---

[1] μνημονεύω can take a direct object in the genitive or accusative.

[2] ὑμέτερος, α, ον, *your(s)* (11).

[3] The augment shows this is the imperfect of ἔχω. However, instead of the usual third plural ending (εἶχον), this word has borrowed the third plural ending from μι verbs. Why did John use the imperfect?

[4] πρόφασις, εως, ἡ, *motive, reason, valid excuse; falsely alleged motive, pretext* (6).

---

(29)   15:19   ἐξελεξάμην. Parse the tense of ἐξελεξάμην and μισεῖ carefully. They are significant to the theology of the verse.

(30)   15:20   οὗ. Did you notice that the relative pronoun οὗ was *attracted* (BBG, §14.15) to the case of its antecedent? In what case "should" it have been?

(31)   15:22   V 22. Is ignorance of God's law permission to sin?

(32)   15:22   μή. Did you notice that μή is followed by an indicative verb? This is unusual and is due to the fact that it occurs in a contrary-to-fact conditional sentence (cf. *BDF* §428.2). See also v 24.

ἐποίησεν, ἁμαρτίαν οὐκ εἴχοσαν· νῦν δὲ καὶ ἑωράκασιν καὶ μεμισήκασιν καὶ

ἐμὲ καὶ τὸν πατέρα μου. **15:25** ἀλλ᾿ ἵνα πληρωθῇ ὁ λόγος ὁ[1] ἐν τῷ νόμῳ αὐτῶν

γεγραμμένος ὅτι **Ἐμίσησάν με δωρεάν**.[2]

The Holy Spirit (15:26-27)

15:26[3] Ὅταν ἔλθῃ ὁ <u>παράκλητος</u>[4] ὃν ἐγὼ πέμψω ὑμῖν παρὰ τοῦ πατρός,

τὸ πνεῦμα τῆς ἀληθείας ὃ παρὰ τοῦ πατρὸς ἐκπορεύεται, <u>ἐκεῖνος</u> μαρτυρήσει

περὶ ἐμοῦ· **15:27** καὶ ὑμεῖς δὲ μαρτυρεῖτε, ὅτι ἀπ᾿ ἀρχῆς μετ᾿ ἐμοῦ ἐστε.

---

1   Locate the word this article is modifying.

2   δωρεάν, *as a gift, gratis; undeservedly* (19). It is the accusative singular form of
     δωρεά, which was used adverbially and eventually became an adverb. The bold
     type indicates that the editors feel an Old Testament passage is being quoted.

3   The structure of v 26 can be a little difficult to see. Identify the subject. Remem-
     ber, the subject of a subordinate clause, such as a relative clause, grammatically
     cannot be the subject of the main verb. Phrasing will help you here.

4   παράκλητος, ου, ὁ, *intercessor, mediator, advocate* (5).

---

(33) 15:26   παράκλητος. Be sure to do a word study on παράκλητος. See Morris,
               662-66. We have already meet this word in 1 John 2:1.

(34) 15:26   ἐκεῖνος. Why is ἐκεῖνος masculine and not neuter as might be expected
               from τὸ πνεῦμα.

Grammar Summary

1. The *iterative present* describes an on-going action as a series of events.

2. The *gnomic present* describes something that is always true.

3. A word that occurs only once in the New Testament is called a *hapax legomenon* (ἅπαξ λεγόμενον), or simply a *"hapax."*

4. The *intensive perfect* tense places its emphasis on the on-going results of the action.

5. The *immediate past (dramatic) aorist* is the use of the aorist to describe an event that just occurred.

6. A *customary present* describes (1) an event that regularly occurs or (2) an ongoing state.

7. A *transitive* verb is one that takes a direct object. An *intransitive* verb does not take a direct object.

8. The *dative of advantage* is used when the action of the word, which the dative form modifies, is done for the advantage of the word in the dative. When the same construction specifies that an action is done for the disadvantage of something, the dative is called the *dative of disadvantage.*

9. The *gnomic aorist* describes something that is eternally true.

10. Some words are always followed by a genitive and you use the key word *than.* This genitive is called the *genitive of comparison.*

11. Some verbs require two direct objects to make complete sense, and the two objects are called *double accusatives,* indicating a person and a thing or two things.

On Bearing Fruit

John 15:4-5

Introduction

Much of what we learn in life we learn by analogy.

Jesus was a master teacher.

He teaches about Christian maturity and outreach by using an analogy of the relationship between a vine and its branches.

A. Exhortation (v. 4a)

Maintain a relationship of continuing awareness of and fellowship with the person of Christ.

B. Explanation (v. 4b-c)

Note the graciousness of God in explaining why we are to remain in Christ.

1. An obvious truth from nature.
    Branches don't have the power in themselves to bear fruit. They must remain attached to the vine.

2. An obvious corollary in the spiritual realm.
    We cannot bear fruit unless we remain "attached" to Christ.

C. Expansion (v. 5)

1. Vine and branches identified (v. 5a).
    Christ is the vine.
    We are the branches.

2. Believers who bear "much fruit" identified (v. 5b).
    Those who "remain" in Christ.
    (Goes without saying that Christ will "remain" in them.)

Note: NIV makes 5b a conditional sentence. The Greek text merely describes the kind of person who bears fruit.

Conclusion

A warning and an encouragement (v. 5c).

No one can bear fruit unless that person is abiding in Christ.

Corollary: Those who do abide will bear much fruit.

Chapter 3

ΚΑΤΑ ΜΑΡΚΟΝ 1:1-28

Many of the exercises in *The Basics of Biblical Greek* were drawn from the initial chapters of Mark. There are a large number of comments in the *Exegetical Discussion* section for this chapter, but the text is narrative and quite easy. There is no phrasing for this chapter, as it is mostly narrative. Commentary references are to C.F.D. Moule, *The Gospel According to Saint Mark*, in The Cambridge Greek Testament Commentary (Cambridge, 1977).

John the Baptist (1:1-8)

1:1 Ἀρχὴ τοῦ εὐαγγελίου Ἰησοῦ Χριστοῦ [[1]υἱοῦ θεοῦ]. **1:2** Καθὼς

---

[1] The square brackets means there is a question as to whether the enclosed words belong in the text, but the editors agree that they probably do. Sometimes the textual apparatus discusses the manuscript evidence of bracketed words, but sometimes not. See discussion in Moule, 38.

Exegetical Discussion

(1) 1:1 Ἀρχή. Notice the lack of the definite article. This is typical in titles, salutations, and common phrases. Does that give you a hint as to the function of v 1? For a discussion of the relationship of v 1 to the following see Moule, 34-35.

(2) 1:1 εὐαγγελίου. For an interesting word study see Moule, 35-36.

(3) **1:1** * Ἰησοῦ could be either a subjective genitive or an objective genitive. These are extremely important categories to master. If a word is a **subjective genitive**, it is the *subject* of the action implied by the word it is modifying and therefore *produces* the action. It is the gospel that Jesus proclaims. If a word is an **objective genitive**, it is the *object* of the action implied by the word it is modifying and therefore *receives* the action (cf. *Workbook BBG*, 170n5). The gospel proclaims Jesus.

Sometimes it is not an "either/or" situation but a "both/and." Moule comments, "We take it therefore that the basic idea in εὐαγγέλιον here is that of the announcement of good news by Jesus (Ἰησοῦ Χριστοῦ subjective genitive). But Jesus was not only the herald of good tidings; he was also himself the content of the good tidings he announced, as every section of Mark is eloquent to proclaim.... Ἰησοῦ Χριστοῦ is best explained as a subjective genitive; but an objective genitive is in fact implicit here" (36).

γέγραπται ἐν τῷ Ἠσαΐᾳ τῷ προφήτῃ,

Ἰδοὺ ἀποστέλλω τὸν ἄγγελόν[1] μου πρὸ προσώπου σου,

ὃς κατασκευάσει[2] τὴν ὁδόν σου·

1:3   φωνὴ βοῶντος[3] ἐν τῇ ἐρήμῳ,

Ἑτοιμάσατε τὴν ὁδὸν κυρίου,

εὐθείας[4] ποιεῖτε τὰς τρίβους[5] αὐτοῦ.

---

[1]   Note the range of meaning of this word in a lexicon. Which one is correct here?

[2]   κατασκευάζω, *I prepare, make ready; build* (11).

[3]   βοάω, *I break forth and shout; declare* (12). Did you notice that this word cannot be modifying φωνή since it is not the same gender or case? You need to assume something like "a voice *of a person* (ἀθρώπου)" that βοῶντος modifies.

[4]   εὐθύς, εῖα, ύ, genitive έως, *straight* (8). This is not the adverb εὐθύς, meaning *immediately*.

[5]   τρίβος, ου, ἡ, *(beaten) path* (3).

Moule also comments how this common name dropped out of use at the beginning of the second century, "Jews avoiding it out of hatred for Jesus, and Christians avoiding it as a common name out of reverence for him" (37).

(4)   **1:2 ***   γέγραπται. Why is γέγραπται in this tense? Is the emphasis more on the completion of the action or the ongoing effects of the action? How would your translation differ, depending on your answer?

When the perfect emphasizes the inception of the action, it is called an **consummative perfect** and is here translated *has been written*. As we saw in the last chapter (John 15:3), when the perfect emphasizes the ongoing implications of the action, it is called an *intensive perfect*. In this context an intensive perfect would be translated *is written*.

(5)   1:3   φωνή. Why is φωνή nominative?

(6)   1:3   ἐν. Does this prepositional phrase go with the preceding or following? What would be the difference. See Moule, 40.

(7)   1:3   ποιεῖτε. Is ποιεῖτε indicative or imperative? Does the parallel structure of the verse help? ποιέω has a wide range of meaning. Spend some time looking through the options in your lexicon.

1:4 ἐγένετο[1] Ἰωάννης [ὁ] βαπτίζων ἐν τῇ ἐρήμῳ καὶ κηρύσσων

βάπτισμα[2] μετανοίας εἰς[3] ἄφεσιν[4] ἁμαρτιῶν. **1:5**[5] καὶ ἐξεπορεύετο πρὸς αὐτὸν

πᾶσα ἡ Ἰουδαία χώρα καὶ οἱ Ἰεροσολυμῖται[6] πάντες, καὶ ἐβαπτίζοντο ὑπ᾽ αὐτοῦ

ἐν τῷ Ἰορδάνῃ[7] ποταμῷ[8] ἐξομολογούμενοι[9] τὰς ἁμαρτίας αὐτῶν. **1:6** καὶ ἦν ὁ

---

[1]   γίνομαι basically means *to be* (in the sense of existing), or *to come into being*. Most specific usages fall into one of these two basic meanings.

[2]   βάπτισμα, ματος, τό, *baptism* (19).

[3]   One of the meanings of εἰς is *with reference to*.

[4]   ἄφεσις, έσεως, ἡ, *release; pardon, forgiveness* (17).

[5]   It might help you to diagram this sentence. Be sure to identify the subject, main verb, and qualifiers.

[6]   This word is not Ἰεροσόλυμα. It is from Ἰεροσολυμίτης, ου, ὁ, a word occurring only twice in the New Testament meaning *a native of Jerusalem*.

[7]   Ἰορδάνης, ου, ὁ, *Jordan* (15).

[8]   ποταμός, οῦ, ὁ, *river* (17).

[9]   ἐξομολογέω, *I promise*; in the middle, *I confess, admit* (10).

Did you notice the shift in tense between ἑτοιμάσατε and ποιεῖτε? A shift in tense is usually significant, but is it here? Remember the nature of Hebraic poetry and parallelism. Remember that these are not finite verbs, so their only significance is aspect, not time!

(8)   **1:4** *   [ὁ]. If the article is part of the text, the participle is probably attributive and belongs in the subject as a title: "John the Baptizer." If the article is not original, then the participle is **circumstantial** and belongs in the predicate: "John appeared baptizing...." A "circumstantial" participle describes a circumstance that accompanies another event.

(9)   1:4   βάπτισμα μετανοίας. A study on the origin of John's baptism and the significance of requiring God's "chosen" people to be baptized can be fascinating (Moule, 43-44). You should also do a word study on "repentance" (Moule, 44-46).

(10)   1:5   ἐξεπορεύετο. What is the significance of the tense of ἐξεπορεύετο? What picture is it creating in your mind's eye?

(11)   **1:5** *   ἐξομολογούμενοι is a participle of **attendant circumstances**, a strange term that means the participle tells you the circumstances surrounding the action of the verb. You usually must translate this type of participle with a finite verb.

Ἰωάννης <u>ἐνδεδυμένος</u> τρίχας[1] καμήλου[2] καὶ ζώνην[3] δερματίνην[4] περὶ τὴν

ὀσφὺν[5] αὐτοῦ καὶ ἐσθίων ἀκρίδας[6] καὶ μέλι[7] ἄγριον.[8] **1:7** καὶ ἐκήρυσσεν

<u>λέγων</u>, Ἔρχεται ὁ <u>ἰσχυρότερός</u> μου ὀπίσω μου, <u>οὗ</u> οὐκ εἰμὶ ἱκανὸς <u>κύψας</u>[9]

---

[1] θρίξ, τριχός, ἡ, *hair* (15). The θ becomes a τ in every case except dative plural (θρίξι). The Greeks did not like the two θ ... ξ sounds in a row. The stem is actually *θριξ (*MBG*, p. 193n1).

[2] κάμηλος, ου, ὁ and ἡ, *camel* (6).

[3] ζώνη, ης, ἡ, *belt* (8).

[4] δερμάτινος, η, ον, *leather* (2).

[5] ὀσφῦς, ύος, ἡ, *waist* (8).

[6] ἀκρίς, ίδος, ἡ, *locust, grasshopper,* (4).

[7] μέλι, ιτος, τό, *honey* (4).

[8] ἄγριος, ία, ιον, *wild* (3).

[9] κύπτω, *I bend (myself) down* (2).

---

(12)   1:6   ἐνδεδυμένος. Did you notice how Greek can separate the two words in a periphrastic construction with several words? Is there any significance as to how John was dressed? See Moule, 47.

(13)   **1:7** *   λέγων. It is common to find a finite verb that describes some sort of speaking activity followed by λέγων. It is a reflection of a Hebraic idiom. The participle can be translated as an English participle or a finite verb. Check with your teacher. It is called a **redundant participle**.

(14)   **1:7** *   ἰσχυρότερος. Adjectives have a **positive**, **comparative**, and **superlative** form, or what is called its *degree*. Some are formed regularly (e.g., in English, *big, bigger, biggest*), while others modify their stems (e.g., in English, *good, better, best*).

-τερος is added to a Greek adjective to form the comparative degree (e.g., ἰσχυρότερος). In biblical times the superlative form could be used for the comparative, and vice versa. -τατος is added to a Greek adjective to form the superlative degree (e.g., ἁγιώτατος). See *MBG*, pp. 219-21.

Comparative and superlative adjectives that are formed regularly are often not listed in lexicons, so you must look up the normal adjective. ἰσχυρότερός is from ἰσχυρός, which means *strong, mighty, powerful*.

Notice also that the accent from μου has come forward onto ἰσχυρότερός. This is because μου is an **enclitic**, has no accent of its own, and so it "leans back" on the preceding word (*MBG*, §28.23).

(15)   1:7   οὗ. What is the antecedent of οὗ?

λῦσαι τὸν ἱμάντα[1] τῶν ὑποδημάτων[2] αὐτοῦ. **1:8** <u>ἐγὼ</u> ἐβάπτισα ὑμᾶς <u>ὕδατι</u>,

αὐτὸς δὲ βαπτίσει ὑμᾶς <u>ἐν πνεύματι ἁγίῳ</u>.

Jesus' Baptism and Temptation (1:9-13)

1:9 <u>Καὶ ἐγένετο</u> ἐν ἐκείναις ταῖς ἡμέραις ἦλθεν Ἰησοῦς <u>ἀπὸ Ναζαρὲτ</u>[3]

τῆς Γαλιλαίας καὶ ἐβαπτίσθη <u>εἰς</u> τὸν Ἰορδάνην ὑπὸ Ἰωάννου. **1:10**[4] καὶ εὐθὺς

---

[1] ἱμάς, ἱμάντος, ὁ, *strap, thong* (4).

[2] ὑπόδημα, ματος, τό, *sandal* (10).

[3] Ναζαρέτ, *Nazareth* (4). It is indeclinable and has several spellings (cf. *BAGD*, 532).

[4] It would be helpful to diagram this sentence. Find its subject and two direct objects.

---

(16) **1:7** *   κύψας. The aorist (undefined) participle denotes an undefined action occurring before the time described by the main verb. In some cases, even though this **relative time significance** makes sense, it does not make proper sounding English and you can translate with a finite verb (*BBG*, §28.17-18).

Moule (48) cites Rabbi Joshua b. Levi, "All services which a slave does for his master a pupil should do for his teacher, with the exception of undoing his shoes" (*b Ket. 96a*).

(17) **1:8** *   ἐγώ. This verse is a good example of the emphatic use of pronouns to provide contrast. On the relationship between the two baptisms see Moule, 50-51.

(18) **1:8** *   ὕδατι. Is ὕδατι **dative of place** ("in"), or **dative of means** ("by") indicating the means or instrument by which something happens?

(19) **1:8** *   ἐν πνεύματι ἁγίῳ. Note that there is no article in the prepositional phrase ἐν πνεύματι ἁγίῳ. The article frequently drops out in prepositional phrases.

(20) **1:9**   Καὶ ἐγένετο is a common construction in the NT (sixty times) that usually introduces a new topic. It may be a reflection of the similarly common Hebraic וַיְהִי.

(21) **1:9**   ἀπὸ Ναζαρέτ. Does the prepositional phrase ἀπὸ Ναζαρέτ modify ἦλθεν or Ἰησοῦς? How does your decision here affect the theological meaning of the verse?

(22) **1:9**   εἰς. What does εἰς mean in this context? Can it mean *into*? By biblical time, εἰς was taking over the function of ἐν.

ἀναβαίνων ἐκ τοῦ ὕδατος εἶδεν <u>σχιζομένους</u>¹ τοὺς οὐρανοὺς καὶ τὸ πνεῦμα ὡς

περιστερὰν² καταβαῖνον εἰς αὐτόν· **1:11** καὶ φωνὴ ἐγένετο ἐκ τῶν οὐρανῶν, Σὺ

εἶ ὁ υἱός μου ὁ <u>ἀγαπητός</u>, ἐν σοὶ <u>εὐδόκησα</u>.

1:12 Καὶ εὐθὺς τὸ πνεῦμα αὐτὸν <u>ἐκβάλλει</u> εἰς τὴν ἔρημον. **1:13** καὶ ἦν

ἐν τῇ ἐρήμῳ τεσσεράκοντα <u>ἡμέρας</u> <u>πειραζόμενος</u> ὑπὸ τοῦ Σατανᾶ, καὶ ἦν μετὰ

τῶν θηρίων, καὶ οἱ ἄγγελοι <u>διηκόνουν</u> αὐτῷ.

---

¹ σχίζω, *I split, divide* (11).
² περιστερά, ᾶς, ἡ, *dove, pigeon* (10).

---

(23) 1:10   σχιζόμενους. What word is σχιζόμενους modifying? Usually participles come after the word they modify.

(24) 1:11   ἀγαπητός. Why is ἀγαπητός in this case? Is it appositional used as a title or adjectival?

(25) **1:11** *   εὐδόκησα. Can you translate εὐδόκησα as a simple aorist? The context says "No!" If you learned that the main significance of a verb is its temporal meaning (past, present, and future), then you are not going to be able to explain why this verb is in the aorist. Does this mean that God was pleased with Jesus in the past, but not in the present? Even in the indicative mood, the main significance of the Greek verb is its aspect.

It is debatable as to the specific meaning of the aorist here. It could be a **constative aorist**, in which the aorist is used to summarize the totality of Christ's life up to this point–since the aorist looks at the action as a whole–and over all of it God pronounces his pleasure. It could also be a reflection of a Semitic idiom with a stative meaning (cf. Fanning, *Verbal Aspect*, 278).

(26) 1:12   ἐκβάλλει. Did you notice the time shift in ἐκβάλλει from the previous verses? It is an historic present (cf. John 15:27). Moule says this word describes a "strong compulsion" (56). What does he mean?

(27) **1:13** *   ἡμέρας. When Greek wants to specify how long an action occurs, it puts the time designation in the accusative. This is called **accusative of measure**.

The Calling of the Disciples (1:14-20)

1:14 Μετὰ δὲ τὸ <u>παραδοθῆναι</u> τὸν Ἰωάννην ἦλθεν ὁ Ἰησοῦς εἰς τὴν

Γαλιλαίαν <u>κηρύσσων</u> τὸ εὐαγγέλιον τοῦ θεου **1:15** καὶ λέγων <u>ὅτι</u> <u>Πεπλήρωται</u>

ὁ καιρὸς καὶ ἤγγικεν[1] <u>ἡ βασιλεία τοῦ θεοῦ·</u> μετανοεῖτε καὶ πιστεύετε ἐν τῷ

εὐαγγελίῳ.

---

[1] This is an -ιζω verb (cf. *BBG* §20.11 and *MBG* §43.6). Moule (67-68) discusses the difference between "has come" and "has come near."

---

(28) **1:13 *** πειραζόμενος. This is an excellent example illustrating the flexibility of the participle. How is it used here? To name three possibilities, it could be *attendant circumstance,* **purpose** ("in order to be tested"), or *periphrastic* with the preceding ἦν. Is there anything in the context that would help you decide?

(29) **1:13 *** διηκόνουν. The imperfect can be used to describe the beginning of a continuous action. This is called an **inceptive imperfect** (also **inchoative**). You can use the key phrase "begin to" to help carry this nuance into English. This is as opposed to the **durative imperfect**, which is the name we use for the "normal" use of the imperfect to describe continuous past action. Your decision here might help to understand the difference between this verse and Matt 4:11 (cf. Moule, 60).

(30) 1:14 παραδοθῆναι. Is there any theological significance to the fact that παραδοθῆναι is passive? See Moule (62) and the *Exegetical Insight* in *BBG* (207) by J. Ramsey Michaels.

(31) 1:14 κηρύσσων is what type of participle?

(32) **1:15 *** ὅτι can be followed by either *indirect discourse* or *direct discourse* (cf. 1 John 3:2). If it is indirect, translate ὅτι as *that.* If it is direct, use quotations marks. This is called **ὅτι recitativum** (cf. *BDF* §470.1). The capital Π in the next word tells you that the editors of the Greek text think ὅτι is being used with direct discourse.

(33) 1:15 πεπλήρωται. What is the significance of the tense of πεπλήρωται and ἤγγικεν?

(34) 1:15 ἡ βασιλεία τοῦ θεοῦ. Be sure to do a background study on this concept (Moule, 63-67).

1:16 Καὶ <u>παράγων</u>[1] παρὰ τὴν θάλασσαν τῆς Γαλιλαίας εἶδεν Σίμωνα

καὶ Ἀνδρέαν τὸν ἀδελφὸν Σίμωνος ἀμφιβάλλοντας[2] <u>ἐν</u> τῇ θαλάσσῃ· ἦσαν γὰρ

ἁλιεῖς.[3] **1:17** καὶ εἶπεν αὐτοῖς ὁ Ἰησοῦς, Δεῦτε[4] ὀπίσω μου, καὶ ποιήσω ὑμᾶς

γενέσθαι ἁλιεῖς ἀνθρώπων. **1:18** καὶ εὐθὺς ἀφέντες[5] τὰ δίκτυα[6] ἠκολούθησαν[7]

αὐτῷ. **1:19** Καὶ προβὰς[8] ὀλίγον εἶδεν Ἰάκωβον <u>τὸν τοῦ Ζεβεδαίου</u> καὶ Ἰωάννην

τὸν ἀδελφὸν αὐτοῦ <u>καὶ</u> αὐτοὺς ἐν τῷ πλοίῳ καταρτίζοντας[9] τὰ δίκτυα, **1:20** καὶ

---

[1] παράγω, *I pass by* (10).

[2] ἀμφιβάλλω, *I cast (a fishing net)* (1).

[3] ἁλιεύς, έως, ὁ, *fisherman* (5).

[4] δεῦτε, *come!* (12).

[5] This is a participle from ἀφίημι (*MBG*, §93.4). Remember to watch just for ἀφ because sometimes that is all you will recognize.

[6] δίκτυον, ου, τό, *net* (12).

[7] ἀκολουθέω is the only common word (but cf. 1:27) where the "θη" is not a sign of the aorist passive but is part of the verbal stem.

[8] προβαίνω, *I go on, advance* (5). *βα is the stem. What happened to the tense formative (*MBG*, p. 310)?

[9] καταρτίζω, *I restore, prepare, make* (13).

---

(35) 1:16 παράγων. It is considered good Greek style to repeat the preposition after the compound verb (παράγων παρά); it was not seen as redundant.

(36) 1:16 ἐν. In classical Greek ἐν and εἰς had distinctly different meanings, but notice here how their meanings in Koine Greek overlap.

(37) **1:19** * τὸν τοῦ Ζεβεδαίου. Back in v 16 the word following the article in a similar construction was supplied. Here the word after the article has been dropped. What is it? This construction is somewhat common, and you can usually determine which word has been dropped. It is usually υἱόν or ἀδελφόν. τοῦ is called a **genitive of relationship.**

(38) **1:19** * καί. One function of καί is called **epexegetical** (*BDF* §442.9). In this use it means "that is to say," or "namely." If that is the case here, then αὐτοὺς ἐν τῷ πλοίῳ is the same group as previously described (i.e., James and John). If the καί is not epexegetical, then αὐτοὺς ἐν τῷ πλοίῳ describes another group of people, which is the **copulative** use of καί indicating a simple connective.

εὐθὺς <u>ἐκάλεσεν</u> αὐτούς. καὶ ἀφέντες τὸν πατέρα αὐτῶν Ζεβεδαῖον ἐν τῷ πλοίῳ

μετὰ τῶν μισθωτῶν[1] ἀπῆλθον ὀπίσω αὐτοῦ.

An Exorcism (1:21-28)

1:21 Καὶ εἰσπορεύονται[2] εἰς Καφαρναούμ· καὶ εὐθὺς <u>τοῖς σάββασιν</u>

εἰσελθὼν εἰς τὴν συναγωγὴν <u>ἐδίδασκεν</u>. **1:22** καὶ <u>ἐξεπλήσσοντο</u>[3] ἐπὶ τῇ διδαχῇ

αὐτοῦ· ἦν γὰρ διδάσκων αὐτοὺς ὡς ἐξουσίαν ἔχων καὶ οὐχ ὡς οἱ γραμματεῖς.

---

[1] μισθωτός, οῦ, ὁ, *hired help* (3). It is an adjective, but in our literature it is used only as a noun.

[2] εἰσπορεύομαι, *I go (in)* (18).

[3] ἐκπλήσσω, *I amaze;* passive, *am amazed, overwhelmed* (13). For a summary of this reaction to Jesus see Moule, 73.

---

(39) 1:20   ἐκάλεσεν. Notice that the contract vowel in ἐκάλεσεν does not lengthen. Cf. v-1d(2b) in *MBG*.

(40) **1:21** *   τοῖς σάββασιν. When Greek wants to specify *when* an action occurs, it puts the time designation in the dative. This is called the **dative of time (when)**. σάββασιν is normally plural, as are other names of Jewish holidays, but it can also occur as a true plural (Acts 17:2).

(41) **1:21** *   ἐδίδασκεν. What would the different meanings be if ἐδίδασκεν were an *inceptive, iterative,* or *durative* imperfect? An **iterative imperfect** describes a repeated action occurring in the past.

(42) **1:22** *   ἐξεπλήσσοντο. Whenever a compound formed with ἐκ receives an augment, the κ becomes ξ. Actually, it was a ξ to begin with, and was changed to a κ because it was followed by a consonant (*MBG*, §19.3).

What is the significance of the tense?

1:23 καὶ εὐθὺς <u>ἦν</u> ἐν τῇ συναγωγῇ αὐτῶν ἄνθρωπος <u>ἐν</u> <u>πνεύματι</u> ἀκαθάρτῳ καὶ

ἀνέκραξεν[1] **1:24** λέγων, <u>Τί ἡμῖν καὶ σοί</u>, Ἰησοῦ Ναζαρηνέ;[2] ἦλθες <u>ἀπολέσαι</u>

ἡμᾶς; <u>οἶδά</u> σε τίς εἶ, ὁ ἅγιος τοῦ θεοῦ. **1:25** καὶ <u>ἐπετίμησεν</u> αὐτῷ ὁ Ἰησοῦς

λέγων, Φιμώθητι[3] καὶ ἔξελθε ἐξ αὐτοῦ. **1:26**[4] καὶ σπαράξαν[5] αὐτὸν τὸ πνεῦμα

τὸ ἀκάθαρτον καὶ φωνῆσαν φωνῇ μεγάλῃ ἐξῆλθεν ἐξ αὐτοῦ. **1:27** καὶ

---

[1] ἀνακράζω, *I cry out* (5).

[2] Ναζαρηνός, ή, όν is an adjective, used as a masculine noun meaning *Nazarene* (6). What case is it here?

[3] φιμόω, *I muzzle*; passive, *I am silenced* or *silent* (7). You can see the tense formative, but there is no augment.

[4] Locate the subject and verb.

[5] σπαράσσω, *I tear, convulse* (3).

---

(43) **1:23** * ἦν. Sometimes it is easier to insert a "there" before the translation of εἰμί. This is called the **preparatory use of "there."**

(44) 1:23 ἐν. This may sound like an awkward construction. It is a Semitism (Moule, 74). Luke reads, ἔχων.

(45) 1:23 πνεύματι. Moule (75) has an interesting discussion on the idea that some people's "confident certainty" that demons do not exist is in fact the demons' greatest triumph. While demons are defeated they must be taken seriously, as people in ministry often discover soon after leaving school.

(46) 1:24 Τί ἡμῖν καὶ σοί. This awkward construction is an idiom found both in the LXX and Classical Greek literature (Moule, 75).

(47) **1:24** * ἀπολέσαι. This is an **infinitive of purpose**, "in order that." See *BBG* (§32.12) for a discussion of various ways to make a statement of purpose.

(48) 1:24 οἶδα. Did you notice the switch from the plural ἡμῖν to the singular οἶδα? How do you explain this? (Hint: the answer is not grammatical.)

(49) 1:25 ἐπετίμησεν. How strong a word is ἐπετίμησεν? Moule calls it "the divine word of rebuke" (77) and gives some interesting OT background.

ἐθαμβήθησαν[1] ἅπαντες <u>ὥστε</u> συζητεῖν[2] πρὸς ἑαυτοὺς λέγοντας, Τί[3] ἐστιν τοῦτο; διδαχὴ <u>καινὴ</u> κατ᾽ ἐξουσίαν· καὶ[4] τοῖς πνεύμασι τοῖς ἀκαθάρτοις ἐπιτάσσει,[5] καὶ <u>ὑπακούουσιν</u> αὐτῷ. **1:28** καὶ ἐξῆλθεν ἡ ἀκοὴ αὐτοῦ εὐθὺς πανταχοῦ[6] εἰς ὅλην[7] τὴν περίχωρον[8] τῆς Γαλιλαίας.

---

[1] θαμβέω, *I astound, amaze* (3).

[2] συζητέω, *I discuss; dispute, debate* (10).

[3] Should this be "who" or "what"?

[4] Do not translate καί as "and."

[5] ἐπιτάσσω, *I command, order* (10). It takes a direct object in the dative. How "strong" of a command does this word denote?

[6] πανταχοῦ, *everywhere* (7).

[7] This word, like πᾶς, usually occurs before the word it modifies.

[8] περίχωρος, ον, *neighboring*; as a feminine noun, *surrounding region*, (9).

---

(50)   1:27   ὥστε. Did you remember that ὥστε with an infinitive is used to express result (*BBG*, §32.13)? Since we do not have the same idiom in English, you must translate the infinitive as a finite verb.

(51)   1:27   καινή. This passage maintains the classical distinction between καινός meaning "new" in relation to quality, and νέος meaning "new in relation to time. This distinction is not always maintained in Koine Greek.

(52)   **1:27** *   ὑπακούουσιν. Classical Greek strongly adhered to the rule of using a singular verb with a plural neuter subject. In Koine Greek you can also find plural verbs in the same context (Moule, 81).

Grammar Summary

1. If a word is a *subjective genitive*, it is the subject of the action implied by the word it is modifying and therefore produces the action. If a word is an *objective genitive*, it is the object of the action implied by the word it is modifying and therefore receives the action.

2. When the perfect emphasizes the inception of the action, it is called a *consummative perfect*.

3. A *circumstantial participle* describes a circumstance that accompanies another event.

4. The participle of *attendant circumstances* tells you the circumstances surrounding the action of the verb.

5. It is common to find a finite verb that describes some sort of speaking activity followed by λέγων. The participle can be translated as an English participle or a finite verb and is termed a *redundant participle.*

6. Adjectives have a *positive* ("big"), *comparative* ("bigger"; -τερος), and *superlative* ("biggest"; -τατος) form, or what is called its *degree.*

7. An *enclitic* has no accent of its own and "leans back" on the preceding word.

8. The aorist (undefined) participle denotes an undefined action occurring before the time described by the main verb (*relative time* significance).

9. Personal pronouns are often used to state an *emphasis*, normally a contrasting emphasis.

10. The *dative of place* indicates "in" and the *dative of means* indicates the means or instrument by which something happens ("by").

11. The article frequently *drops out in prepositional phrases.*

12. The *constative aorist* summarizes the totality of an event. In English we use the present tense.

13. When Greek wants to specify how long an action occurs, it puts the time designation in the *accusative of measure.*

14. Participles can indicate *purpose* ("in order to").

15. The *inceptive imperfect* (*inchoative*) describes the beginning of a continuous action ("began to").

16. The *durative imperfect* is the usual category for the imperfect, describing continuous past action.

17. ὅτι can be followed by either *indirect discourse* or *direct discourse* (ὅτι *recitativum*).

18. The *genitive of relationship* describes a familial relationship.

19. *Epexegetical* καί is used to further clarify something ("that is to say," "namely").

20. The normal connective use of καί is called the *copulative* use.

21. *Dative of time* specifies when an action occurs.

22. The *iterative imperfect* describes a repeated action occurring in the past.

23. Whenever a compound formed with ἐκ receives an augment, the κ becomes ξ.

24. The *preparatory use of "there"* allows you to insert a "there" before the translation of εἰμί.

25. The *infinitive of purpose* indicates purpose ("in order that").

26. In Koine Greek you can find plural verbs with a plural neuter subject.

Seven "Immediate" Lessons

Mark 1:1-28

Introduction

Papias (about AD 140) indicates that Mark was a close associate of Peter and that the gospel of Mark consists largely of Peter's preaching organized by John Mark. Knowing what we do about Peter's personality, is it any wonder that the Greek word εὐθύς ("immediately") occurs 42 times in Mark alone? Although εὐθύς is occasionally used in a weakened form, it basically carries a sense of urgency and refers to an action that takes place without delay.

Seven lessons from the seven "immediately's" in Mark 1:1-28

1. *When we do what is right, God's approval is immediate.*

   Jesus was baptized and his Father spoke from heaven, declaring his love for him and that he was well pleased with what he had done (vv. 10-11).

2. *Times of testing often follow times of great spiritual blessing.*

   While it was the Spirit who sent Jesus into the desert, Satan seized the opportunity to tempt him to sin (vv. 12-13).

3. *Our response to Jesus' requests must be immediate.*

   Simon and Andrew were at work fishing, but when Jesus said, "Come, follow me," they left their nets immediately and did exactly what he said (vv. 16-18).

4. *The call of God takes priority over all other relationships.*

   James and John were important to their father's fishing business (note: there were also hired men), but when called by Jesus they obeyed without delay (vv. 19-20).

5. *Worshiping God is our number one priority.*

   The first thing Jesus did on the Sabbath was to go to the synagogue (v. 21).

6. *The word of God taught with authority stirs up immediate opposition.*

   When Jesus taught, the evil spirit immediately cried out in opposition (vv. 22-24).

7. *Whenever Jesus is actively at work the news spreads immediately.*

   The entire region of Galilee quickly learned what Jesus had said and done in the synagogue at Capernaum (vv. 27-28).

Conclusion

If God has spoken to you through these texts in a specific way, will you respond "immediately"?

Chapter 4

KATA MAPKON 8:27-9:8

Like the previous chapter, much of this passage is narrative but with a larger theology component. 8:34-38 are good verses to phrase, although hopefully by now you are phrasing the entire passage. Commentary references are to C.F.D. Moule, *The Gospel According to Saint Mark,* in The Cambridge Greek Testament Commentary (Cambridge, 1977).

Peter's Confession (8:27-9:1)

8:27 Καὶ ἐξῆλθεν ὁ Ἰησοῦς καὶ οἱ μαθηταὶ αὐτοῦ εἰς τὰς κώμας

Καισαρείας τῆς Φιλίππου·[1] καὶ ἐν τῇ ὁδῷ ἐπηρώτα τοὺς μαθητὰς αὐτοῦ λέγων

αὐτοῖς, [2]Τίνα με λέγουσιν οἱ ἄνθρωποι εἶναι; **8:28** οἱ δὲ εἶπαν αὐτῷ λέγοντες

---

[1] The city and personal name are the same word.

[2] As written, the following phrase is an indirect question.

Exegetical Discussion

(1) **8:27** * ἐξῆλθεν. If a Greek verb has a compound subject, it is not necessarily plural as it is in English. The verb takes the number of the subject that is closest to it. In this sentence, Ἰησοῦς is singular and is closer to ἐξῆλθεν than is μαθηταί, so the verb is singular.

(2) 8:27 ἐν introduces a dative of time when. The same basic idea could have been expressed with just the dative case, so the preposition is not necessary.

(3) 8:27 ἐπηρώτα is what type of imperfect?

(4) **8:27** * Τίνα με. To understand Τίνα με, you should turn the question into an indirect statement. The same type of construction occurs in v 29.

με is an **accusative subject of the infinitive** (Wallace's phrase; many call it the **accusative of respect/reference**). See discussion in Moule, 268.

(5) **8:28** * οἱ δέ. In the phrase οἱ δέ, the article functions as a personal pronoun.

[ὅτι] Ἰωάννην τὸν βαπτιστήν,[1] καὶ ἄλλοι, Ἠλίαν, ἄλλοι δὲ ὅτι εἷς τῶν

προφητῶν. **8:29** καὶ αὐτὸς ἐπηρώτα αὐτούς, Ὑμεῖς δὲ τίνα με λέγετε εἶναι;

ἀποκριθεὶς ὁ Πέτρος λέγει αὐτῷ, Σὺ εἶ ὁ Χριστός. **8:30** καὶ ἐπετίμησεν αὐτοῖς

ἵνα μηδενὶ λέγωσιν περὶ αὐτοῦ.

8:31 Καὶ ἤρξατο διδάσκειν αὐτοὺς ὅτι δεῖ τὸν υἱὸν τοῦ ἀνθρώπου πολλὰ

παθεῖν καὶ ἀποδοκιμασθῆναι[2] ὑπὸ τῶν πρεσβυτέρων καὶ τῶν ἀρχιερέων καὶ

τῶν γραμματέων καὶ ἀποκτανθῆναι καὶ μετὰ τρεῖς ἡμέρας ἀναστῆναι· **8:32** καὶ

---

[1] βαπτιστής, οῦ, ὁ, *Baptist, baptizer* (12).

[2] ἀποδοκιμάζω, *I reject* (9).

---

(6)   8:28   εἷς. Did you notice that Mark switches from the accusative (Ἰωάννην, Ἠλίαν) to the nominative (εἷς)? The sentence construction changed to a ὅτι clause with an implied verb that requires the nominative. What is the verb?

(7)   **8:28** *   προφητῶν is a **partitive genitive**. The partitive genitive describes the larger group, and the word it modifies specifies a smaller subgroup. εἷς is the subgroup of the larger group προφητῶν.

(8)   8:29   Ὑμεῖς. Grammatically, what has Mark done to put Ὑμεῖς in an emphatic position (Moule, 269)?

(9)   8:29   Χριστός is a good candidate for a word study (Moule, 269-71).

(10)   8:30   ἐπιτιμάω. What is the precise meaning of ἐπιτιμάω? Is it different from τιμάω? How strong a word is it? Is this a request or a strong rebuke? *BAGD* shows that the verb takes a direct object in the dative.

(11)   **8:31** *   ἄρχω is usually followed by a **complementary infinitive**. On complementary infinitives see *BBG* §32.10.

(12)   8:31   δεῖ. Why was Jesus' death necessary? See Moule's discussion of δεῖ (272).

(13)   8:31   τὸν υἱὸν τοῦ ἀνθρώπου. Be sure to do a background study on this phrase (Moule, 272-77).

(14)   8:31   πολλά. As a neuter plural, πολλύς can function adverbially or adjectivally. What would the difference be here?

παρρησίᾳ τὸν λόγον ἐλάλει. καὶ προσλαβόμενος[1] ὁ <u>Πέτρος</u> αὐτὸν ἤρξατο

ἐπιτιμᾶν αὐτῷ. **8:33** ὁ δὲ ἐπιστραφεὶς[2] καὶ ἰδὼν τοὺς μαθητὰς αὐτοῦ <u>ἐπετίμησεν</u>

Πέτρῳ καὶ <u>λέγει</u>, Ὕπαγε ὀπίσω μου, Σατανᾶ, ὅτι οὐ <u>φρονεῖς</u> τὰ[3] τοῦ θεοῦ ἀλλὰ

τὰ τῶν ἀνθρώπων. **8:34** Καὶ προσκαλεσάμενος τὸν ὄχλον σὺν τοῖς μαθηταῖς

αὐτοῦ εἶπεν αὐτοῖς, Εἴ τις θέλει ὀπίσω μου ἀκολουθεῖν, <u>ἀπαρνησάσθω</u>[4] ἑαυτὸν

---

[1]   προσλαμβάνω, active: *I take*; middle: *I take aside* (12).

[2]   ἐπιστρέφω, in the middle and passive, means *I turn around*, which is basically the
      same as its meaning in the active. The α should tell you what tense the word is
      in (*MBG* §95.1).

[3]   τά is not the same case as the following τοῦ θεοῦ. The article is being used sub-
      stantively, not as a modifier. Moule says τά τινος φρονεῖν is an idiom meaning
      to take someone's side, espouse someone's cause (281).

[4]   ἀπαρνέομαι, *I deny* (11).

---

(15)   8:32   Πέτρος. It is common for a New Testament writer to place the subject
               of the sentence inside an adverbial participial clause (προσλαβόμενος
               ... αὐτόν). Do not be confused and think that the noun is part of the
               clause; a participle cannot take a subject.

(16)   8:33   ἐπετίμησεν. Have you noticed how this word helps to tie the discussion
               together? Remember, Scripture is also literature and uses literary
               devices. See Moule, 279 and v 30.

(17)   **8:33** *   λέγει is a **historical present**, in which the present tense is used to por-
               tray a past event vividly. We have the same idiom in English.

(18)   8:33   φρονεῖς. There are different words meaning *to think* in Greek; what is
               the specific nuance of φρονέω?

(19)   **8:34** *   ἀπαρνησάσθω. Did you notice the tense shifts in the three imperatives
               in this verse (ἀπαρνησάσθω ... ἀράτω ... ἀκολουθείτω)? Since they are
               nonindicative verb forms, their aspect must be important.

               In Luke's account (9:23), the aorist ἀράτω is joined with καθ᾽ ἡμέραν to
               show that the action is to be done "daily." How does this affect your
               understanding of the aorist tense in general? This is an extremely
               important issue to understand, and do not go on until you can explain
               grammatically why an aorist verb can describe a daily action. Cf *BBG*
               §15.6-7.

καὶ <u>ἀράτω</u> τὸν σταυρὸν αὐτοῦ καὶ ἀκολουθείτω μοι. **8:35** ὃς γὰρ ἐὰν[1] θέλῃ τὴν

ψυχὴν αὐτοῦ σῶσαι ἀπολέσει[2] αὐτήν· ὃς δ' ἂν ἀπολέσει τὴν ψυχὴν αὐτοῦ

ἕνεκεν ἐμοῦ καὶ τοῦ εὐαγγελίου σώσει αὐτήν. **8:36** τί γὰρ ὠφελεῖ[3] ἄνθρωπον

κερδῆσαι[4] τὸν κόσμον ὅλον[5] καὶ ζημιωθῆναι[6] τὴν ψυχὴν αὐτοῦ; **8:37** τί γὰρ

<u>δοῖ</u>[7] ἄνθρωπος ἀντάλλαγμα[8] τῆς ψυχῆς αὐτοῦ; **8:38** ὃς γὰρ ἐὰν ἐπαισχυνθῇ[9]

με καὶ τοὺς ἐμοὺς λόγους ἐν τῇ γενεᾷ ταύτῃ τῇ μοιχαλίδι[10] καὶ ἁμαρτωλῷ,[11]

καὶ ὁ υἱὸς τοῦ ἀνθρώπου ἐπαισχυνθήσεται αὐτόν, ὅταν ἔλθῃ ἐν τῇ δόξῃ τοῦ

πατρὸς αὐτοῦ μετὰ τῶν ἀγγέλων τῶν ἁγίων. **9:1** Καὶ ἔλεγεν αὐτοῖς, Ἀμὴν λέγω

---

[1]   γάρ comes between ὅς and ἐάν because it is a postpositive, but this does not mean that the meaning of ὅς ἐάν has changed.

[2]   The future form of ἀπόλλυμι. The double lambda occurs only in the present tense (*MBG*, cv-3c[2]; p. 309).

[3]   ὠφελέω, *I help, benefit, am of use (to)* (15).

[4]   κερδαίνω, *I gain* (17).

[5]   ὅλος always is in the predicate position when it modifies a word.

[6]   ζημιόω, *I suffer damage* or *loss, am punished* (6). The verb is always passive in form in our literature but active in meaning.

[7]   The verbal root of this verb is *δο. It is a second aorist active subjunctive form. It is the uncontracted form of δῷ (*MBG* §52.4). See the textual variants in your Greek Bible.

[8]   ἀντάλλαγμα, ατος, τό, *something given in exchange* (2).

[9]   ἐπαισχύνομαι, *I am ashamed* (11).

[10]   μοιχαλίς, ίδος, ἡ, *adulteress* (7).

[11]   This is not a noun.

---

(20)   8:34   ἀράτω. What does it actually mean to "take up one's cross"? See Moule, 282.

(21)   **8:37** *   δοῖ is a **deliberative subjunctive**. This means that there is some uncertainty on the part of the speaker as to the answer. (In this context, Jesus is speaking on someone else's behalf.) See *BBG* §31.13.

(22)   9:1   V 1. On this verse as a whole see Moule, 285-89. Is he right in seeing the Transfiguration as the fulfillment of the prophecy?

ὑμῖν ὅτι εἰσίν τινες ὧδε τῶν <u>ἐστηκότων</u> οἵτινες <u>οὐ μὴ γεύσωνται</u>[1] θανάτου ἕως

ἂν ἴδωσιν τὴν βασιλείαν τοῦ θεοῦ ἐληλυθυῖαν[2] ἐν δυνάμει.

Transfiguration (9:2-8)

9:2 Καὶ μετὰ ἡμέρας ἕξ[3] παραλαμβάνει ὁ Ἰησοῦς τὸν Πέτρον καὶ τὸν

Ἰάκωβον καὶ τὸν Ἰωάννην καὶ ἀναφέρει[4] αὐτοὺς εἰς ὄρος ὑψηλὸν[5] <u>κατ᾽ ἰδίαν</u>

μόνους. καὶ μετεμορφώθη[6] ἔμπροσθεν αὐτῶν, **9:3** καὶ τὰ ἱμάτια αὐτοῦ ἐγένετο

στίλβοντα[7] λευκὰ λίαν,[8] οἷα[9] γναφεὺς[10] ἐπὶ τῆς γῆς οὐ δύναται οὕτως

λευκᾶναι.[11] **9:4** καὶ ὤφθη αὐτοῖς Ἡλίας σὺν Μωϋσεῖ καὶ ἦσαν

---

[1] γεύομαι, *I taste, enjoy; come to know* (15). It is followed by the genitive or accusative of the thing tasted.

[2] This is a participle (*MBG* §94.1).

[3] ἕξ, *six* (indeclinable; 13).

[4] ἀναφέρω, *I bring/take up* (10).

[5] ὑψηλός, ή, όν, *high* (11).

[6] μεταμορφόω, *I transform, change in form* (4).

[7] στίλβω, *I shine* (1).

[8] λίαν, *very (much), exceedingly.* An adverb also used with verbs and adjectives (12).

[9] οἷος, α, ον, *of what sort, (such) as* (relative pronoun; 14).

[10] γναφεύς, έως, ὁ, *bleacher, fuller* (1). A person who cleans woolen cloth.

[11] λευκαίνω, *I make white* (2).

---

(23) 9:1   ἐστηκότων is what type of genitive (cf. 8:28)?

(24) **9:1** * οὐ μὴ γεύσωνται. How strongly is the negation οὐ μὴ γεύσωνται worded? Cf. *BBG* §33.15. In Wallace it is discussed under **Subjunctive/Emphatic negation.**

(25) 9:2   κατ᾽ ἰδίαν is an idiom meaning *privately* (*BAGD*, #4).

συλλαλοῦντες[1] τῷ Ἰησοῦ. **9:5** καὶ ἀποκριθεὶς ὁ Πέτρος λέγει τῷ Ἰησοῦ, Ῥαββί,[2]

καλόν ἐστιν ἡμᾶς ὧδε εἶναι, καὶ ποιήσωμεν τρεῖς σκηνάς, σοὶ μίαν καὶ Μωϋσεῖ

μίαν καὶ Ἠλίᾳ μίαν. **9:6** οὐ γὰρ ᾔδει[3] τί ἀποκριθῇ, ἔκφοβοι[4] γὰρ ἐγένοντο.

9:7 καὶ ἐγένετο νεφέλη ἐπισκιάζουσα[5] αὐτοῖς, καὶ ἐγένετο φωνὴ ἐκ τῆς νεφέλης,

Οὗτός ἐστιν ὁ υἱός μου ὁ ἀγαπητός, ἀκούετε αὐτοῦ. **9:8** καὶ ἐξάπινα[6]

περιβλεψάμενοι[7] οὐκέτι οὐδένα εἶδον ἀλλὰ τὸν Ἰησοῦν μόνον μεθ' ἑαυτῶν.

---

[1] συλλαλέω, *I talk/discuss with* (6).

[2] Ῥαββί, *rabbi* (indeclinable; 15).

[3] ᾔδει is actually the pluperfect of οἶδα, which is really a perfect. ᾔδει functions as an aorist (*MBG*, p. 263).

[4] ἔκφοβος, ον, *terrified* (2). ἐκ can be an intensifier. The disciples were not just frightened; they were terrified. See the *Exegetical Discussion* below.

[5] ἐπισκιάζω, *I overshadow; cover* (5).

[6] ἐξάπινα, *suddenly, unexpectedly* (1).

[7] περιβλέπω, *I look around; look for, hunt* (7).

---

(26)   9:4   συλλαλέω is a compound verb formed from σύν and λαλέω. Remember that when ν and λ occur together, the ν becomes λ (cf. *MBG* §24.7).

(27)   9:5 *   ποιήσωμεν is a hortatory subjunctive, the subjunctive used as an exhortation, "Let us ..." (*BBG* §31.12).

(28)   **9:6** *   ἔκφοβοι. This is called the **perfective** use of the preposition in which the preposition intensifies the action of the verb/noun to which it is attached (ἐκ + φόβος). It is what turns "eat" (ἐσθίω) into "devour" (κατεσθίω). Bruce Metzger lists ἀπό, διά, ἐκ, κατά, and σύν as all being capable of having this meaning (*Lexical Aids for Students of New Testament Greek* [Theological Book Agency (Princeton, New Jersey: 1973) pp. 81-85]). You cannot always assume in Koine Greek that the author intends the force of the perfective preposition. Is it intended in ἐπιτιμάω in 8:30?

(29)   9:7   νεφέλη. See Moule (292) for the OT significance of the cloud.

Grammar Summary

1. If a Greek verb has a *compound subject,* it is not necessarily plural as it is in English. The verb takes the number of the subject that is closest to it.

2. Wallace uses the phrase *accusative subject of the infinitive* to describe the word in the accusative functioning as if it were the subject of the infinitive. Others call it the *accusative of respect/reference.*

3. In the phrase οἱ δέ, the article functions as a personal pronoun.

4. The *partitive genitive* describes the larger group, and the word it is linked with specifies a smaller subgroup.

5. Certain verbs are followed by a *complementary infinitive,* which completes the thought of the infinitive.

6. The *historical present* portrays a past event vividly.

7. How can an aorist be used to describe an ongoing action?

8. A *deliberative subjunctive* is used when the speaker asks a question that requires deliberation, when there is some uncertainty as to the answer.

9. The aorist subjunctive is used with οὐ μη to make an *emphatic negation.*

10. A *hortatory subjunctive* is used to state an exhortation, "Let us ...."

11. Certain prepositions (ἀπό, διά, ἐκ, κατά, σύν) can be added to words to make the word emphatic. This is called the *perfective* use.

The Price of Discipleship

Mark 8:34-38

Introduction

The Christian faith is not psychological insights into successful living. It calls for unconditional surrender to Jesus Christ. To "follow" Christ means to become his disciple.

A. What it takes to be a disciple of Christ (v. 34)

1. "Deny" yourself
   Not deny yourself things but give up all right to yourself.
2. Take up your cross
   Die to your own desires and ambitions.
3. Follow Christ
   He gave himself without reserve for the benefit of others.

B. The ultimate paradox (v. 35)

1. *Save* your life (=live for yourself)
   Result: You will lose your life (fail to experience what life is all about and sacrifice eternal life)
2. *Lose* your life (=live for the benefit of others)
   Result: You will save your life (experience the real meaning of life now and enter into life eternal)

C. Two questions with obvious answers (vv. 36-37)

1. What advantage would there be in getting everything the world has to offer if it cost you your soul? (No advantage!)
2. For what would you exchange your soul? (There is nothing!)

D. The consequence of refusing discipleship (v. 38)

To be "ashamed" of Christ and his words in this context means to decide against following him and acknowledging his lordship before others.

The consequence of not acknowledging him in this sinful world is that he will not acknowledge you when he returns in glory.

Conclusion

The decision to follow or not to follow Christ has eternal consequences. Granted, the latter is too terrible to contemplate. But the former is almost too glorious to comprehend. Jesus is saying to you, "Follow me." What is your response?

Chapter 5

ΠΡΟΣ ΚΟΛΟΣΣΑΕΙΣ 1:1-23

Colossians 1 is a great passage for studying Paul's writing style and the connection of his thoughts. Concentrate especially on the precise meanings of the prepositions and the participles. Do not be content merely using the generic meaning of the preposition or the "-ing" translation of the participle.

Be sure to spend time working on your phrasing and you will see again why this discipline is vital for exegesis. We recommend that you phrase the entire passage. If you can only do a smaller amount of text, phrase either vv 3-8 or vv 9-12.

Commentary references are to Peter T. O'Brien, *Colossians, Philemon*, in Word Biblical Commentary (Word, 1982). See also Murray Harris, *Colossians & Philemon*, in Exegetical Guide of the Greek New Testament (Eerdmans, 1991).

Salutation (1:1-2)

1:1 Παῦλος ἀπόστολος Χριστοῦ Ἰησοῦ διὰ θελήματος θεοῦ καὶ

Τιμόθεος ὁ ἀδελφὸς **1:2** τοῖς ἐν Κολοσσαῖς[1] ἁγίοις <u>καὶ</u> πιστοῖς ἀδελφοῖς ἐν

Χριστῷ, <u>χάρις</u> ὑμῖν καὶ <u>εἰρήνη</u> ἀπὸ θεοῦ πατρὸς ἡμῶν.

---

[1] Κολοσσαῖ, ῶν, αἱ, *Colossae* (1).

Exegetical Discussion

(1) 1:2 καί. The question is whether Paul is addressing one or two groups of people. It is possible that καί is copulative and Paul is addressing two groups: "To the saints in Colossae and the faithful brothers in Christ." It is also possible that καί is epexegetical and Paul is addressing one group of people: "To the saints in Colossae, namely, the faithful brothers in Christ." Which do you think is correct? See O'Brien, 3.

(2) 1:2 χάρις is a good word on which to do a word study (O'Brien, 4-5).

(3) 1:2 εἰρήνη is another good word on which to do a word study (O'Brien, 5-6). Note especially the role of the LXX in defining the word.

Thanksgiving (1:3-8)

<u>1:3</u> Εὐχαριστοῦμεν τῷ θεῷ πατρὶ τοῦ κυρίου ἡμῶν Ἰησοῦ Χριστοῦ

<u>πάντοτε</u> περὶ ὑμῶν προσευχόμενοι, **1:4** <u>ἀκούσαντες</u> τὴν πίστιν ὑμῶν ἐν Χριστῷ

Ἰησοῦ καὶ τὴν ἀγάπην ἣν ἔχετε εἰς πάντας τοὺς ἁγίους **1:5** διὰ τὴν <u>ἐλπίδα</u> τὴν

<u>ἀποκειμένην</u>[1] ὑμῖν ἐν τοῖς <u>οὐρανοῖς,</u> ἣν προηκούσατε[2] ἐν τῷ λόγῳ τῆς

---

[1] ἀπόκειμαι, *I put away, stored up* (4).
[2] προακούω, *I hear beforehand* (1).

---

(4)   **1:3** *   Vv 3-8 form one sentence. It will be helpful to phrase the basic structure of the verses.

(5)   1:3   πάντοτε. Does πάντοτε modify the preceding verb or the following participle?

(6)   1:4   ἀκούσαντες. What is/are the direct object(s) of ἀκούσαντες? What kind of participle is it?

(7)   1:5   ἐλπίδα is a great word for a word study. It is a good example of how the English equivalent is significantly different from the Greek (O'Brien, 11-12).

(8)   1:5   ἀποκειμένην. How does the aspect of ἀποκειμένην affect the meaning of the verse?

(9)   1:5   οὐρανοῖς. Because of the Hebrew idiom, we usually see οὐρανοῖς in the plural, but sometimes in the singular. It should always be translated in the singular unless the speaker is thinking of multiple heavens, such as in 2 Corinthians 12:2.

ἀληθείας[1] τοῦ εὐαγγελίου **1:6** τοῦ παρόντος[2] εἰς ὑμᾶς, καθὼς καὶ ἐν παντὶ τῷ

κόσμῳ ἐστὶν καρποφορούμενον[3] καὶ αὐξανόμενον καθὼς καὶ ἐν ὑμῖν, ἀφ᾽ ἧς

ἡμέρας[4] ἠκούσατε καὶ ἐπέγνωτε[5] τὴν χάριν τοῦ θεοῦ ἐν ἀληθείᾳ· **1:7** καθὼς

ἐμάθετε ἀπὸ Ἐπαφρᾶ[6] τοῦ ἀγαπητοῦ συνδούλου[7] ἡμῶν, ὅς ἐστιν πιστὸς[8] ὑπὲρ

ὑμῶν διάκονος τοῦ Χριστοῦ, **1:8** ὁ καὶ δηλώσας[9] ἡμῖν τὴν ὑμῶν ἀγάπην ἐν

πνεύματι.

---

[1] This is most likely an **Hebraic genitive**. (Wallace lists it under the **Attributive genitive.**) It is the use of a noun to function as an adjective. Instead of saying the "truthful word," in Hebrew you say the "word of truth," and that idiomatic way of speaking can come directly into Greek.

[2] This is a compound verb. Recognizing the verbal morpheme οντος should help you see what the verbal part of the compound is. It looks like you have just the prepositional part of the compound verb, and the verbal part looks just like the participle morpheme.

[3] καρποφορέω, *I bear fruit* or *crops* (8).

[4] ἀφ᾽ ἧς ἡμέρας is a rather awkward construction. *BAGD* say that it is a shortened form of ἀπὸ τῆς ἡμέρας, ᾗ. The antecedent of the relative pronoun actually comes after it. The same construction occurs in v. 9.

[5] This is a compound verb with the verbal root of *γνο.

[6] Ἐπαφρᾶς, ᾶ, ὁ, *Epaphras* (3). It is a partially declined noun. See *MBG*, n-1e.

[7] σύνδουλος, ου, ὁ, *fellow-slave/servant* (10).

[8] πιστός is a second declension adjective. Do not confuse it with πίστις, a third declension noun.

[9] δηλόω, *I show* (7).

---

(10) 1:5   εὐαγγελίου. What is the specific relationship between εὐαγγελίου and ἀληθείας?

(11) 1:6   παντί. In what sense is this true? Is Paul saying that every single individual has heard the gospel? What are the theological ramifications of your answer? See O'Brien, 13, and v 23.

(12) **1:6** *   ἐπέγνωτε. This could be an **inceptive aorist** (also called **ingressive**), which emphasizes the beginning of the action. You can use the key phrase "began to" to bring out its significance.

How much difference, if any, is there between ἐπέγνωτε and the simple γινώσκω? What would be the different meanings and how would it affect your exegesis? Its noun cognate appears again in v. 9.

Prayer (1:9-14)

<u>**1:9**</u> Διὰ τοῦτο καὶ ἡμεῖς, ἀφ᾽ ἧς ἡμέρας ἠκούσαμεν, οὐ <u>παυόμεθα</u>[1] ὑπὲρ

ὑμῶν <u>προσευχόμενοι</u>[2] καὶ <u>αἰτούμενοι</u>, <u>ἵνα</u>[3] <u>πληρωθῆτε</u> τὴν <u>ἐπίγνωσιν</u> τοῦ

θελήματος αὐτοῦ ἐν πάσῃ σοφίᾳ καὶ συνέσει[4] πνευματικῇ, **1:10** <u>περιπατῆσαι</u>

<u>ἀξίως</u>[5] τοῦ κυρίου εἰς πᾶσαν <u>ἀρεσκείαν</u>,[6] ἐν παντὶ ἔργῳ ἀγαθῷ

---

[1] παύω, active: *I stop, cause to cease;* middle: *I stop* (myself), *cease* (15).

[2] προσευχόμενοι takes the case of the word it is modifying, even though the word is assumed in the verb. What is it modifying?

[3] Your phrasing at this point becomes very important. What is the relationship among πληρωθῆτε (v 9), περιπατῆσαι (v 10a), καρποφοροῦντες, αὐξανόμενοι, and δυναμούμενοι (vv 10b-11), and εὐχαριστοῦντες (v 12)?

[4] σύνεσις, εως, ἡ, *intelligence; understanding* (7).

[5] ἀξίως, *worthily* (6). With the genitive of the person following.

[6] ἀρεσκεία, ας, ἡ, *willing service, desire to please* (1). It is usually used in the bad sense of *obsequiousness.*

---

(13)   **1:9** *   V 9. Phrase the basic structure of vv 9-12 and see how they relate to vv 13-14. See O'Brien, 19-20.

(14)   1:9   παυόμεθα. What is the meaning of παυόμεθα in the middle? See *BBG,* p. 225n15.

(15)   1:9   αἰτούμενοι. Is αἰτούμενοι a middle or passive? What is its significance?

(16)   1:9   πληρωθῆτε. What is the theological significance of the passive?

(17)   **1:9** *   ἐπίγνωσιν is an **accusative of respect** (also **reference**). It limits the force of the verb (which is passive and cannot have a direct object here). You can use the key phrase *with respect to* or in this case *with.*

      Does this prayer square with your own experience? What is the role of knowledge in your own spiritual growth, and how does knowledge relate to wisdom and to application?

(18)   1:10   περιπατῆσαι is what type of infinitive? Do not just translate it with "to." What does it modify?

καρποφοροῦντες καὶ αὐξανόμενοι τῇ ἐπιγνώσει τοῦ θεοῦ, **1:11** ἐν πάσῃ δυνάμει

δυναμούμενοι[1] κατὰ τὸ κράτος[2] τῆς δόξης αὐτοῦ εἰς πᾶσαν ὑπομονὴν καὶ

μακροθυμίαν.[3] μετὰ χαρᾶς **1:12** εὐχαριστοῦντες τῷ πατρὶ τῷ ἱκανώσαντι[4] ὑμᾶς

εἰς τὴν μερίδα[5] τοῦ κλήρου[6] τῶν ἁγίων ἐν τῷ φωτί· **1:13** ὃς ἐρρύσατο[7] ἡμᾶς ἐκ

---

[1] δυναμόω, *I strengthen* (2).

[2] κράτος, ους, τό, *power, might* (12).

[3] μακροθυμία, ας, ἡ, *patience, steadfastness, endurance* (14).

[4] ἱκανόω, *I make sufficient* (2). How does τῷ ἱκανώσαντι function?

[5] μερίς, μερίδος, ἡ, *part; portion* (5).

[6] κλῆρος, ου, ὁ, *lot; portion, share* (i.e., that which is assigned by lot; 11).

[7] ῥύομαι, *I save, rescue* (17). Verbs beginning with ρ often duplicate the ρ when they augment (*MBG* §31.2b).

---

(19) 1:10   καρποφοροῦντες. What kind of participles are καρποφοροῦντες and αὐξανόμενοι? O'Brien has a good discussion of the relationship of the words (23).

(20) 1·10   αὐξανόμενοι can be middle or passive. How does this affect the meaning of the verse?

(21) **1:10** *   ἐπιγνώσει is a **dative of reference** (also **respect**). You can use the key phrase *with respect to*. Notice how the textual variants suggest this meaning.

(22) 1:11   ἐν carries what precise meaning?

(23) 1:11   δόξης is what type of genitive?

(24) 1:11   μακροθυμίαν. Do a word study of μακροθυμία, paying special attention to its use in the LXX (O'Brien, 24-25).

(25) 1:11   μετά. Does the prepositional phrase μετὰ χαρᾶς go with the preceding or following? Remember, punctuation was not part of the original text.

(26) 1:12   εὐχαριστοῦντες. The period after the earlier μακροθυμίαν is puzzling. If μετά begins a new sentence, there is no finite verb that can be the main verb. This forces the participle εὐχαριστοῦντες to be an "independent participle," an unusual construction. If you replace the period with a comma, as do the *NIV* and the *NRSV*, what does εὐχαριστοῦντες modify?

(27) 1:12   ἁγίων. Does ἁγίων refer to angels or saints? See O'Brien, 26-27.

τῆς ἐξουσίας τοῦ σκότους καὶ μετέστησεν[1] εἰς τὴν βασιλείαν τοῦ υἱοῦ τῆς

<u>ἀγάπης</u> αὐτοῦ, **1:14** ἐν <u>ᾧ</u> <u>ἔχομεν</u> τὴν ἀπολύτρωσιν,[2] τὴν <u>ἄφεσιν</u>[3] τῶν ἁμαρτιῶν·

Christ (1:15-20)

1:15 ὅς ἐστιν εἰκὼν τοῦ θεοῦ τοῦ <u>ἀοράτου</u>,[4] <u>πρωτότοκος</u>[5] πάσης

κτίσεως,[6] **1:16** ὅτι ἐν[7] αὐτῷ <u>ἐκτίσθη</u>[8] τὰ πάντα ἐν τοῖς οὐρανοῖς καὶ ἐπὶ τῆς γῆς,

---

[1] μεθίστημι, *I change, remove* (5). You must assume a direct object from elsewhere in the verse.

[2] ἀπολύτρωσις, εως, ἡ, *release, redemption* (10).

[3] ἄφεσις, ἀφέσεως, ἡ, *release, pardon, forgiveness* (17).

[4] ἀόρατος, ον, *unseen, invisible* (5).

[5] πρωτότοκος, ον, *firstborn* (8).

[6] κτίσις, εως, ἡ, *creation* (19).

[7] Did you notice that ἐν here could not be translated with the usual "in." Always check your translation of prepositions carefully, that they make sense in each particular context. Always ask yourself, what precisely does this preposition mean.

[8] κτίζω, *I create* (15).

---

(28) 1:13 ἀγάπης is what type of genitive?

(29) 1:14 ᾧ. Identify the antecedent of ᾧ. There has been a shift in subject.

(30) 1:14 ἔχομεν. Did you notice that the preceding three verbs are aorists and here Paul shifts to the present? What is the significance of the aorist and of the tense shift? See O'Brien, 26.

(31) 1:14 ἄφεσιν. What is the relationship between ἀπολύτρωσιν and ἄφεσιν? How does this affect your theology?

(32) **1:15** * ἀοράτου. English uses the prefixes "ir" and "un" to negate a word. Greek uses α. This is called the **alpha privative**. Normally, when the word begins with a vowel, Greek uses ἀν. However, here the ν is omitted, perhaps because ὁρατός begins with a rough breathing.

(33) **1:15** * πρωτότοκος. What case is πρωτότοκος and why? By saying that Christ was the "firstborn," does this mean he was created? See O'Brien, 44-45.

(34) 1:16 ἐκτίσθη. Who is doing the creating, and how does this affect your understanding of Genesis 1?

τὰ ὁρατὰ[1] καὶ τὰ ἀόρατα, εἴτε θρόνοι εἴτε κυριότητες[2] εἴτε ἀρχαὶ εἴτε ἐξουσίαι·

τὰ πάντα δι᾽ αὐτοῦ καὶ εἰς[3] αὐτὸν ἔκτισται·[4] **1:17** καὶ αὐτός ἐστιν πρὸ <u>πάντων</u>

καὶ τὰ πάντα ἐν αὐτῷ συνέστηκεν,[5] **1:18** καὶ αὐτός ἐστιν ἡ κεφαλὴ τοῦ σώματος

τῆς <u>ἐκκλησίας</u>· ὅς ἐστιν ἀρχή, πρωτότοκος ἐκ τῶν νεκρῶν, ἵνα γένηται[6] ἐν

πᾶσιν αὐτὸς πρωτεύων,[7] **1:19** ὅτι ἐν αὐτῷ εὐδόκησεν πᾶν τὸ <u>πλήρωμα</u>[8]

<u>κατοικῆσαι</u> **1:20** καὶ δι᾽ αὐτοῦ ἀποκαταλλάξαι[9] τὰ πάντα εἰς αὐτόν,

---

[1] ὁρατός, ή, όν, *visible* (1).

[2] κυριότης, ητος, ἡ, *lordship, dominion* (4). "The essential nature of the κύριος, esp. the majestic power."

[3] εἰς here denotes "goal," and you translate it as "for."

[4] Parse this form carefully. What are some of the clues? (1) There is no connecting vowel. That should tell you right away what it is. (2) There is vocalic reduplication. (3) What is that sigma doing there? It is a v-2a(1) verb.

Did you also notice the shift in tense from the preceding occurrence of the same word? What is the significance, if any?

[5] συνίστημι, transitive: *I bring together*; intransitive: *I consist, continue, exist*. The intransitive occurs only in the present middle and the perfect active.

[6] Remember that this verb takes a predicate nominative and not a direct object.

[7] πρωτεύω, *I am preeminent* (1).

[8] πλήρωμα, ατος, τό, *fullness, fulfillment* (17).

[9] ἀποκαταλλάσσω, *I reconcile* (3). Does this compound form have any difference in meaning from the simple καταλλάσσω?

---

(35) 1:17   πάντων. What is this word's gender, and how does your answer affect your interpretation of the verse?

(36) 1:18   ἐκκλησίας. What is the relationship of ἐκκλησίας to σώματος? For a word study see O'Brien, 57-61.

(37) 1:19   πλήρωμα. Fullness of what? See O'Brien, 51-53.

(38) 1:19   κατοικῆσαι. To what does κατοικῆσαι and the following infinitive ἀποκαταλλάξαι refer? What type of infinitives are they?

εἰρηνοποιήσας¹ διὰ τοῦ αἵματος τοῦ σταυροῦ αὐτοῦ, [δι᾽ αὐτοῦ] εἴτε τὰ ἐπὶ τῆς

γῆς εἴτε τὰ ἐν τοῖς οὐρανοῖς.

Reconciliation (1:21-23)

1:21 Καὶ ὑμᾶς ποτε ὄντας ἀπηλλοτριωμένους² καὶ ἐχθροὺς τῇ διανοίᾳ³

ἐν τοῖς ἔργοις τοῖς πονηροῖς, **1:22** νυνὶ δὲ ἀποκατήλλαξεν ἐν τῷ σώματι τῆς

<u>σαρκὸς</u> αὐτοῦ διὰ τοῦ θανάτου <u>παραστῆσαι</u> ὑμᾶς ἁγίους καὶ ἀμώμους⁴ καὶ

ἀνεγκλήτους⁵ κατενώπιον⁶ αὐτοῦ, **1:23** <u>εἴ</u> γε <u>ἐπιμένετε</u>⁷ τῇ πίστει

---

1 εἰρηνοποιέω, *I make peace* (1).

2 ἀπαλλοτριόω, *I estrange, alienate* (3). There is vocalic reduplication, no connecting vowel, the participle morpheme, but no tense formative. This can only be one tense and voice.

3 διάνοια, ας, ἡ, *understanding, intelligence, mind* (12).

4 ἄμωμος, ον, *unblemished, blameless* (8).

5 ἀνέγκλητος, ον, *blameless, irreproachable* (5).

6 κατενώπιον, *before, in the presence of* (3). An improper preposition with the genitive. In our literature it is always used in relation to God.

7 ἐπιμένω, *I stay, remain; persevere* (16).

---

(39) 1:21 V 21. Be sure to locate the basic parts of this sentence, the subject and verb, and then locate the basic modifying clauses.

(40) 1:22 σαρκός is what type of genitive?

(41) 1:22 παραστῆσαι. What type of infinitive is παραστῆσαι? What does it modify? It takes a double accusative.

(42) **1:23** * εἴ. What does εἴ signify? What is the relationship between vv 21-22 and v 23? O'Brien comments, "But continuance is the test of reality. If it is true that the saints *will* persevere to the end, then it is equally true that the saints *must* persevere to the end. And one of the means which the apostle uses to insure that his readers within the various congregations of his apostolic mission do not fall into a state of false security is to stir them up with warnings such as this" (69). Do you agree?

(43) 1:23 ἐπιμένετε. What is the force of its aspect? The verb has three modifying words. What are they?

τεθεμελιωμένοι[1] καὶ ἑδραῖοι[2] καὶ μὴ μετακινούμενοι[3] ἀπὸ τῆς ἐλπίδος τοῦ

εὐαγγελίου οὗ ἠκούσατε, τοῦ κηρυχθέντος ἐν πάσῃ κτίσει τῇ ὑπὸ τὸν οὐρανόν,

οὗ ἐγενόμην ἐγὼ Παῦλος διάκονος.

Grammar Summary

1. Hebrew can use a noun in a construct relationship as if it were an adjective, and this usage comes into Greek as the *Hebraic genitive* (*attributive*; "body of sin").

2. An *inceptive aorist* (*ingressive*) emphasizes the beginning of the action ("began to").

3. An *accusative of respect* (*reference*) limits the force of the verb ("with respect to").

4. A *dative of reference* (*respect*) uses the key phrase "with respect to."

5. The alpha privative negates a word by adding α (ἀν) before it.

---

[1] θεμελιόω, *I found, lay the foundation of; establish, strengthen* (5).

[2] ἑδραῖος, (αία), αῖον, *firm, steadfast* (3). The parentheses indicate that sometimes this word has a separate feminine form and at other times the masculine and feminine are the same. For other words like this, see category a-3b(1) in *MBG*.

[3] μετακινέω, *I shift, remove*; middle (?) *move away, remove* (1).

---

(44) 1:23 τεθεμελιωμένοι. How does the passive definition of this word differ from its active? What does it modify?

(45) 1:23 εὐαγγελίου has three phrases modifying it. What are they?

(46) 1:23 οὗ. Did you notice how attraction has changed the case of this relative pronoun οὗ. What case "should" it have been?

A Model Prayer

Colossians 1:9-12

Introduction

To succeed in any field one must "study the Masters." Paul's prayer differs greatly from our usual prayers for physical protection and health. A study of his prayer life will help reorient our prayers to concerns that lie closer to the heart of God.

A. The occassion (v. 9a)

1. What led Paul to pray for the Colossians?

   He had heard about their faith and love (cf. vv. 3-5)
   (Moule translates διὰ τοῦτο καί as "that is precisely why.")

2. What characterized Paul's prayer life?
   Unceasing prayer from the moment he learned about the believers at Colosse (cf. 1 Thess 5:17, "Pray continually").

B. The content (v. 9b)

1. Stated.
   That God might fill them with the knowledge of his will, "which comes through all true spiritual wisdom and insight" (TCNT).

2. Why this kind of prayer?
   Faith and love must be informed by spiritual wisdom. People's emotive and active side must be balanced by spiritual discernment.

C. The purpose (vv. 10-12)

1. That they might lead a life …

   a. Worthy of the Lord, and
   b. That brings him complete satisfaction.

2. This kind of life is described as…

   (Note the four present tense participles!)

   a. Fruitful in everything you do.
   b. Growing continually in the knowledge of God.
   c. Strengthened by his glorious power to go through whatever might happen.
   d. Thanking God with joy for enabling you to take part in what he has planned.

Conclusion

The theology of prayer has less to do with what happens to us as to what happens in us and through us. The Christian faith is less a great idea than a great way to live. It is active and life-transforming.

Chapter 6

ΚΑΤΑ ΜΑΘΘΑΙΟΝ 6:5-34

In case you were wondering if you really did know Greek since the previous passage was a little difficult, this narrative will boost your confidence. There is a lot of unusual vocabulary but most is footnoted.

Be sure you spend time thinking about the theology of the passage, reflecting not only on what the Greek means but mostly on what Jesus means. It also is a good passage to spend time doing word studies. A good word study will help make this passage clearer, less open to misunderstanding, and more exciting to read.

We are also going to start learning how to use *BAGD* in translation of difficult constructions. Because these points are so important, they will be placed in the footnotes and not in the *Exegetical Discussion* section. Commentary references are to Donald. A. Hagner, *Matthew 1-13*, in Word Biblical Commentary (Word, 1993).

By now you should be phrasing the entire passage. If you cannot, then vv 7-15 and vv 25-34 are fun to phrase, especially the latter.

The Position of Prayer (6:5-6)

6:5 Καὶ ὅταν προσεύχησθε, οὐκ <u>ἔσεσθε</u> ὡς οἱ ὑποκριταί,[1] ὅτι φιλοῦσιν[2]

ἐν ταῖς συναγωγαῖς καὶ ἐν ταῖς γωνίαις[3] τῶν πλατειῶν[4] ἑστῶτες[5]

---

[1] ὑποκριτής, οῦ, ὁ, *hypocrite* (17).

[2] If it helps at first, skip the intervening phrases and find the next word that follows this verb.

[3] γωνία, ας, ἡ, *corner* (9).

[4] πλατεῖα, ας, ἡ, *wide road, street* (9). It can refer to main intersections.

[5] The verbal stem is *στα and it is a participle. Hagner comments, "The perfect participle … has the nuance of having taken a position and continuing to stand in it, and this implies the enjoyment of public attention" (142).

Exegetical Discussion

(1)   **6:5 *** ἔσεσθε is an **imperatival future**. This is the use of the future in place of an imperative. For example, "Thou shalt not steal."

προσεύχεσθαι, ὅπως φανῶσιν[1] τοῖς <u>ἀνθρώποις</u>· ἀμὴν λέγω ὑμῖν, ἀπέχουσιν[2]

τὸν μισθὸν αὐτῶν. **6:6** σὺ δὲ ὅταν προσεύχῃ, εἴσελθε[3] εἰς τὸ ταμεῖόν[4] σου καὶ

κλείσας[5] τὴν θύραν σου πρόσευξαι τῷ πατρί σου τῷ ἐν τῷ κρυπτῷ·[6] καὶ ὁ

πατήρ σου ὁ βλέπων ἐν τῷ κρυπτῷ ἀποδώσει[7] σοι.

The Lord's Prayer (6:7-15)

    6:7 Προσευχόμενοι δὲ μὴ <u>βατταλογήσητε</u>[8] ὥσπερ οἱ ἐθνικοί,[9] δοκοῦσιν

---

[1]   The preceding word should be a big clue as to the mood of this form. The stem vowel has also undergone ablaut.

[2]   ἀπέχω, a technical term meaning *I receive in full, I receive a receipt* (19). Can you bring out the full force of the linear aspect in your translation?

[3]   This is a compound verb, and it is not present or indicative.

[4]   ταμεῖον, ου, τό, *innermost* or *secret room* (4). It refers to a storeroom, or any room inside a house.

[5]   κλείω, *I shut, lock* (16). Note that it does not have an augment.

[6]   κρυπτός, ή, όν, *hidden, secret* (17).

[7]   This is a compound verb whose simple root is *δο.

[8]   βατταλογέω, *I babble* (1).

[9]   ἐθνικός, ή, όν, *Gentile* (4).

---

(2)   6:5   προσεύχεσθαι can be a complementary infinitive because it completes the thought of the verb φιλοῦσιν. It could also be the simple use of the infinitive as a noun, acting as the direct object of the verb.

(3)   **6:5** *   ἀνθρώποις may be a **dative of agency** since the dative indicates the personal agent by whom the action described by the verb is accomplished. You can use the key word *by*. However, see Wallace's qualifications for this category.

(4)   6:7   βατταλογήσητε is an aorist active subjunctive used with μή to express a strong negation; see *BBG* §33.15 and Wallace. There is another one in v 8.

γὰρ ὅτι <u>ἐν</u> τῇ πολυλογίᾳ[1] αὐτῶν εἰσακουσθήσονται.[2] **6:8** μὴ οὖν ὁμοιωθῆτε[3]

αὐτοῖς·[4] <u>οἶδεν</u> γὰρ ὁ πατὴρ ὑμῶν ὧν[5] χρείαν ἔχετε πρὸ[6] τοῦ ὑμᾶς αἰτῆσαι

αὐτόν. **6:9** Οὕτως οὖν προσεύχεσθε ὑμεῖς·

---

1. πολυλογία, ας, ἡ, *wordiness* (1). This compound word has maintained the meaning of its two parts.

2. εἰσακούω, *I obey* (5). When God is the subject, it means *I hear.*

3. ὁμοιόω, active: *I make* τινά *like* τινί, *make someone like a person* or *thing;* passive: *I become like, am like* τινί, *someone.*

4. *BAGD lesson #1.* How do you know if ὁμοιωθῆτε takes a direct object in the dative, or if αὐτοῖς is a special use of the dative apart from the verb?

   Look up ὁμοιόω in *BAGD* and you will find the following: *"make like* τινά τινί *make someone like a person or thing."* What this means is that when ὁμοιόω means *make someone like someone/thing,* the *someone* will be in the accusative (τινά) and the *someone/thing* (τινί) will be in the dative. In other words, *BAGD* use τις to indicate the case of the words that will be used in the actual verse.

   ὁμοιόω of course can have other meanings and can occur in other constructions. In this verse, the person that would normally be in the accusative (τινά) is not expressed (it is implied in the subject), but αὐτοῖς is in the dative (τινί).

5. *BAGD lesson #2.* Why is the relative pronoun in the genitive? If you look up χρείαν in *BAGD,* you will find the following: χρείαν ἔχειν τινός *(have) need (of) someone or someth.* The word that describes the need will be in the genitive (τινός). "You have need *of things.*"

   But there is an additional problem here. What is the antecedent of the relative pronoun? We have seen how Greek omits words. Here it has omitted the relative pronoun's antecedent, and you have to guess as to what it is from the context. In this verse ἐκεῖνα is a good guess. "For your Father knows *those things* of which you have need." In other words, sometimes you have to reconstruct the full form of a sentence and then see what words have been omitted.

6. This preposition is followed by an articular infinitive (*BBG* §32.11).

---

(5) **6:7 *** ἐν can have an **instrumental** meaning, *by.*

(6) 6:8 οἶδεν. If God already knows, then why do we pray?

Πάτερ ἡμῶν ὁ ἐν τοῖς οὐρανοῖς·

ἁγιασθήτω τὸ ὄνομά σου·

6:10   ἐλθέτω ἡ βασιλεία σου·

γενηθήτω τὸ θέλημά σου,

ὡς ἐν οὐρανῷ καὶ ἐπὶ γῆς·

6:11   τὸν ἄρτον ἡμῶν τὸν ἐπιούσιον[1] δὸς[2] ἡμῖν σήμερον·

---

[1]   ἐπιούσιος, ον, *daily* (2).

[2]   The parallel structure of the prayer should give you a clue as to the parsing of this word. Its root is *δο, but it is not third person as are the previous three verbal forms.

---

(7)   6:9   Πάτερ. What is the inherent contrast in this phrase? See Hagner, 147.

(8)   **6:9** *   ἁγιασθήτω. Note carefully the precise meaning of ἁγιασθήτω and the following two verbs. Why does Jesus use this mood and voice? Does this change your understanding of the Lord's prayer?

   ἁγιασθήτω is an **imperative of entreaty**. You cannot tell God what to do, but you can petition him, and that requires the imperative. The same is true of petitioning those in power in general, not just petitioning God. What do you think of Hagner's comments about the disciples' involvement in this activity (148-49)?

(9)   6:11   ἐπιούσιος. Check out ἐπιούσιος in the lexicons and Hagner (144 note g, and especially pp. 149-50). What is so unusual about it? What is its range of meaning? What do you think it means?

6:12   καὶ ἄφες¹ ἡμῖν τὰ ὀφειλήματα² ἡμῶν,

ὡς καὶ <u>ἡμεῖς</u> <u>ἀφήκαμεν</u> τοῖς ὀφειλέταις³ ἡμῶν·

6:13   καὶ μὴ εἰσενέγκῃς⁴ ἡμᾶς εἰς <u>πειρασμόν</u>,

ἀλλὰ ῥῦσαι⁵ ἡμᾶς ἀπὸ τοῦ <u>πονηροῦ</u>.

---

1   You may just need to memorize this form. It is a second person singular imperative meaning *forgive!* as you probably guessed from the context. It is from ἀφίημι.

   BAGD lesson #3. BAGD states that ἀφίημι takes the dative of the person and the accusative of the thing. This means that the person being forgiven will be in the dative (ἡμῖν) and what is being forgiven will be in the accusative (τὰ ὀφειλήματα).

2   ὀφείλημα, ατος, τό, *debt* (2).

3   ὀφειλέτης, ου, ὁ, *debtor* (7).

4   εἰσφέρω, *I bring in, carry on* (8).

5   ῥύομαι, *I deliver, rescue* (17).

---

(10) 6:12   ἡμεῖς is a good example of the emphatic use of the pronoun. It emphasizes the contrast between what God will do (ἄφες) and what we are to do as well (ἡμεῖς).

(11) 6:12   ἀφήκαμεν. Parse ἀφήκαμεν carefully. How does its tense help you to understand the verse?

(12) 6:13   πειρασμόν. But James tells us that God does not tempt anyone (1:13). What does this verse mean? See Hagner, 151. Part of the answer lies in your translation of πειρασμόν here and of πονηροῦ (below).

(13) 6:13   πονηροῦ is substantival, as shown by the presence of the article. But it can be personal ("the evil one") or impersonal ("the evil"). What is the difference? See Hagner, 151-52.

6:14 Ἐὰν γὰρ ἀφῆτε[1] τοῖς ἀνθρώποις τὰ παραπτώματα[2] αὐτῶν, ἀφήσει καὶ ὑμῖν ὁ πατὴρ ὑμῶν ὁ οὐράνιος·[3] **6:15** ἐὰν δὲ μὴ ἀφῆτε τοῖς ἀνθρώποις, οὐδὲ ὁ πατὴρ ὑμῶν ἀφήσει τὰ παραπτώματα ὑμῶν.

Fasting (6:16-18)

6:16 Ὅταν δὲ νηστεύητε, μὴ γίνεσθε ὡς οἱ ὑποκριταὶ σκυθρωποί,[4] ἀφανίζουσιν[5] γὰρ τὰ πρόσωπα αὐτῶν ὅπως φανῶσιν τοῖς ἀνθρώποις νηστεύοντες· ἀμὴν λέγω ὑμῖν, ἀπέχουσιν τὸν μισθὸν αὐτῶν. **6:17** σὺ δὲ νηστεύων ἄλειψαί[6] σου τὴν κεφαλὴν καὶ τὸ πρόσωπόν σου νίψαι,[7] **6:18** ὅπως

---

[1]   This is a compound verb formed with a preposition, altered verbal root, tense formative, connecting vowel, and personal ending. In other words, if you can identify the root, the rest of the verb is regular.

[2]   παράπτωμα, ματος, τό, *transgression, sin* (19).

[3]   οὐράνιος, ον, *heavenly* (9).

[4]   σκυθρωπός, (ή), όν, *with a sad* or *gloomy look* (2).

[5]   ἀφανίζω, *I disfigure, make unrecognizable* (5).

[6]   ἀλείφω, *I anoint* (9).

[7]   νίπτω, *I wash* (17).

---

(14)   6:14   V 14. On the textual issues on the verse see Hagner, 144-45, note k.

                Do vv 14-15 mean what they appear to mean? Is a believer who holds a grudge condemned to hell? See Hagner, 152.

(15)   6:16   ἀφανίζουσιν is formed with the alpha privative. Words constructed with the alpha privative usually maintain the meaning of the two parts, unlike other types of compound word formations where the resulting word can have little to do with the meaning of the parts. It creates a word play with the following φανῶσιν.

(16)   6:16   νηστεύοντες is what type of participle? Is it adjectival or adverbial? Why is it nominative?

μὴ φανῇς τοῖς ἀνθρώποις νηστεύων ἀλλὰ τῷ πατρί σου τῷ ἐν τῷ κρυφαίῳ·[1] καὶ

ὁ πατήρ σου ὁ βλέπων ἐν τῷ κρυφαίῳ ἀποδώσει[2] σοι.

The Pursuit of God and Wealth (6:19-24)

6:19 Μὴ θησαυρίζετε[3] ὑμῖν θησαυροὺς[4] ἐπὶ τῆς γῆς, ὅπου σὴς[5] καὶ

βρῶσις[6] ἀφανίζει[7] καὶ ὅπου κλέπται[8] διορύσσουσιν[9] καὶ κλέπτουσιν·[10]

6:20 θησαυρίζετε δὲ ὑμῖν θησαυροὺς ἐν οὐρανῷ, ὅπου οὔτε σὴς οὔτε βρῶσις

ἀφανίζει καὶ ὅπου κλέπται οὐ διορύσσουσιν οὐδὲ κλέπτουσιν· **6:21** ὅπου γάρ

ἐστιν ὁ θησαυρός σου, ἐκεῖ ἔσται καὶ ἡ καρδία σου.

---

[1] κρυφαῖος, αία, αῖον, *hidden* (2). The idiom ἐν τῷ κρυφαίῳ means *in secret*.

[2] ἀποδώσει is a compound verb and the root is clearly visible.

[3] θησαυρίζω, *I store up, save* (8).

[4] θησαυρός, οῦ, ὁ, *storehouse, treasure* (17).

[5] σής, σητός, ὁ, *moth* (3).

[6] βρῶσις, εως, ἡ, *eating*, when used in conjunction with σής it means *corrosion, rust* (11). See Hagner, 157.

[7] ἀφανίζω, *I destroy* (5). This is the same verb we saw in v 16. However, when it is used in relationship to treasure it means *destroy*. This is a good illustration why it is important to know the full range of a word's meaning. It is a strong word denoting ruin and destruction (Hagner, 157).

[8] κλέπτης, ου, ὁ, *thief* (16).

[9] διορύσσω, *I dig/break through* (4).

[10] κλέπτω, *I steal* (13).

---

(17) 6:19   V 19. Pay special attention to the aspect of the verbs in this verse. How does knowing the aspect affect your presentation of the verse?

(18) 6:20   διορύσσουσιν. Check out the full definition of διορύσσω. What is the imagery that Jesus is creating?

6:22 Ὁ λύχνος[1] τοῦ σώματός ἐστιν ὁ <u>ὀφθαλμός</u>. ἐὰν οὖν ᾖ[2] ὁ ὀφθαλμός

σου ἁπλοῦς,[3] ὅλον τὸ σῶμά σου φωτεινὸν[4] ἔσται· **6:23** ἐὰν δὲ ὁ ὀφθαλμός σου

πονηρὸς ᾖ, ὅλον τὸ σῶμά σου σκοτεινὸν[5] ἔσται. εἰ οὖν τὸ <u>φῶς</u> τὸ ἐν σοὶ σκότος

ἐστίν, τὸ σκότος πόσον.[6]

6:24 Οὐδεὶς δύναται δυσὶ[7] κυρίοις δουλεύειν· ἢ γὰρ τὸν ἕνα <u>μισήσει</u>

καὶ τὸν ἕτερον ἀγαπήσει, ἢ ἑνὸς ἀνθέξεται[8] καὶ τοῦ ἑτέρου καταφρονήσει.[9] οὐ

δύνασθε θεῷ δουλεύειν καὶ μαμωνᾷ.[10]

---

[1] λύχνος, ου, ὁ, *light, lamp, candle* (14).

[2] The two most important hints for this form are its smooth breathing and the fact that it follows ἐάν.

[3] ἁπλοῦς, ῆ, οῦν, *sound, clear, healthy* (2).

[4] φωτεινός, ή, όν, *radiant, shining, bright* (5).

[5] σκοτεινός, ή, όν, *dark* (3).

[6] πόσος is idiomatic and you have some degree of freedom in translation.

[7] What case is δυσί? If you do not know see *MBG* a-5a.

[8] ἀντέχω, *I hold fast, am devoted* (4). In our literature ἀντέχω is always middle so some list the word as ἀντέχομαι. When the χ turns into a ξ because of the tense formative, the τ of the stem turns into a θ. See cv-1b(2) in *MBG*.

[9] καταφρονέω *I look down on, despise* (9).

[10] μαμωνᾶς, ᾶ, ὁ, *wealth, property* (4).

---

(19) 6:22   ὀφθαλμός. "Eyes" are the gateway into the inside of a person. Does this help clarify the meaning of the passage? Hagner (158) thinks of the "evil (i.e., covetous) eye" as opposed to the "good (i.e., generous or singleminded) eye," defining vv 22-23 by the surrounding pericopes.

(20) 6:23   φῶς is metonymy standing for the eye itself. See Hagner, 157.

(21) **6:24** *   μισήσει is a **gnomic future**. When a speaker wants to express a time-less truth, one that is always true, the future can be used. There also is a gnomic present and gnomic aorist. See *Wallace* for a discussion of the differences. (Wallace does not discuss the gnomic future because it is a minor category; see Young, 119.) Hagner (159) discusses translating "hate vs love" as "neglect vs prefer." Be sure to check it out, or you may think that elsewhere (Luke 14:26) God calls us to hate our parents.

Anxiety and Seeking God (6:25-34)

6:25 Διὰ τοῦτο λέγω ὑμῖν, μὴ μεριμνᾶτε[1] τῇ ψυχῇ ὑμῶν τί φάγητε [ἢ τί

πίητε], μηδὲ τῷ σώματι ὑμῶν τί ἐνδύσησθε. οὐχὶ ἡ ψυχὴ πλεῖόν[2] ἐστιν τῆς

τροφῆς[3] καὶ τὸ σῶμα τοῦ ἐνδύματος;[4] **6:26** ἐμβλέψατε[5] εἰς τὰ πετεινὰ[6] τοῦ

οὐρανοῦ ὅτι οὐ σπείρουσιν οὐδὲ θερίζουσιν οὐδὲ συνάγουσιν εἰς ἀποθήκας,[7]

καὶ ὁ πατὴρ ὑμῶν ὁ οὐράνιος τρέφει[8] αὐτά· οὐχ ὑμεῖς μᾶλλον διαφέρετε[9]

---

[1] μεριμνάω, *I care for, am concerned about; am anxious, overly concerned* (19).

[2] πλεῖον is followed by the genitive of comparison.

[3] τροφή, ῆς, ἡ, *food* (16).

[4] ἔνδυμα, ματος, τό, *garment, clothing* (8).

[5] ἐμβλέπω, *I look at, consider* (11). See *BAGD* §2.

[6] πετεινόν, οῦ, τό, *bird* (14).

[7] ἀποθήκη, ης, ἡ, *storehouse, barn, cellar* (6).

[8] τρέφω, *I feed, nourish* (9).

[9] διαφέρω, *I am worth more* (13). When used as an intransitive verb it means *I am different from*. When it is used in a good sense, it therefore means *I am worth more*.

---

(22) 6:25   Διὰ τοῦτο refers back to what?

(23) 6:25   μεριμνᾶτε. What is the force of the verbal aspect of μεριμνᾶτε?

(24) 6:25   φάγητε is what type of subjunctive?

(25) 6:25   ἐνδύσησθε. Why is ἐνδύσησθε middle?

(26) 6:26   ἐμβλέψατε. Notice that ἐμβλέπω is a compound verb. Does it have a different nuance than the simple βλέπω? How does the context help make this decision?

(27) 6:26   τρέφω, when used with reference to a child, means *I rear, train*. Do you think that Jesus intended a double meaning here?

αὐτῶν; **6:27** τίς δὲ ἐξ ὑμῶν <u>μεριμνῶν</u> δύναται προσθεῖναι[1] ἐπὶ τὴν <u>ἡλικίαν</u>[2]

αὐτοῦ πῆχυν[3] ἕνα; **6:28** καὶ περὶ ἐνδύματος τί μεριμνᾶτε; <u>καταμάθετε</u>[4] τὰ

κρίνα[5] τοῦ ἀγροῦ πῶς αὐξάνουσιν· οὐ κοπιῶσιν οὐδὲ νήθουσιν·[6] **6:29** λέγω δὲ

ὑμῖν ὅτι οὐδὲ Σολομὼν[7] ἐν πάσῃ τῇ δόξῃ αὐτοῦ <u>περιεβάλετο</u> ὡς ἓν τούτων.

6:30[8] εἰ δὲ τὸν χόρτον[9] τοῦ ἀγροῦ σήμερον ὄντα καὶ αὔριον[10] εἰς κλίβανον[11]

---

[1]   προστίθημι, *I add* (18).

[2]   ἡλικία, ας, ἡ, *age, stature* (8).

[3]   πῆχυς, εως, ὁ, *hour, cubit* (4). It originally meant a measurement of length, specifically the length of a forearm, hence *cubit*. It can also be used of time, hence *hour*.

[4]   καταμανθάνω, *I learn well* (1).

[5]   κρίνον, ου, τό, *lily* (2).

[6]   νήθω, *I spin* (2).

[7]   Σολομών, ῶνος, ὁ, *Solomon* (12). There is an alternate formation Σολομών, ῶντος, ὁ. This type of variation with foreign names brought into Greek is common. The accent in our text shows that our editors prefer the former spelling.

[8]   Find the subject, verb, and direct object for this sentence. What kind of conditional sentence is it? Will you translate εἰ as *if* or *since*? Why?

[9]   χόρτος, ου, ὁ, *grass, hay* (15).

[10]   αὔριον, *tomorrow; soon, in a short time* (14). An adverb.

[11]   κλίβανος, ου, ὁ, *furnace* (2).

---

(28)   **6:27** *   μεριμῶν is an **instrumental participle**. (Wallace calls it an **adverbial participle of means**.) This means that the participle is the means through which a person is attempting to perform an action. The verse creates a silly picture of "worry" being a personified instrument incapable of performing a task.

(29)   6:27   ἡλικίαν. Notice how ἡλίκια and πῆχυς together can create two different pictures in this passage. Which makes the best sense here? See Hagner, 164.

(30)   6:28   καταμανθάνω. Have you noticed how many compound words in this passage use the intensifying force of a preposition? That should give you a clue as to the precise meaning of this word.

(31)   **6:29** *   περιεβάλετο is a **direct middle** (also called **reflexive**). The subject acts on itself. How can its nuance be brought out in your translation? This is a rare use of the middle (see Wallace).

βαλλόμενον ὁ θεὸς οὕτως ἀμφιέννυσιν,[1] οὐ πολλῷ μᾶλλον ὑμᾶς, ὀλιγόπιστοι;[2]

6:31 μὴ οὖν <u>μεριμνήσητε</u> λέγοντες, Τί φάγωμεν; ἤ, Τί πίωμεν; ἤ, Τί περι-

βαλώμεθα; **6:32** πάντα γὰρ <u>ταῦτα</u> τὰ ἔθνη <u>ἐπιζητοῦσιν</u>·[3] οἶδεν γὰρ ὁ πατὴρ

ὑμῶν ὁ οὐράνιος ὅτι χρῄζετε[4] τούτων ἁπάντων. **6:33** <u>ζητεῖτε</u> δὲ <u>πρῶτον</u> τὴν

βασιλείαν [τοῦ θεοῦ] καὶ τὴν δικαιοσύνην αὐτοῦ, καὶ ταῦτα πάντα

προστεθήσεται ὑμῖν. **6:34** μὴ οὖν μεριμνήσητε εἰς τὴν αὔριον,[5] ἡ γὰρ αὔριον

μεριμνήσει ἑαυτῆς·[6] <u>ἀρκετὸν</u>[7] τῇ ἡμέρᾳ ἡ κακία[8] αὐτῆς.[9]

---

[1] ἀμφιέννυμι, *I clothe, dress* (3). What is the subject and direct object of this verb? Some list the lexical form as ἀμφιάζω.

[2] ὀλιγόπιστος, ον, *of little faith* (5). What case is this word and what type of adjective is it (*BBG* §9.14)?

[3] ἐπιζητέω, *I (earnestly) search for, (earnestly) strive for* (13).

[4] χρῄζω, *I have need* (5).

[5] *BAGD lesson #4.* As we saw above, αὔριον is an adverb (and therefore does not inflect). However, here it appears to be used as an adjective because of the preceding article. If you look up αὔριον in *BAGD*, you will find the following: "W. art., w. ἡμέρα to be supplied." This means that Greek allowed the idiomatic construction of using the adverb αὔριον to mean "next day," and you are to supply "day" after it.

The same construction occurs in the next clause, but notice there it is used as the subject, so the article is ἡ.

---

(32) 6:31 μεριμνήσητε. How strongly is the prohibition μὴ μεριμνήσητε stated? See *BBG* §33.15 and Wallace.

(33) **6:32** * ταῦτα. When Greek wants to refer back not to one word but to a preceding clause or general idea, the pronoun is placed in the neuter. This is why ταῦτα is neuter.

(34) 6:32 ἐπιζητοῦσιν. What is the difference in meaning between the simple ζητέω (v 33) and the compound ἐπιζητέω? Does the compound carry its full meaning in this context?

(35) 6:33 ζητεῖτε. Exegetically, what is the significance of the aspect of ζητεῖτε?

(36) 6:33 πρῶτον. Is πρῶτον functioning as an adjective or an adverb? Remember, all Greek adjectives can function adverbially.

Grammar Summary

1. The *imperatival future* can be used in place of an imperative.

2. The dative of agency indicates the personal agent by whom the action described by the verb is accomplished ("by").

3. ἐν can have an instrumental meaning, "by."

4. An *imperative of entreaty* is used to entreat or request a person who is in power over the speaker to do something.

5. The *gnomic future* expresses a timeless truth.

6. The *instrumental participle* (*means*) expresses the means through which a person is attempting to perform an action.

7. In a *direct middle* (*reflexive*), the subject acts on itself.

8. When Greek wants to refer back not to one word but to a preceding clause or general idea, the pronoun is placed in the neuter.

---

6   *BAGD lesson #5.* In *BAGD* we see that μεριμνάω is used with "περί τινος," as illustrated in v 28. Therefore, when we arrive at v 34b, since ἑαυτῆς is in the genitive, we can assume that the περί was omitted.

7   ἀρκετός, ή, όν, *enough, sufficient* (3).

8   κακία, ας, ἡ. In a moral sense it means *depravity, wickedness.* It can also mean *trouble* or *misfortune* (11). See *BAGD.*

9   Why is αὐτῆς genitive? Sometimes you need to reconstruct the sentence, placing it in more of a "normal" word order, to see why a word is in the case it is: "The trouble that belongs to (viewing αὐτῆς as a possessive) the day is (understood verb) sufficient."

---

(37)   6:34   ἀρκετόν. Did you notice that ἀρκετόν is neuter, even though it is a predicate nominative referring to κακία, which is feminine? *BDF* explains that when the subject is "conceived as a class in the abstract" (i.e., not any specific trouble but trouble in general), then as in Classical Greek the predicate is put in the neuter singular (§131; see also Hagner, 166).

Jesus Teaches on Prayer

Matthew 6:5-13

Introduction

In the first 18 verses of Matthew 6 Jesus deals with the three most prominent obligations of Jewish piety–almsgiving, prayer, and fasting. In each case there is a right way and a wrong way. Who better than Jesus himself to serve as our teacher on the subject of prayer?

A. Don't be like the hypocrites when you pray (v 5)

They use prayer as an occasion to call attention to themselves. Such prayers won't be answered because they've already received their "reward"–i.e., the attention of others!

B. Genuine prayer calls for a personal relationship with God (v 6)

Prayer is intended as a highly personal conversation between you and your God. Obviously there is a place for "public" prayer, but even there the leader is not so much praying on behalf of those listening as he is leading them as they themselves encounter God on an individual basis.

C. It is not the length of your prayer that counts (vv 7-8)

Those who don't know any better apparently think that God is impressed by long prayers. The repetition of empty phrases is a pagan practice. Since our heavenly Father knows what we need before we ask, we certainly don't need to tell him again and again.

D. Jesus tells us how to pray (vv 9-13)

1. First for those things that concern God, his character, and his redemptive program in the world.
    - that his name may be held in honor.
    - that his eternal kingdom may come.
    - that his will may be done.

2. Second that our own needs be met.
    - that we will receive each day that which is necessary for life.
    - that we will be forgiven for daily sins.
    - that we will be kept from failing in our responsibilities to God.

Conclusion

The basis for true prayer is a recognition of the greatness of God and our absolute dependence on him. The one place where pious subterfuge has no place is in our relation to him.

Chapter 7

ΠΡΟΣ ΡΩΜΑΙΟΥΣ
3:21-26; 5:1-11; 8:1-17

This could be one of your favorite passages. The vocabulary is not very difficult, nor is the grammar. But it is beautiful theology that will remind you why you learned Greek and why it is fun and rewarding to use it. There are several good word studies. We have included more verses than normal. This is an especially good chapter to phrase.

There are several genitive absolutes that may give you trouble if you do not recognize them as such. Be careful also to watch Paul's use of ἐν; is it temporal or instrumental? In fact, this is a good passage to be careful in translating cases and prepositions. Try to be exact and do not use approximate English translations.

By the end of this chapter you will have been exposed to the majority of the significant grammatical categories. You may want to consider reading through a full grammar like Wallace; you may be surprised at how much you already know.

Commentary references are to C.E.B. Cranfield, *A Critical and Exegetical Commentary on The Epistle to the Romans,* in The International Critical Commentary (T&T Clark, 1977), vol 1.

The Righteousness of God (3:21-26)

3:21 <u>Νυνὶ δὲ</u> χωρὶς <u>νόμου</u> δικαιοσύνη <u>θεοῦ</u> πεφανέρωται μαρτυρουμένη

Exegetical Discussion

(1)   3:21   Νυνὶ δέ creates a strong contrast with the preceding. From your general knowledge of Paul's argument in Romans, what is the contrast?

(2)   **3:21** *   νόμου. Notice that νόμου is anarthrous while the following τοῦ νόμου is not. What is the significance? Read the *Gram Sum*, "Absence of the Article."

(3)   **3:21** *   θεοῦ. Most commentaries will have handled the debate of what kind of genitive we see in θεοῦ back in Rom 1:17. Is it describing an activity of God (i.e., a "subjective genitive") or our righteous status (i.e., an "objective genitive" or perhaps "genitive of origin"), or a combination of these and perhaps other options? This is a good place to confirm that you can differentiate these different genitives. They are discussed in depth by Cranfield (91-99, 203), by Wallace, and in the *BBG Workbook* (170n5 on 1 John 2:15).

ὑπὸ τοῦ νόμου καὶ τῶν προφητῶν,   **3:22** δικαιοσύνη δὲ θεοῦ διὰ πίστεως Ἰησοῦ

<u>Χριστοῦ</u> εἰς πάντας τοὺς πιστεύοντας. οὐ γάρ ἐστιν διαστολή,[1] **3:23** πάντες

γὰρ ἥμαρτον καὶ <u>ὑστεροῦνται</u>[2] τῆς <u>δόξης τοῦ θεοῦ</u> **3:24** δικαιούμενοι <u>δωρεὰν</u>[3]

τῇ αὐτοῦ χάριτι διὰ τῆς <u>ἀπολυτρώσεως</u>[4] τῆς ἐν Χριστῷ Ἰησοῦ· **3:25** ὃν

---

[1]   διαστολή, ῆς, ἡ, *difference, distinction* (3).

[2]   ὑστερέω, active: *I come too late, lack, fail;* passive: *I lack, come short of,* followed by
      the genitive of the thing (16).

[3]   δωρεάν, *freely, as a free gift, undeservedly* (9).

[4]   ἀπολύτρωσις, εως, ἡ, *redemption, acquittal* (10).

---

(4)   3:22   Ἰησοῦ Χριστοῦ is what type of genitive?

(5)   3:23   ὑστεροῦνται. Did you notice the tense shift between ἥμαρτον and
              ὑστεροῦνται? How would you paraphrase the verse to bring out the
              difference? Cranfield has a detailed discussion of ἥμαρτον (on Rom
              2:12, citing Burton §54).

(6)   3:23   δόξης τοῦ θεοῦ presents an interesting exegetical question. If people
              never sinned, would they ever attain to God's own glory? Of course
              not. Even human perfection is no match for God's own glory. So what
              is this verse saying? What kind of glory does our sin cause us to fall
              short of? Part of the answer lies in the ambiguity of the genitive. What
              type of genitive is θεοῦ? See Cranfield, 204-5.

(7)   3:24   δικαιούμενοι has three modifiers. What are they? δικαιούμενοι gram-
              matically is tied to πάντες, but does this mean that all are justified?

(8)   3:24   δωρεάν is actually the accusative of the noun δωρεά. Some therefore
              class this usage as an "adverbial accusative." Because δωρεάν is used
              frequently adverbially, others prefer to classify δωρεάν as an adverb.

(9)   3:24   ἀπολυτρώσεως has a rich set of meanings that will help this passage
              come alive. It is worth a word study. Is the emphasis here on "freedom
              gained" or the "price that was paid"? See Cranfield, 206-8.

προέθετο¹ ὁ θεὸς ἱλαστήριον² διὰ [τῆς] πίστεως ἐν τῷ αὐτοῦ αἵματι εἰς ἔνδειξιν³

τῆς δικαιοσύνης αὐτοῦ διὰ τὴν πάρεσιν⁴ τῶν προγεγονότων⁵ ἁμαρτημάτων⁶

3:26 ἐν τῇ ἀνοχῇ⁷ τοῦ θεοῦ, πρὸς τὴν ἔνδειξιν τῆς δικαιοσύνης αὐτοῦ ἐν τῷ νῦν

καιρῷ, εἰς τὸ εἶναι αὐτὸν δίκαιον καὶ δικαιοῦντα τὸν⁸ ἐκ πίστεως Ἰησοῦ.

---

1. προτίθημι, active: *I set before;* middle: *I display publicly; propose, intend* (3). This verb takes a double accusative here.
2. ἱλαστήριον, ου, τό, *place of propitiation, propitiation, expiation* (2). It can describe both the means and the place of propitiation/expiation.
3. ἔνδειξις, εως, ἡ, *sign, omen; proof* (4).
4. πάρεσις, εως, ἡ, *passing over, letting go unpunished* (1).
5. προγίνομαι, *I happen previously, previously commit* (1).
6. ἁμάρτημα, ματος, τό, *sin, transgression* (4).
7. ἀνοχή, ῆς, ἡ, *delay, forbearance, clemency* (2).
8. It is helpful to think of a word missing here.

---

(10) 3:25   προέθετο. People differ on which of the two basic meanings of προτίθημι is present here. Is Paul referring to what God did (i.e., "publicly show"), or is Paul discussing what God's eternal intentions were (i.e., "intend")? What do you think, and what is the significance of the question? See Cranfield, 208-10.

(11) 3:25   ἱλαστήριον is another excellent choice for a word study. In doing one, be sure you can clearly explain to laypeople the difference between "expiation" and "propitiation" and why it is an important issue. See Cranfield, 214-18.

(12) 3:25   πάρεσιν. If God "passed over" sins committed before the time of Christ, what does that teach you about the nature of Old Testament sacrifices? How does it affect your understanding of the refrain that runs through Leviticus, "and he will be forgiven" (4:31, et al.)?

(13) **3:26** *   τὴν ἔνδειξιν. Did you notice that the first time Paul speaks of ἔνδειξιν it is anarthrous but here it is articular? This is a common use of the article where the author, when using a word the second time, points the reader back to the first use of the word, as if to say, "the sign, i.e., the one that I introduced earlier...." Another example is John 3. When Nicodemus is first introduced his name is anarthrous (v. 1), but the next time it is ὁ Νικόδημος (v. 4). This is called the **anaphoric** use of the article.

Life of Peace with God (5:1-11)

5:1 <u>Δικαιωθέντες οὖν</u> ἐκ πίστεως <u>εἰρήνην</u> <u>ἔχομεν</u> πρὸς τὸν θεὸν διὰ τοῦ

κυρίου ἡμῶν Ἰησοῦ Χριστοῦ **5:2** δι' οὗ καὶ τὴν προσαγωγὴν[1] ἐσχήκαμεν[2] [τῇ

πίστει] εἰς τὴν χάριν ταύτην ἐν ᾗ ἑστήκαμεν[3] καὶ καυχώμεθα ἐπ' ἐλπίδι τῆς

δόξης τοῦ θεοῦ. **5:3** οὐ μόνον δέ, ἀλλὰ καὶ καυχώμεθα <u>ἐν</u> ταῖς θλίψεσιν, εἰδότες

---

[1] προσαγωγή, ῆς, ἡ, *access, approach* (3).

[2] The root of this verb is *σεχ. This is a good illustration of the theological significance of this tense. See *MBG*, v-1b(2).

[3] The root of this verb is *στα. If you check this verb's entry in *BAGD,* you will see that in the perfect it has a present tense meaning, as you might suspect from the needs of this passage. See *MBG*, v-6a.

---

(14) 5:1   Δικαιωθέντες οὖν is an extremely important connective phrase, showing the relationship between the argument in chapter 5 with the argument in 3:21 - 4:25 (some argue the preceding section runs from 1:17, or 1:19). What is the connection? See Cranfield, 257.

(15) 5:1   εἰρήνη provides another marvelous opportunity to do a word study. Does the biblical doctrine of "peace" basically mean the feeling of peace? Is it something more? See Cranfield, 258.

(16) 5:1   ἔχομεν. Instead of the indicative ἔχομεν most manuscripts read the subjunctive ἔχωμεν. What would the difference be theologically? This is one of the few places where the editors of our text prefer a reading that is substantially weaker (i.e., the indicative) because of internal reasons (i.e., the theology and grammar of the passage). What are the arguments for both? See Metzger, *Textual,* 452, and Cranfield, 257n1.

This would be a good opportunity for your teacher to explain the basics of textual criticism, including what "weaker," "stronger," and "reading" mean.

(17) **5:3** *   ἐν. Is ἐν here temporal or causal? While the latter may sound almost morbid, it has support from the context. See Cranfield, 260.

ὅτι ἡ θλῖψις <u>ὑπομονὴν</u> <u>κατεργάζεται</u>, **5:4** ἡ δὲ ὑπομονὴ δοκιμήν,[1] ἡ δὲ δοκιμὴ

ἐλπίδα. **5:5** ἡ δὲ ἐλπὶς οὐ καταισχύνει,[2] ὅτι ἡ ἀγάπη τοῦ <u>θεοῦ</u> ἐκκέχυται[3] ἐν

ταῖς καρδίαις ἡμῶν διὰ πνεύματος ἁγίου τοῦ δοθέντος[4] ἡμῖν. **5:6** ἔτι γὰρ

Χριστὸς <u>ὄντων ἡμῶν ἀσθενῶν</u> ἔτι κατὰ καιρὸν[5] ὑπὲρ ἀσεβῶν[6] ἀπέθανεν.

5:7 μόλις[7] γὰρ ὑπὲρ δικαίου τις ἀποθανεῖται· ὑπὲρ γὰρ τοῦ <u>ἀγαθοῦ</u> τάχα[8] τις

καὶ τολμᾷ[9] ἀποθανεῖν· **5:8** συνίστησιν[10] δὲ τὴν ἑαυτοῦ ἀγάπην εἰς ἡμᾶς ὁ θεός,

---

[1] δοκιμή, ῆς, ἡ, *approvedness, character* (as the result of being approved); *test, ordeal* (7).

[2] καταισχύνω, active: *I put to shame, disgrace, dishonor*; passive: *I am disappointed* (13).

[3] There is no connecting vowel in this form. *MBG*, cv-1a(1).

[4] The verbal root is *δο and the important morpheme is ντ. *MBG*, v-6a.

[5] κατά can be used in many specific uses, such as in a time designation. See *BAGD* II 2 a.

[6] ἀσεβής, ές, *godless, impious* (9).

[7] μόλις, *with difficulty; not readily, only rarely* (6).

[8] τάχα, *possibly, perhaps* (2).

[9] τολμάω, *I dare, have the courage*; abs.: *I am courageous*, followed by an infinitive (16).

[10] συνίστημι, *I bring together, collect; introduce, demonstrate* (16).

---

(18)   5:3   ὑπομονή deserves a word study. Is it an "active" or "passive" concept, and what is the difference?

(19)   5:3   κατεργάζω also deserves a word study. It does not just mean to do something. It has a special nuance that is helpful in interpreting this passage.

(20)   5:5   θεοῦ. Is θεοῦ an objective or subjective genitive? See Cranfield, 262.

(21)   5:6   ὄντων ἡμῶν ἀσθενῶν. How many times have you heard people claim that the "Bible says" that "God helps those who help themselves"? Does it? Who does? How does the phrase ὄντων ἡμῶν ἀσθενῶν help you in this discussion? See Cranfield, 263-64.

(22)   5:7   ἀγαθοῦ. It is an interesting debate as to the difference, if any, between δικαίου and ἀγαθοῦ. What do you think Paul means by this verse? See Cranfield, 264-65.

ὅτι ἔτι ἁμαρτωλῶν ὄντων ἡμῶν Χριστὸς ὑπὲρ ἡμῶν ἀπέθανεν. **5:9** πολλῷ οὖν

μᾶλλον δικαιωθέντες νῦν ἐν τῷ αἵματι αὐτοῦ σωθησόμεθα δι᾽ αὐτοῦ ἀπὸ τῆς

ὀργῆς. **5:10** εἰ γὰρ ἐχθροὶ ὄντες κατηλλάγημεν[1] τῷ θεῷ διὰ τοῦ θανάτου τοῦ

υἱοῦ αὐτοῦ, πολλῷ μᾶλλον καταλλαγέντες σωθησόμεθα ἐν τῇ ζωῇ αὐτοῦ·

5:11 οὐ μόνον δέ, ἀλλὰ καὶ καυχώμενοι[2] ἐν τῷ θεῷ διὰ τοῦ κυρίου ἡμῶν Ἰησοῦ

Χριστοῦ δι᾽ οὗ νῦν τὴν καταλλαγὴν[3] ἐλάβομεν.

The Indwelling of the Holy Spirit (8:1-17)

8:1 Οὐδὲν <u>ἄρα</u> νῦν κατάκριμα[4] τοῖς ἐν Χριστῷ Ἰησοῦ· **8:2** ὁ γὰρ <u>νόμος</u>

<u>τοῦ πνεύματος</u> τῆς ζωῆς ἐν Χριστῷ Ἰησοῦ ἠλευθέρωσέν[5] σε ἀπὸ τοῦ νόμου τῆς

ἁμαρτίας καὶ τοῦ θανάτου. **8:3** τὸ γὰρ ἀδύνατον[6] τοῦ νόμου ἐν ᾧ ἠσθένει διὰ

---

[1]   καταλλάσσω, active: *I reconcile*; passive: *I am/become reconciled* (6). You may be
     tempted to translate this as an active form, but notice the long η before the per-
     sonal ending. See Cranfield, 267, on the relational aspect of this verb.

[2]   Did you notice that this verse does not have a finite verb? καυχώμενοι is an
     independent participle functioning as a finite verb.

[3]   καταλλαγή, ῆς, ἡ, *reconciliation* (4).

[4]   κατάκριμα, ατος, τό, *punishment* (3).

[5]   ἐλευθερόω, *I (set) free* (7). How can the believer be set free and still be under the
     law of the Spirit? See Cranfield, 377-78.

[6]   ἀδύνατος, ον, *powerless, unable; impossible* (10). See Cranfield, 379-82, for a gram-
     matical discussion.

---

(23)   5:9   V 9. Paul's argument here and in v 10 reflects the Jewish argument of
               the "light and heavy," the "difficult and easy." What is this argument?
               See Cranfield, 265-66.

(24)   8:1   ἄρα. We have seen similar connectives in 3:21 and 5:1. What is the con-
               nection in this verse to the preceding argument?

(25)   8:2   νόμος τοῦ πνεύματος. What is this law? See Cranfield, 375-76, and
               Rom 7:23.

τῆς σαρκός, ὁ θεὸς τὸν ἑαυτοῦ υἱὸν πέμψας ἐν ὁμοιώματι[1] σαρκὸς ἁμαρτίας καὶ

περὶ ἁμαρτίας <u>κατέκρινεν</u>[2] τὴν ἁμαρτίαν ἐν τῇ σαρκί, **8:4** ἵνα τὸ δικαίωμα[3] τοῦ

νόμου πληρωθῇ ἐν ἡμῖν τοῖς μὴ κατὰ σάρκα περιπατοῦσιν ἀλλὰ κατὰ πνεῦμα.

8:5 οἱ γὰρ κατὰ σάρκα ὄντες τὰ τῆς σαρκὸς <u>φρονοῦσιν</u>, οἱ δὲ κατὰ πνεῦμα τὰ

τοῦ πνεύματος. **8:6** τὸ γὰρ φρόνημα[4] τῆς σαρκὸς θάνατος, τὸ δὲ φρόνημα τοῦ

πνεύματος ζωὴ καὶ εἰρήνη· **8:7** διότι τὸ φρόνημα τῆς σαρκὸς ἔχθρα[5] εἰς θεόν, τῷ

γὰρ νόμῳ τοῦ θεοῦ οὐχ ὑποτάσσεται, οὐδὲ γὰρ δύναται· **8:8** οἱ δὲ ἐν σαρκὶ

ὄντες θεῷ ἀρέσαι[6] οὐ δύνανται. **8:9** ὑμεῖς δὲ οὐκ ἐστὲ ἐν σαρκὶ ἀλλὰ ἐν

πνεύματι, <u>εἴπερ</u>[7] πνεῦμα θεοῦ οἰκεῖ ἐν ὑμῖν. εἰ δέ τις πνεῦμα Χριστοῦ οὐκ ἔχει,

---

[1] ὁμοίωμα, ατος, τό, *likeness; image, copy; form, appearance* (6).

[2] κατακρίνω, *I punish, condemn* (16). See Cranfield, 382-83.

[3] δικαίωμα, ατος, τό, *regulation, commandment; righteous deed* (10). See Cranfield, 383-84.

[4] φρόνημα, ατος, τό, *mind-set, way of thinking; aspiration* (4).

[5] ἔχθρα, ας, ἡ, *enmity* (6).

[6] ἀρέσκω, *I strive to please; please, am pleasing* (17).

[7] εἴπερ, *if indeed; since* (6). Choose carefully. See Cranfield, 388, and εἰ in v 10.

---

(26) 8:3 κατέκρινεν. *BAGD* and Cranfield define κατακρίνω as describing both the sentence ("I condemn") and the execution ("I punish"). But interestingly *BAGD* states that the cognate noun κατάκριμα used earlier in 8:1 only means "punishment," not "condemnation."

This would be yet another helpful word study, especially as it involves learning about the relationships between cognates and how sometimes they have the same basic meaning and at other times they are different.

(27) 8:5 φρονοῦσιν. What is the precise meaning of φρονέω? Does it have the same nuance as its cognate noun used below?

(28) 8:9 εἴπερ is often used in combination with other words. You should look through the discussion in *BAGD* (VI.11).

οὗτος οὐκ ἔστιν <u>αὐτοῦ</u>. **8:10** εἰ δὲ Χριστὸς ἐν ὑμῖν, τὸ <u>μὲν</u> σῶμα νεκρὸν διὰ

ἁμαρτίαν τὸ δὲ <u>πνεῦμα</u> ζωὴ διὰ δικαιοσύνην. **8:11** εἰ δὲ τὸ πνεῦμα τοῦ

ἐγείραντος τὸν Ἰησοῦν ἐκ νεκρῶν οἰκεῖ ἐν ὑμῖν, ὁ ἐγείρας Χριστὸν ἐκ νεκρῶν

ζωοποιήσει[1] καὶ τὰ θνητὰ[2] σώματα ὑμῶν διὰ τοῦ ἐνοικοῦντος[3] αὐτοῦ

πνεύματος ἐν ὑμῖν.

8:12 Ἄρα οὖν, ἀδελφοί, ὀφειλέται[4] ἐσμὲν οὐ τῇ σαρκὶ τοῦ κατὰ σάρκα

ζῆν,[5] **8:13** εἰ γὰρ κατὰ σάρκα ζῆτε, <u>μέλλετε ἀποθνῄσκειν</u>· εἰ δὲ πνεύματι τὰς

πράξεις[6] τοῦ σώματος θανατοῦτε,[7] ζήσεσθε. **8:14** ὅσοι γὰρ πνεύματι θεοῦ

---

1 ζῳοποιέω, *I make alive, give life to* (11).

2 θνητός, ή, όν, *mortal* (6).

3 ἐνοικέω, *I live, dwell (in)* (5).

4 ὀφειλέτης, ου, ὁ, *debtor, one who is obligated/guilty* (7).

5 ζῆν is not a noun. Check out the needs of the sentence and the irregular contractions of verbal forms (*BBG* §32.4).

6 πρᾶξις, εως, ἡ, *activity; way/course of acting; plan of action; action, deed* (6).

7 θανατόω, *I kill, put to death* (11).

---

(29) **8:9** * αὐτοῦ is a **possessive genitive**, since the genitive possesses the noun to which it is related. Notice how Paul shifts between speaking of "Christ," the "Spirit of Christ," and the "Spirit of God." What can you learn from this?

(30) **8:10** μὲν. Cranfield, 389, says μὲν is concessive and is an example of parataxis.

(31) **8:10** πνεῦμα. Is πνεῦμα here the Holy Spirit or the human spirit? Note that ζωή means *life,* not *alive.* See Cranfield, 390.

(32) **8:13** μέλλετε ἀποθνῄσκειν. Cranfield says μέλλετε ἀποθνῄσκειν is a periphrastic future used to "emphasize that the consequence is necessary and certain" (394).

ἄγονται, οὗτοι υἱοὶ θεοῦ εἰσιν. **8:15** οὐ γὰρ ἐλάβετε πνεῦμα δουλείας[1] πάλιν

εἰς φόβον ἀλλὰ ἐλάβετε πνεῦμα υἱοθεσίας[2] ἐν ᾧ κράζομεν, Αββα[3] ὁ πατήρ.

8:16 αὐτὸ τὸ πνεῦμα συμμαρτυρεῖ[4] τῷ πνεύματι ἡμῶν ὅτι ἐσμὲν τέκνα θεοῦ.

8:17 εἰ δὲ τέκνα, καὶ κληρονόμοι·[5] κληρονόμοι μὲν θεοῦ, <u>συγκληρονόμοι</u>[6] δὲ

Χριστοῦ, εἴπερ <u>συμπάσχομεν</u>[7] ἵνα καὶ συνδοξασθῶμεν.[8]

Grammar Summary

1. The *article* in Greek is not strictly analogous to the definite article in English. Its presence and absence often have significant if not subtle differences in meaning. Read a thorough discussion on the Greek article.

2. Be clear as to the difference among the *objective genitive, genitive of origin,* and the *subjective genitive.*

3. The *anaphoric* use of the article refers the reader back to a previous use of the same word.

4. An *independent participle* can function as a finite verb.

5. A *possessive genitive* possesses the noun to which it is related.

---

[1]   δουλεία, ας, ἡ, *slavery* (5).

[2]   υἱοθεσία, ας, ἡ, *adoption* (5). This word is used both of the nation of Israel and of individual Christians.

[3]   Ἀββά, *father* (3).

[4]   συμμαρτυρέω, *I bear witness with; confirm* (3).

[5]   κληρονόμος, ου, ὁ, *heir* (15).

[6]   συγκληρονόμος, ον, *inheriting together with* (4).

[7]   συμπάσχω, *I suffer together* (2).

[8]   συνδοξάζω, *I glorify together* (1).

---

(33)   8:17   συγκληρονόμος. You may have guessed it, but συγκληρονόμος is a combination of σύν and κληρονόμος. When ν appears before a velar (κ γ χ ξ), it becomes a gamma-nasal (συν ‣ συγ; *MBG* §24.2).

(34)   **8:17** *   συμπάσχομεν. What are the theological implications of this verse if in life a Christian does not suffer?

It Doesn't Get Any Better Than This

Romans 5:1-5

Introduction

By nature the human race is at war with God.

The "good news" is that God has won the battle but now wants to make us children instead of prisoners of war.

It simply doesn't get any better than this!

A. The crucial battle is over (vv. 1-2)

1. The armistice has been signed.

   "We have peace with God."

   "Peace" (εἰρήνη) is not so much personal tranquility as it is *shalom* (Hebrew concept of "positive well-being").

2. Twofold basis:
   a. What Christ did for us on the cross.
      "Through our Lord Jesus Christ."
   b. We responded in faith.
      "We have been justified through faith."

B. It is time to celebrate the victory (vv. 3-5)

Two reasons why we should celebrate:

   (Taking καυχώμεθα as hortatory subjunctive, "let us exult.")
   1. We now have the hope of "attaining God's glorious ideal" (TCNT).
   2. We now understand God's purpose in the suffering that comes our way.

      - Suffering develops endurance.
      - Endurance demonstrates strength of character.
      - Character give rise to hope.

C. How do we know for sure we're not "whistling Dixie"? (v. 5).

1. Because God "has poured out his love into our hearts."
2. Because God has given us "the Holy Spirit."

Conclusion

It's time to celebrate God's incredible victory over sin and Satan!

It's great to be on the winning side!

Chapter 8

ΙΑΚΩΒΟΥ 1:1-21

The Greek in James is decidedly different from the type of Greek you have been reading so far. The vocabulary is more difficult, although most of the new words occur less than twenty times and are therefore footnoted. The grammar is quite good.

We would encourage you to spend some serious time with your exegesis of this passage. This is real life in the ministry.

This is your eighth chapter in the *Graded Reader*. By now you should be getting comfortable with translating the text. Therefore, we will start giving you fewer hints and helps. Both you and your teacher need to know for sure how you are doing. At chapter thirteen we will start giving you only the minimum necessary. Our hope is that by now you have seen the importance of phrasing and will do it on your own. We will not be doing any more.

Commentary references are to Peter H. Davids, *The Epistle of James,* in The New International Greek Testament Commentary (Eerdmans, 1982).

Introduction (1:1)

1:1 Ἰάκωβος θεοῦ καὶ κυρίου Ἰησοῦ Χριστοῦ δοῦλος ταῖς δώδεκα

φυλαῖς ταῖς ἐν τῇ <u>διασπορᾷ</u>[1] χαίρειν.[2]

---

[1] διασπορά, ᾶς, ἡ, *dispersion* (3). It is used of both the people and the location.

[2] χαίρειν, the infinitive form of the verb, is the standard greeting in ancient letters (cf. *BAGD*, 2b). *Greeting.*

Exegetical Discussion

(1)   1:1   διασπορᾷ. Is this to be understood literally or figuratively? See Davids, 64.

Testing, Wisdom, and Wealth (1:2-11)

1:2 <u>Πᾶσαν</u> χαρὰν ἡγήσασθε, ἀδελφοί μου, ὅταν πειρασμοῖς περιπέσητε[1]

ποικίλοις,[2] **1:3** γινώσκοντες ὅτι τὸ δοκίμιον[3] ὑμῶν τῆς πίστεως <u>κατεργάζεται</u>

<u>ὑπομονήν</u>. **1:4** ἡ δὲ ὑπομονὴ ἔργον τέλειον[4] ἐχέτω, ἵνα ἦτε τέλειοι καὶ

ὁλόκληροι[5] ἐν μηδενὶ λειπόμενοι.[6]

1:5 Εἰ δέ τις ὑμῶν λείπεται σοφίας, αἰτείτω παρὰ τοῦ διδόντος θεοῦ

πᾶσιν ἁπλῶς[7] καὶ μὴ ὀνειδίζοντος[8] καὶ δοθήσεται αὐτῷ. **1:6** αἰτείτω δὲ ἐν

---

[1]   περιπίπτω, *I fall in with, encounter* (3).
[2]   ποικίλος, η, ον, *various kinds, diversified* (10).
[3]   δοκίμιον, ου, τό, *testing* (2).
[4]   τέλειος, α, ον, *perfect, mature, having achieved the purpose* (19). See Davids, 69-70.
[5]   ὁλόκληρος, ον, *complete, whole* (2).
[6]   λείπω, transitive: *I leave*; intransitive mid. and pass.: *lack, fall short of* (6).
[7]   ἁπλῶς, *simply, sincerely*, with δίδωμι, *generously, without reserve* (1).
[8]   ὀνειδίζω, *I reproach, revile, find fault* (9).

---

(2)   1:2   πᾶσαν. James' use of πᾶσαν has caused a myriad of problems for exegetes who are trying to apply the text to real life. What exactly does πᾶσαν mean? If you are preparing for the ministry, you must be able to deal with this issue. And when you think you have understood it, can you explain it to a widow who is dying of cancer and cannot find a family to adopt her three children? If you cannot, then you have not properly exegeted πᾶσαν.

(3)   1:3   κατεργάζεται. What does κατεργάζεται actually mean? A word study is helpful.

(4)   1:3   ὑπομονή. Does testing actually produce ὑπομονή? If so, then everybody who has been tested would have endurance! Don't let your exegesis stop at the bare meaning of the word. Always step back and look at the context. See Davids, 68-69.

πίστει <u>μηδὲν</u> διακρινόμενος·[1] ὁ γὰρ διακρινόμενος ἔοικεν[2] κλύδωνι[3] θαλάσσης

ἀνεμιζομένῳ[4] καὶ ῥιπιζομένῳ.[5] **1:7** μὴ γὰρ οἰέσθω[6] ὁ ἄνθρωπος ἐκεῖνος ὅτι

λήμψεταί τι παρὰ τοῦ κυρίου, **1:8** ἀνὴρ δίψυχος,[7] ἀκατάστατος[8] ἐν πάσαις

ταῖς ὁδοῖς αὐτοῦ.

1:9 Καυχάσθω δὲ ὁ ἀδελφὸς ὁ ταπεινὸς[9] ἐν τῷ ὕψει[10] αὐτοῦ, **1:10** ὁ δὲ

<u>πλούσιος</u> ἐν τῇ <u>ταπεινώσει</u>[11] αὐτοῦ, ὅτι ὡς ἄνθος[12] χόρτου[13] παρελεύσεται.

---

[1] διακρίνω, active: *I separate; differentiate; judge;* middle: *doubt, waver* (19).

[2] ἔοικα, *I am like, resemble* (2). Is actually a perfect with a present meaning and it takes an object in the dative.

[3] κλύδων, ωνος, ὁ, *rough water, wave* (2).

[4] ἀνεμίζω, passive: *I am moved by the wind* (1).

[5] ῥιπίζω, *I blow here and there, toss* (1).

[6] οἴομαι, *I suppose, expect, imagine* (3). Think of the verbal root as being *οι and the parsing should be clear.

[7] δίψυχος, ον, *double-minded; doubting, hesitating* (2). On its Jewish background see Davids, 74-75.

[8] ἀκατάστατος, ον, *unstable, restless* (2).

[9] ταπεινός, ή, όν, *lowly, poor; subservient* (8).

[10] ὕψος, ους, τό, *height, high place* (6).

[11] ταπείνωσις, εως, ἡ, *humiliation, humility; self-abasement* (4).

[12] ἄνθος, ους, τό, *flower, blossom; fragrance* (4).

[13] χόρτος, ου, ὁ, *grass, hay* (15).

---

(5)   1:6   μηδείς is technically an adjective, but as you can see in *BAGD* (2b) the form μηδέν developed an almost adverbial sense of *not ... at all, in no way.*

(6)   1:10   πλούσιος. Is this person a Christian or not? See Davids, 76-77.

(7)   1:10   ταπεινώσει. How is it possible to boast in one's ταπείνωσις?

1:11 ἀνέτειλεν[1] γὰρ ὁ ἥλιος σὺν τῷ καύσωνι[2] καὶ ἐξήρανεν[3] τὸν χόρτον καὶ τὸ

ἄνθος αὐτοῦ ἐξέπεσεν[4] καὶ ἡ εὐπρέπεια[5] τοῦ προσώπου αὐτοῦ ἀπώλετο· οὕτως

καὶ ὁ πλούσιος ἐν ταῖς πορείαις[6] αὐτοῦ μαρανθήσεται.[7]

Testing and Speech (1:12-21)

1:12 Μακάριος ἀνὴρ ὃς ὑπομένει[8] πειρασμόν, ὅτι δόκιμος[9] γενόμενος

λήμψεται τὸν στέφανον[10] τῆς ζωῆς ὃν ἐπηγγείλατο[11] τοῖς ἀγαπῶσιν αὐτόν.

1:13 μηδεὶς πειραζόμενος λεγέτω ὅτι Ἀπὸ θεοῦ πειράζομαι· ὁ γὰρ θεὸς

ἀπείραστός[12] ἐστιν κακῶν, <u>πειράζει</u> δὲ αὐτὸς οὐδένα. **1:14** ἕκαστος δὲ

πειράζεται ὑπὸ τῆς ἰδίας <u>ἐπιθυμίας</u> ἐξελκόμενος[13] καὶ δελεαζόμενος·[14]

---

[1] ἀνατέλλω, transitive: *I cause to rise/spring up*; intransitive: *rise* (9).

[2] καύσων, ωνος, ὁ, *heat, burning* sun (3).

[3] ξηραίνω, active: *I dry out*; passive: *become dry, wither* (15).

[4] ἐκπίπτω, *I fall off; drift off course; lose* (10).

[5] εὐπρέπεια, ας, ἡ, *fine appearance, beauty* (1).

[6] πορεία, ας, ἡ, *journey; way of life, conduct* (2).

[7] μαραίνω, active: *I quench; destroy*; always passive in our literature: *(gradually) die
     out, fade, disappear* (1).

[8] ὑπομένω, *I remain, bear, endure* (17).

[9] δόκιμος, ον, *approved* (by test); *genuine; respected* (7).

[10] στέφανος, ου, ὁ, *wreath, crown* (18).

[11] ἐπαγγέλλομαι, *I promise; profess* (15).

[12] ἀπείραστος, ον, *without temptation* (1).

[13] ἐξέλκω, *I drag away* (1).

[14] δελεάζω, *I lure, entice* (3).

---

(8) 1:13   πειράζει. But does not "God" appear as the subject of πειράζω in the
            LXX? See Davids, 82-83.

(9) 1:14   ἐπιθυμίας is singular. Why? See Davids, 83.

1:15 εἶτα[1] ἡ ἐπιθυμία συλλαβοῦσα[2] τίκτει[3] ἁμαρτίαν, ἡ δὲ ἁμαρτία

ἀποτελεσθεῖσα[4] ἀποκύει[5] θάνατον.

1:16 Μὴ πλανᾶσθε, ἀδελφοί μου ἀγαπητοί. **1:17** πᾶσα δόσις[6] ἀγαθὴ καὶ

πᾶν δώρημα[7] τέλειον ἄνωθέν[8] ἐστιν καταβαῖνον ἀπὸ τοῦ πατρὸς τῶν φώτων,

παρ' ᾧ οὐκ ἔνι[9] παραλλαγὴ[10] ἢ τροπῆς[11] ἀποσκίασμα.[12] **1:18** βουληθεὶς

ἀπεκύησεν ἡμᾶς λόγῳ ἀληθείας εἰς τὸ εἶναι ἡμᾶς ἀπαρχήν[13] τινα[14] τῶν αὐτοῦ

κτισμάτων.[15]

---

[1] εἶτα, *then, next* (13).

[2] συλλαμβάνω, active: *I seize, grasp; conceive; help;* middle: *seize, arrest* (16).

[3] τίκτω, *bear, I give birth* (18).

[4] ἀποτελέω, *I bring to completion, finish; perform* (2).

[5] ἀποκυέω, *I bring forth, give birth to* (2).

[6] δόσις, εως, ἡ, *gift, giving* (2).

[7] δώρημα, ατος, τό, *gift, present* (2).

[8] ἄνωθεν, *from above; from the beginning; again* (13).

[9] ἔνι, *there is* (6). An abbreviated form of ἔνεστιν.

[10] παραλλαγή, ῆς, ἡ, *change, variation* (1).

[11] τροπή, ῆς, ἡ, *turning; variation, change* (1).

[12] ἀποσκίασμα, ματος, τό, *shadow* (1). This is a difficult phrase. You may want to check Davids, 87-88.

[13] ἀπαρχή, ῆς, ἡ, *firstfruits* (9).

[14] τίς can be used to "soften the metaphorical expression" and is translated "so to say," "a kind of" (*BDF* §301.1). *BAGD* says τίς is used "to moderate an expr. that is too definite" (2.b.α).

[15] κτίσμα, ματος, τό, *creature, that which is created* (4).

Speech and Anger (1:19-21)

1:19 Ἴστε,[1] ἀδελφοί μου ἀγαπητοί· ἔστω δὲ πᾶς ἄνθρωπος ταχὺς[2] εἰς τὸ

ἀκοῦσαι, βραδὺς[3] εἰς τὸ λαλῆσαι, βραδὺς εἰς ὀργήν· **1:20** ὀργὴ γὰρ ἀνδρὸς

δικαιοσύνην θεοῦ οὐκ ἐργάζεται. **1:21** διὸ ἀποθέμενοι[4] πᾶσαν ῥυπαρίαν[5] καὶ

περισσείαν[6] κακίας[7] ἐν πραΰτητι,[8] δέξασθε τὸν ἔμφυτον[9] λόγον τὸν δυνάμενον

σῶσαι τὰς ψυχὰς ὑμῶν.

---

[1] Ἴστε is the perfect active imperative of οἶδα. You may just want to memorize it.

[2] ταχύς, εῖα, ύ, *swift, quick* (1). The neuter singular ταχύ is used twelve times adverbially, meaning *quickly*.

[3] βραδύς, εῖα, ύ, *slow* (3).

[4] ἀποτίθημι, *I take off; lay down, put away* (9).

[5] ῥυπαρία, ας, ἡ, *dirt, filth; greediness, avarice* (1).

[6] περισσεία, ας, ἡ, *surplus, abundance* (4).

[7] κακία, ας, ἡ, *depravity, wickedness; misfortune* (11).

[8] πραΰτης, ητος, ἡ, *gentleness, humility, meekness* (11).

[9] ἔμφυτος, ον, *implanted* (1).

Chapter 9

ΠΡΟΣ ΦΙΛΙΠΠΗΣΙΟΥΣ 1:27-2:13

This is a short passage but theologically one of the most significant in the Pauline literature. Be sure to read at least one commentary on the passage. There are theological and word study issues that are essential to discuss if you are to understand what the passage means.

Be sure to phrase especially the "hymn" in 2:6-11 and study Fee's comments about whether or not these verses are a hymn, especially pp. 40-43 and p. 193n4. Fee includes a visual representation of the text similar to phrasing in his commentary, where you can see his emphasis on the connectives (pp. 194-95). Notice the lack of articles in 2:5-11.

Commentary references are to Gordon D. Fee, *Paul's Letter to the Philippians*, in The New International Commentary on the New Testament (Eerdmans, 1995), and Gerald F. Hawthorne, *Philippians*, in Word Biblical Commentary (Word, 1983). See also Peter T. O'Brien, *Commentary on Philippians*, in New International Greek Testament Commentary (Eerdmans, 1991). Although we will not prompt you to do so, this is a good time to read several commentaries and enter into their dialogue and debate. For example, what do you think of Fee's discussion of the "trinitarian substructure" in 2:1 (pp. 179-82)?

Appeal to Unity (1:27-30)

1:27 Μόνον ἀξίως[1] τοῦ εὐαγγελίου τοῦ Χριστοῦ πολιτεύεσθε,[2] ἵνα εἴτε

ἐλθὼν καὶ ἰδὼν ὑμᾶς εἴτε ἀπὼν[3] ἀκούω τὰ περὶ ὑμῶν, ὅτι στήκετε[4] ἐν ἑνὶ

---

[1] ἀξίως, *worthily, in a manner worthy of* (6)

[2] πολιτεύομαι, *I have my citizenship* or *home; live, conduct myself, lead my life* (2). See Fee, 161-62.

[3] ἄπειμι, *I am absent, away* (8).

[4] στήκω, *I stand; stand firm, am steadfast* (9).

Exegetical Discussion

(1) 1:27 Vv 27-30 form one sentence. Find the implied subject, main verb, and the four following main thoughts. See Fee's "phrasing" on pp. 159-60.

πνεύματι, μιᾷ ψυχῇ συναθλοῦντες[1] τῇ πίστει <u>τοῦ εὐαγγελίου</u> **1:28** καὶ μὴ

πτυρόμενοι[2] ἐν μηδενὶ ὑπὸ τῶν ἀντικειμένων,[3] <u>ἥτις</u> ἐστὶν αὐτοῖς ἔνδειξις[4]

ἀπωλείας,[5] ὑμῶν δὲ σωτηρίας, καὶ τοῦτο ἀπὸ θεοῦ· **1:29** ὅτι ὑμῖν <u>ἐχαρίσθη</u> τὸ

ὑπὲρ Χριστοῦ, οὐ μόνον τὸ εἰς αὐτὸν πιστεύειν ἀλλὰ καὶ τὸ ὑπὲρ αὐτοῦ

πάσχειν, **1:30** τὸν αὐτὸν ἀγῶνα[6] ἔχοντες, οἷον[7] εἴδετε ἐν ἐμοὶ καὶ νῦν ἀκούετε

ἐν ἐμοί.

---

[1] συναθλέω, *I contend* or *struggle along with* τινί *someone* (2).
[2] πτύρω, *I frighten, scare* (1).
[3] ἀντίκειμαι, *I am opposed, in opposition* τινί *to someone* (8).
[4] ἔνδειξις, εως, ἡ, *sign; proof* (4).
[5] ἀπώλεια, ας, ἡ, *destruction, annihilation* (18).
[6] ἀγών, ἀγῶνος, ὁ, *contest; struggle, fight* (6).
[7] οἷος, α, ον, relative pronoun, *of what sort, (such) as* (14).

---

(2)   1:27   πνεύματι. Is πνεύματι "spirit" or "Spirit"? See Fee, 163-66.

(3)   **1:27 *** τοῦ εὐαγγελίου is a **genitive of apposition** (also **epexegetical geni-tive**). We have already seen how you can place a word in apposition to another by putting it in the same case. You can also place a word in apposition by putting it in the genitive regardless of the case of the "head" noun (which can cause confusion when the head noun is also in the genitive). Wallace qualifies the genitive of apposition by saying that the equation between the two is not exact. Normally the head noun is ambiguous and is part of a larger category while the noun in the genitive states a specific example. See Fee, 167.

(4)   1:28   ἥτις. Hawthorne says ἥτις refers back to τῇ πίστει (58-60) while Fee says it refers back to the preceding clause in general and is feminine because it has been attracted to the gender of the following ἔνδειξις (168n53). Who do you think is correct, and what is the significance for exegesis and theology?

(5)   1:29   ἐχαρίσθη is an interesting choice within the context of suffering. What is its significance? How will you preach this?

Unity through Humility (2:1-4)

2:1 Εἴ τις οὖν παράκλησις ἐν Χριστῷ, εἴ τι παραμύθιον[1] ἀγάπης, εἴ τις

κοινωνία[2] πνεύματος, εἴ τις σπλάγχνα[3] καὶ οἰκτιρμοί,[4] **2:2** πληρώσατέ μου τὴν

χαρὰν ἵνα τὸ αὐτὸ φρονῆτε, τὴν αὐτὴν ἀγάπην ἔχοντες, σύμψυχοι,[5] τὸ ἕν

φρονοῦντες, **2:3** μηδὲν κατʼ ἐριθείαν[6] μηδὲ κατὰ κενοδοξίαν[7] ἀλλὰ τῇ

ταπεινοφροσύνῃ[8] ἀλλήλους ἡγούμενοι ὑπερέχοντας[9] ἑαυτῶν, **2:4** μὴ τὰ ἑαυτῶν

ἕκαστος σκοποῦντες[10] ἀλλὰ [καὶ] τὰ ἑτέρων ἕκαστοι.

---

[1] παραμύθιον, ου, τό, *encouragement, consolation* (1).

[2] κοινωνία, ας, ἡ, *fellowship; generosity; participation, close communion* (19).

[3] σπλάγχνον, ου, τό, almost always plural, *entrails; heart* (or the *seat of the emotions*); *love, affection* (11).

[4] οἰκτιρμός, οῦ, ὁ, *pity, mercy, compassion* (5).

[5] σύμψυχος, ον, *harmonious, united in spirit* (1).

[6] ἐριθεία, ας, ἡ, *strife, contentiousness, selfish ambition* (7). Hawthorne says this word can also mean *rivalry*. Aristotle uses it to mean "self-seeking pursuit of political office by unfair means."

[7] κενοδοξία, ας, ἡ, *vanity, conceit, excessive ambition* (1). It refers to a conceit that has no basis, a "kind of 'empty glory' that only the self-blessed can bestow on themselves" (Fee, 187).

[8] ταπεινοφροσύνη, ης, ἡ, *humility, modesty* (7), a "uniquely Christian virtue" (Fee, 187-88).

[9] ὑπερέχω, *I am better than, surpass; have power over* (5).

[10] σκοπέω, *I look out for, notice* (6).

---

(6)   2:1   Εἰ. Paul uses a series of conditional phrases (Εἴ τις …). Be sure that you know what kind of conditions they are and how that affects the nuance of what he is saying.

(7)   2:1   ἀγάπης. What type of genitive is ἀγάπης?

(8)   2:1   πνεύματος. Is πνεύματος objective or subjective? See Fee, 181n40.

(9)   2:2   φρονέω means much more than simply *I think*. See Fee, 184-85.

(10)   2:2   σύμψυχοι. Why is σύμψυχοι nominative?

(11)   2:2   τὸ ἕν is idiomatic, but if you look at what each word means, you can probably figure it out for yourself.

The Example of Christ (2:5-11)

2:5 τοῦτο φρονεῖτε ἐν ὑμῖν ὃ καὶ ἐν Χριστῷ Ἰησοῦ, **2:6** ὃς ἐν μορφῇ[1] θεοῦ

<u>ὑπάρχων</u> οὐχ ἁρπαγμὸν[2] ἡγήσατο[3] τὸ εἶναι ἴσα[4] θεῷ,[5] **2:7** ἀλλὰ ἑαυτὸν

ἐκένωσεν[6] μορφὴν δούλου λαβών, ἐν ὁμοιώματι[7] ἀνθρώπων γενόμενος· καὶ

<u>σχήματι</u>[8] εὑρεθεὶς ὡς ἄνθρωπος **2:8** ἐταπείνωσεν[9] ἑαυτὸν γενόμενος ὑπήκοος[10]

μέχρι[11] θανάτου, θανάτου δὲ <u>σταυροῦ</u>. **2:9** διὸ καὶ ὁ θεὸς αὐτὸν <u>ὑπερύψωσεν</u>[12]

---

[1]   μορφή, ῆς, ἡ, *form, outward appearance, shape* (3). It is essential that you do a word study on μορφή. It is used in v. 7 too. See Fee, 204-5, and Hawthorne, 81-84.

[2]   ἁρπαγμός, οῦ, ὁ, *prize, booty, robbery* (1). See Fee, 205-7.

[3]   ἡγέομαι takes a double accusative here.

[4]   ἴσος, η, ον, *equal* (8). The neuter plural is used adverbially.

[5]   τὸ εἶναι ἴσα θεῷ is a single thought unit. What is its grammatical function?

[6]   κενόω, *I make empty; render void* (5). Did Christ empty himself of anything or did he pour himself out? See Fee, 210-11, and Hawthorne, 85-86. This is a tremendously important decision, as the history of theology illustrates.

[7]   ὁμοίωμα, ματος, τό, *likeness; image, copy; form, appearance* (6). Cf. Rom 8:3.

[8]   σχῆμα, ματος, τό, *outward appearance, form, shape* (2). Be sure you understand the difference between σχῆμα and μορφή. See Hawthorne, 87-88.

[9]   ταπεινόω, *I humble, humiliate* (14).

[10] ὑπήκοος, ον, *obedient* (3).

[11] μέχρι, *until* (17), which is followed by the genitive.

[12] ὑπερυψόω, active: *I raise to the loftiest height;* middle: *I raise myself, rise* (1).

---

(12) **2:6 ***   ὑπάρχων is a **concessive participle**, which carries the idea of "even though." In this context, does this word carry the idea of the pre-existence of Christ? See Fee, 202-3, especially 203n41.

(13) 2:7   σχήματι. What is the relationship between μορφή, σχῆμα, and ὁμοιώματι? Are they synonymous in this context or different?

(14) 2:8   σταυροῦ is anarthrous. How does that help your exegesis? See Fee, 217-187. What type of genitive is it?

(15) 2:9   ὑπερύψωσεν. Is there any exegetical significance to the fact that ὑπερύψωσεν is aorist? Remember, the aorist is the catch-all tense, so just because it is aorist does not mean that the tense is necessarily significant.

καὶ ἐχαρίσατο αὐτῷ τὸ ὄνομα τὸ ὑπὲρ πᾶν ὄνομα, **2:10** ἵνα ἐν τῷ ὀνόματι Ἰησοῦ

πᾶν γόνυ[1] κάμψῃ[2] ἐπουρανίων[3] καὶ ἐπιγείων[4] καὶ καταχθονίων[5] **2:11** καὶ

πᾶσα γλῶσσα ἐξομολογήσηται[6] ὅτι κύριος Ἰησοῦς Χριστὸς εἰς δόξαν θεοῦ

πατρός.

Appeal to Obedience (2:12-13)

2:12 Ὥστε, ἀγαπητοί μου, καθὼς πάντοτε ὑπηκούσατε, μὴ ὡς ἐν τῇ

παρουσίᾳ μου μόνον ἀλλὰ νῦν πολλῷ μᾶλλον ἐν τῇ ἀπουσίᾳ[7] μου, μετὰ φόβου

καὶ τρόμου[8] τὴν ἑαυτῶν σωτηρίαν κατεργάζεσθε· **2:13** θεὸς γάρ ἐστιν ὁ

ἐνεργῶν ἐν ὑμῖν καὶ τὸ θέλειν καὶ τὸ ἐνεργεῖν ὑπὲρ τῆς εὐδοκίας.[9]

---

[1] γόνυ, ατος, τό, *knee* (12).

[2] κάμπτω, *I bend, bow* (4).

[3] ἐπουράνιος, ον, *heavenly* (19). It is often used substantivally, meaning *heavenly things*.

[4] ἐπίγειος, ον, *earthly* (7). It is often used substantivally, meaning *earthly things*.

[5] καταχθόνιος, ον, *under the earth* (1).

[6] ἐξομολογέω, active: *I promise, consent;* middle: *I confess, admit; acknowledge, praise* (10).

[7] ἀπουσία, ας, ἡ, *absence* (1).

[8] τρόμος, ου, ὁ, *trembling, quivering* (5).

[9] εὐδοκία, ας, ἡ, *goodwill; favor, good pleasure; wish, desire* (9).

---

(16) 2:10 ἐπουρανίων. Why is ἐπουρανίων genitive?

(17) 2:12 κατεργάζεσθε. Spend time working through what this means in this context and how it will affect your ministry. See Fee, 234-36.

(18) 2:13 ἐνεργῶν. Did you notice the play on words that ties vv 12-13 together? See Fee, 237.

(19) 2:13 τῆς. What is the precise meaning of τῆς? Of whose good pleasure is Paul speaking? See Fee, 239.

Chapter 10

ΚΑΤΑ ΜΑΘΘΑΙΟΝ 13:1-23

The Parable of the Soils (or as Jesus calls it, τὴν παραβολὴν τοῦ σπείραντος) is a good combination of translation, exegesis, and application. The translation is straight-forward and you should enjoy it. Be sure to discuss why Jesus spoke in parables and how an understanding of Greek helps you to interpret the verses.

Be prepared for a few genitive absolutes, the substantival use of the participle (*BBG* §29.8), especially the articular infinitive, and various uses of the infinitive (*BBG* §32.9ff). The word συνίημι also occurs in various forms; you may want to brush up on its tense stems.

Commentary references are to Donald. A. Hagner, *Matthew 1-13*, in Word Biblical Commentary (Word, 1993).

The Parable of the Soils (13:1-9)

13:1 Ἐν τῇ ἡμέρᾳ ἐκείνῃ ἐξελθὼν ὁ Ἰησοῦς τῆς οἰκίας ἐκάθητο παρὰ τὴν θάλασσαν· **13:2** καὶ συνήχθησαν πρὸς αὐτὸν ὄχλοι πολλοί, ὥστε[1] αὐτὸν εἰς πλοῖον ἐμβάντα[2] καθῆσθαι, καὶ πᾶς ὁ ὄχλος ἐπὶ τὸν αἰγιαλὸν[3] εἱστήκει.[4]

13:3 καὶ ἐλάλησεν αὐτοῖς πολλὰ ἐν παραβολαῖς λέγων, Ἰδοὺ ἐξῆλθεν ὁ σπείρων τοῦ σπείρειν. **13:4** καὶ ἐν τῷ σπείρειν αὐτὸν ἃ μὲν ἔπεσεν παρὰ τὴν ὁδόν, καὶ ἐλθόντα τὰ πετεινὰ[5] κατέφαγεν[6] αὐτά. **13:5** ἄλλα[7] δὲ ἔπεσεν ἐπὶ τὰ πετρώδη[8]

---

[1] ὥστε followed by the infinitive is a special construction. See *BBG* §32.13.

[2] ἐμβαίνω, *I embark* (16).

[3] αἰγιαλός, οῦ, ὁ, *shore* (6).

[4] From a v-6a verb.

[5] πετεινόν, οῦ, τό, *bird* (14).

[6] κατεσθίω, *I eat, consume, devour* (14). Its second aorist is κατέφαγον.

[7] Did you notice that ἄλλα is not the conjunction ἀλλά, which receives its accent on the final syllable?

[8] πετρώδης, ες, *rocky, stony* (4).

ὅπου οὐκ εἶχεν[1] γῆν πολλήν, καὶ εὐθέως ἐξανέτειλεν[2] διὰ τὸ μὴ ἔχειν βάθος[3]

γῆς· **13:6** ἡλίου δὲ ἀνατείλαντος[4] ἐκαυματίσθη[5] καὶ διὰ τὸ μὴ ἔχειν ῥίζαν[6]

ἐξηράνθη.[7] **13:7** ἄλλα δὲ ἔπεσεν ἐπὶ τὰς ἀκάνθας,[8] καὶ ἀνέβησαν αἱ ἄκανθαι

καὶ ἔπνιξαν[9] αὐτά. **13:8** ἄλλα δὲ ἔπεσεν ἐπὶ τὴν γῆν τὴν καλὴν καὶ ἐδίδου

καρπόν, ὃ[10] μὲν ἑκατόν,[11] ὃ δὲ ἑξήκοντα,[12] ὃ δὲ τριάκοντα.[13] **13:9** ὁ ἔχων ὦτα

ἀκουέτω.

The Purpose of Parables (13:10-17)

    13:10 Καὶ προσελθόντες οἱ μαθηταὶ εἶπαν αὐτῷ, Διὰ τί ἐν παραβολαῖς

λαλεῖς αὐτοῖς; **13:11** ὁ δὲ ἀποκριθεὶς εἶπεν αὐτοῖς, Ὅτι ὑμῖν δέδοται γνῶναι τὰ

μυστήρια τῆς βασιλείας τῶν οὐρανῶν, ἐκείνοις δὲ οὐ δέδοται. **13:12** ὅστις γὰρ

---

[1]   On the augment see *MBG* §31.5a.

[2]   ἐξανατέλλω, *I spring up out* (2).

[3]   βάθος, ους, τό, *depth* (8).

[4]   ἀνατέλλω, transitive: *I cause to spring/rise up*; intransitive: *I rise/spring up* (9).

[5]   καυματίζω, *I burn, I scorch* (4).

[6]   ῥίζα, ης, ἡ, *root; source; descendant* (17).

[7]   ξηραίνω, active: *I dry up, parch, wither*; passive: *I become dry* (15).

[8]   ἄκανθα, ης, ἡ, *thorn-plant* (14).

[9]   πνίγω, *I choke, strangle* (3).

[10]   *BAGD* II.2 says that the relative pronoun can also function as the demonstrative pronoun. See the examples they give.

[11]   ἑκατόν, *one hundred* (17). Indeclinable.

[12]   ἑξήκοντα, *sixty* (9). Indeclinable.

[13]   τριάκοντα, *thirty* (11). Indeclinable.

ἔχει, δοθήσεται αὐτῷ καὶ περισσευθήσεται· ὅστις δὲ οὐκ ἔχει, καὶ ὃ ἔχει

ἀρθήσεται[1] ἀπ᾽ αὐτοῦ. **13:13** διὰ τοῦτο ἐν παραβολαῖς αὐτοῖς λαλῶ, ὅτι

βλέποντες οὐ βλέπουσιν καὶ ἀκούοντες οὐκ ἀκούουσιν οὐδὲ συνίουσιν,

13:14 καὶ ἀναπληροῦται[2] αὐτοῖς ἡ προφητεία[3] Ἠσαΐου ἡ λέγουσα,

> Ἀκοῇ[4] ἀκούσετε καὶ οὐ μὴ συνῆτε,

> καὶ βλέποντες βλέψετε καὶ οὐ μὴ ἴδητε.

---

[1] Its verbal root is *αρ and ι was added in the formation of the present tense stem. αρ + ι › αρι › αιρ (cf. *MBG* §33.4).

[2] ἀναπληρόω, *I fulfill* (6).

[3] προφητεία, ας, ἡ, *prophecy, gift of prophecy* (19).

[4] Ἀκοῇ is not a normal Greek construction. It appears that the Septuagint (Isa 6:9) is attempting to imitate the style of the underlying Hebrew. This is why we often find the use of a Greek cognate participle or dative for the Hebrew infinitive absolute. Ἀκοῇ is probably classified as a "dative of reference" since it does not designate what they heard but that they heard with respect to hearing.

Exegetical Discussion

(1)   13:12   ἔχει. Has what? See Hagner, 373.

(2)   13:13   ὅτι. Check out the full range of meanings for ὅτι. Do not assume the verse means something that ὅτι does not allow. Mark has ἵνα. Is there a difference? See Hagner, 375.

(3)   13:13   βλέποντες. What type of participle is βλέποντες and the following ἀκούοντες? See Hagner, 373.

13:15 ἐπαχύνθη[1] γὰρ ἡ καρδία τοῦ λαοῦ τούτου,

       καὶ τοῖς ὠσὶν βαρέως[2] <u>ἤκουσαν</u>

       καὶ τοὺς ὀφθαλμοὺς αὐτῶν ἐκάμμυσαν,[3]

       <u>μήποτε</u> ἴδωσιν τοῖς ὀφθαλμοῖς

       καὶ τοῖς ὠσὶν ἀκούσωσιν

       καὶ τῇ καρδίᾳ συνῶσιν

       καὶ ἐπιστρέψωσιν καὶ ἰάσομαι αὐτούς.

13:16 ὑμῶν δὲ μακάριοι οἱ ὀφθαλμοὶ ὅτι βλέπουσιν καὶ τὰ ὦτα ὑμῶν ὅτι

ἀκούουσιν. **13:17** ἀμὴν γὰρ λέγω ὑμῖν ὅτι πολλοὶ προφῆται καὶ δίκαιοι

ἐπεθύμησαν[4] ἰδεῖν ἃ βλέπετε καὶ οὐκ εἶδαν, καὶ ἀκοῦσαι ἃ ἀκούετε καὶ οὐκ

ἤκουσαν.

---

[1] παχύνω, *I make fat, well-nourished; make impervious, dull* (2).

[2] βαρέως, *heavily, with difficulty* (2). When the adverb is used with ἀκούω it generally denotes "hard of hearing."

[3] καμμύω, *I close* eyes (2).

[4] ἐπιθυμέω, *I desire* (16).

---

(4)   3:15   ἤκουσαν. Did you notice the shift from passive to active with ἤκουσαν? The people addressed by the prophet did not want to understand. How does this help you understand why Jesus spoke in parables? Remember that these kinds of subtle shifts are often the key to understanding the passage.

(5)   13:15   μήποτε. Beginning with μήποτε, is Jesus still describing the dullness of the peoples' hearts? Or to ask it another way, is Jesus still describing the negative consequences in v 15a or has he shifted to something else? If so, what?

The Explanation of the Parable of the Soils (13:18-23)

13:18 Ὑμεῖς οὖν ἀκούσατε τὴν παραβολὴν τοῦ σπείραντος.

13:19 παντὸς ἀκούοντος τὸν λόγον τῆς βασιλείας καὶ μὴ συνιέντος ἔρχεται ὁ πονηρὸς καὶ ἁρπάζει[1] τὸ ἐσπαρμένον ἐν τῇ καρδίᾳ αὐτοῦ, οὗτός ἐστιν ὁ παρὰ τὴν ὁδὸν σπαρείς. **13:20** ὁ δὲ ἐπὶ τὰ πετρώδη σπαρείς, οὗτός ἐστιν ὁ τὸν λόγον ἀκούων καὶ εὐθὺς μετὰ χαρᾶς λαμβάνων αὐτόν, **13:21** οὐκ ἔχει δὲ ῥίζαν ἐν ἑαυτῷ ἀλλὰ πρόσκαιρός[2] ἐστιν, γενομένης δὲ θλίψεως ἢ διωγμοῦ[3] διὰ τὸν λόγον εὐθὺς σκανδαλίζεται. **13:22** ὁ δὲ εἰς τὰς ἀκάνθας σπαρείς, οὗτός ἐστιν ὁ τὸν λόγον ἀκούων, καὶ ἡ μέριμνα[4] τοῦ αἰῶνος καὶ ἡ ἀπάτη[5] τοῦ πλούτου <u>συμπνίγει</u>[6] τὸν λόγον καὶ ἄκαρπος[7] γίνεται. **13:23** ὁ δὲ ἐπὶ τὴν καλὴν γῆν σπαρείς, οὗτός ἐστιν ὁ τὸν λόγον ἀκούων καὶ συνιείς,[8] ὃς δὴ[9] καρποφορεῖ[10] καὶ ποιεῖ ὃ μὲν ἑκατόν, ὃ δὲ ἑξήκοντα, ὃ δὲ τριάκοντα.

---

[1] ἁρπάζω, *I seize, snatch, steal, obtain by robbery* (14).

[2] πρόσκαιρος, ον, *temporary, transitory* (4).

[3] διωγμός, οῦ, ὁ, *persecution* (10). διωγμός is always used in the New Testament of religious persecution.

[4] μέριμνα, ης, ἡ, *anxiety, worry, care* (6).

[5] ἀπάτη, ης, ἡ, *deceit, deception, delight* in a sinful way (7).

[6] συμπνίγω, *I choke utterly; crowd around* (5).

[7] ἄκαρπος, ον, *useless, unfruitful* (7).

[8] συνιείς is a participle.

[9] δή, *indeed, truly* (5). A postpositive particle.

[10] καρποφορέω, *I bear fruit or crops* (8).

---

(6) 13:22 συμπνίγει. What do you think συμπνίγει and ἄκαρπος signify? How does the imagery of "choke" and "fruitless" help us understand the destiny of the seed choked by the cares of the world? Or does the parable tell us anything about the theological issue of eternal security or loss of salvation?

Chapter 11

ΠΕΤΡΟΥ Α΄ 1:1-21

This will be by far the most difficult passage you have translated thus far. But do not let that frighten you; it is a challenge, and a warning. Be sure to allow time to translate it properly. You will want to pay special attention to prepositions and grammar. Do not just translate it quickly but ask yourself why words, cases, and tenses are the way they are. Think through the text.

Peter often separates the article from the word it is modifying by placing a modifier between them (e.g., article + article-adjective + participle). Remember, we do not always give the definitions to proper nouns.

Commentary references are to J. Ramsey Michaels, *1 Peter,* in Word Biblical Commentary (Word, 1988).

Greeting (1:1-2)

1:1 Πέτρος ἀπόστολος Ἰησοῦ Χριστοῦ ἐκλεκτοῖς παρεπιδήμοις[1]

διασπορᾶς[2] Πόντου, Γαλατίας, Καππαδοκίας, Ἀσίας καὶ Βιθυνίας, **1:2** <u>κατὰ</u>

---

[1] παρεπίδημος, ον, *sojourning* (3). Usually used in our literature as a substantive, *stranger, sojourner, exile.*

[2] διασπορά, ᾶς, ἡ, *dispersion* (3). Can be used of both the people and the location.

Exegetical Discussion

(1)   1:1   διασπορᾶς. Is Paul writing to Jewish or Gentile Christians? See Michaels, 6-9.

(2)   1:2   κατά. To what is κατά grammatically connected?

πρόγνωσιν[1] θεοῦ πατρὸς ἐν ἁγιασμῷ[2] <u>πνεύματος</u> εἰς ὑπακοὴν[3] καὶ ῥαντισμὸν[4]

αἵματος Ἰησοῦ Χριστοῦ, χάρις ὑμῖν καὶ εἰρήνη πληθυνθείη.[5]

Rebirth (1:3-5)

1:3 Εὐλογητὸς[6] ὁ θεὸς καὶ πατὴρ τοῦ κυρίου ἡμῶν Ἰησοῦ Χριστοῦ, ὁ

κατὰ τὸ πολὺ αὐτοῦ ἔλεος ἀναγεννήσας[7] ἡμᾶς εἰς ἐλπίδα ζῶσαν δι᾽

ἀναστάσεως Ἰησοῦ Χριστοῦ ἐκ νεκρῶν, **1:4** εἰς κληρονομίαν[8] ἄφθαρτον[9] καὶ

ἀμίαντον[10] καὶ ἀμάραντον,[11] τετηρημένην ἐν οὐρανοῖς εἰς ὑμᾶς **1:5** τοὺς ἐν

δυνάμει θεοῦ φρουρουμένους[12] διὰ πίστεως εἰς σωτηρίαν ἑτοίμην[13]

ἀποκαλυφθῆναι ἐν καιρῷ ἐσχάτῳ.

---

[1] πρόγνωσις, εως, ἡ, *foreknowledge* (2).

[2] ἁγιασμός, οῦ, ὁ, *holiness, sanctification, consecration* (10). To what does it refer?

[3] ὑπακοή, ῆς, ἡ, *obedience* (15).

[4] ῥαντισμός, οῦ, ὁ, *sprinkling* (2).

[5] πληθύνω, active: *I increase, multiply;* passive: *I am multiplied, grow, increase* (12). πληθυνθείη is in the optative mood, aorist passive (cf. *BBG* §35.9). It denotes a wish: "may it be."

[6] εὐλογητός, ή, όν, *blessed* (8).

[7] ἀναγεννάω, *I beget again, cause to be born again* (2). The next time you happen to be in Aberdeen, Scotland, check into the library and read the fascinating, unpublished, Ph.D. dissertation, *The Origin of the New Testament Metaphor of Rebirth,* by William D. Mounce.

[8] κληρονομία, ας, ἡ, *inheritance; possession* (14).

[9] ἄφθαρτος, ον, *imperishable, incorruptible* (8).

[10] ἀμίαντος, ον, *undefiled, pure* (4).

[11] ἀμάραντος, ον, *unfading* (1).

[12] φρουρέω, *I guard; confine* (4).

[13] ἕτοιμος, η, ον, *ready, prepared* (17).

---

(3)   1:2   πνεύματος. Is πνεύματος objective or subjective? See Michaels, 11.

Rejoicing and Faith (1:6-9)

1:6 ἐν ᾧ <u>ἀγαλλιᾶσθε</u>,[1] ὀλίγον ἄρτι εἰ δέον[2] [ἐστὶν] λυπηθέντες ἐν

ποικίλοις[3] πειρασμοῖς, **1:7** ἵνα τὸ δοκίμιον[4] ὑμῶν τῆς πίστεως πολυτιμότερον[5]

χρυσίου[6] τοῦ ἀπολλυμένου διὰ πυρὸς δὲ δοκιμαζομένου, εὑρεθῇ εἰς ἔπαινον[7]

καὶ δόξαν καὶ τιμὴν ἐν ἀποκαλύψει[8] Ἰησοῦ Χριστοῦ. **1:8** ὃν οὐκ ἰδόντες

ἀγαπᾶτε, εἰς ὃν ἄρτι μὴ ὁρῶντες πιστεύοντες δὲ ἀγαλλιᾶσθε χαρᾷ

ἀνεκλαλήτῳ[9] καὶ δεδοξασμένῃ **1:9** κομιζόμενοι[10] τὸ <u>τέλος</u> τῆς πίστεως [ὑμῶν]

σωτηρίαν ψυχῶν.

---

[1] ἀγαλλιάω, usually deponent: *I exult, am glad* (11).

[2] δέον is the present neuter participle of δεῖ.

[3] ποικίλος, η, ον, *various, diversified* (10).

[4] δοκίμιον, ου, τό, *testing, means of testing; genuine(ness)* (2).

[5] πολοτιμότερος, α, ον, comparative form of πολύτιμος, ον, *more precious, of greater price* (3). Remember that comparatives can be followed by the genitive of comparison.

[6] χρυσίον, ου, τό, *gold* (12).

[7] ἔπαινος, ου, ὁ, *praise, approval* (11).

[8] ἀποκάλυψις, εως, ἡ, *revelation* (18).

[9] ἀνεκλάλητος, ον, *inexpressible* (1).

[10] κομίζω, active: *I bring;* middle: *I carry off, receive, recover* (10).

---

(4) 1:6   ᾧ. What is the antecedent of ᾧ? See Michaels, 27-28.

(5) **1:6** *   ἀγαλλιᾶσθε could be a **futuristic present**, in which the present tense is used of a future event in order to add an element of confidence, that the event will most assuredly occur.

(6) 1:9   τέλος. If you have not yet done a word study on τέλος, be sure to do so.

Salvation and the Prophets (1:10-12)

1:10 Περὶ ἧς <u>σωτηρίας</u> ἐξεζήτησαν[1] καὶ ἐξηραύνησαν[2] προφῆται οἱ περὶ

τῆς εἰς ὑμᾶς χάριτος προφητεύσαντες, **1:11** ἐραυνῶντες[3] εἰς τίνα ἢ ποῖον

καιρὸν ἐδήλου[4] τὸ ἐν αὐτοῖς πνεῦμα Χριστοῦ προμαρτυρόμενον[5] τὰ εἰς Χριστὸν

παθήματα[6] καὶ τὰς μετὰ ταῦτα δόξας. **1:12** οἷς ἀπεκαλύφθη ὅτι οὐχ ἑαυτοῖς

ὑμῖν δὲ διηκόνουν αὐτά, ἃ νῦν ἀνηγγέλη[7] ὑμῖν διὰ τῶν εὐαγγελισαμένων ὑμᾶς

[ἐν] πνεύματι ἁγίῳ ἀποσταλέντι ἀπ᾽ οὐρανοῦ, εἰς ἃ ἐπιθυμοῦσιν[8] ἄγγελοι

παρακύψαι.[9]

---

[1] ἐκζητέω, *I seek out, search for; desire* (7).

[2] ἐξεραυνάω, *I inquire carefully* (1).

[3] ἐραυνάω, *I search, examine* (6).

[4] δηλόω, *I reveal, make clear* (7).

[5] προμαρτύρομαι, *I bear witness to beforehand, predict* (1).

[6] πάθημα, ματος, τό, *suffering* (16).

[7] ἀναγγέλλω, *I disclose, announce, proclaim* (14). Its principal parts are, ἀναγγελῶ, ἀνήγγειλα, -, -, ἀνηγγέλην.

[8] ἐπιθυμέω, *I desire* (16).

[9] παρακύπτω, *I bend over; look, gain a clear glance* (5).

---

(7)   1:10   σωτηρίας. περὶ ἧς goes back to σωτηρίαν in v 9, so why is σωτηρίας repeated here? Most likely it is to make clear that the antecedent of ἧς is σωτηρίαν and not the previous πίστεως, both of which are feminine singular.

Hope and Holiness (1:13-21)

1:13 Διὸ ἀναζωσάμενοι¹ τὰς ὀσφύας² τῆς διανοίας³ ὑμῶν νήφοντες⁴

τελείως⁵ <u>ἐλπίσατε</u> ἐπὶ τὴν φερομένην ὑμῖν χάριν ἐν ἀποκαλύψει Ἰησοῦ

Χριστοῦ. **1:14** ὡς τέκνα <u>ὑπακοῆς</u> μὴ συσχηματιζόμενοι⁶ ταῖς πρότερον⁷ ἐν τῇ

ἀγνοίᾳ⁸ ὑμῶν ἐπιθυμίαις **1:15** ἀλλὰ κατὰ τὸν καλέσαντα ὑμᾶς ἅγιον καὶ

αὐτοὶ⁹ ἅγιοι ἐν πάσῃ ἀναστροφῇ¹⁰ γενήθητε, **1:16** διότι γέγραπται [ὅτι] **Ἅγιοι**

ἔσεσθε, ὅτι ἐγὼ ἅγιός [εἰμι].

---

¹ ἀναζώννυμι, *I bind up, gird up* (1).

² ὀσφῦς, ύος, ἡ, *waist, loins* (8).

³ διάνοια, ας, ἡ, *understanding, intelligence; mind, disposition; purpose, plan* (12).

⁴ νήφω, *I am sober, abstain from wine; am self-controlled* (6).

⁵ τελείως, *fully, perfectly, completely* (1).

⁶ συσχηματίζω, *I form* or *mold after something* (2).

⁷ πρότερος, α, ον, *former, earlier; superior, preferable* (11).

⁸ ἄγνοια, ας, ἡ, *ignorance* (4).

⁹ αὐτός has more functions than merely the third person pronoun. Cf. *BBG* §12.9-12.10.

¹⁰ ἀναστροφή, ῆς, ἡ, *way of life, conduct, behavior* (13).

---

(8)   1:13   ἐλπίσατε. See Michaels' comments about the series of aorist imperatives throughout chapters 1 and 2 (55).

(9)   1:14   ὑπακοῆς. What would ὑπακοῆς mean if it were a Hebraic genitive? See
Michaels, 56-57.

1:17 Καὶ εἰ πατέρα ἐπικαλεῖσθε τὸν ἀπροσωπολήμπτως[1] κρίνοντα κατὰ

τὸ ἑκάστου ἔργον, ἐν φόβῳ τὸν τῆς παροικίας[2] ὑμῶν χρόνον ἀναστράφητε,[3]

1:18 εἰδότες ὅτι οὐ φθαρτοῖς,[4] ἀργυρίῳ ἢ χρυσίῳ ἐλυτρώθητε[5] ἐκ τῆς ματαίας[6]

ὑμῶν ἀναστροφῆς πατροπαραδότου[7]   **1:19** ἀλλὰ τιμίῳ[8] αἵματι ὡς ἀμνοῦ[9]

ἀμώμου[10] καὶ ἀσπίλου[11] Χριστοῦ, **1:20** προεγνωσμένου[12] μὲν πρὸ καταβολῆς[13]

κόσμου φανερωθέντος δὲ ἐπ᾽ ἐσχάτου τῶν χρόνων δι᾽ ὑμᾶς **1:21** τοὺς δι᾽ αὐτοῦ

πιστοὺς εἰς θεὸν τὸν ἐγείραντα αὐτὸν ἐκ νεκρῶν καὶ δόξαν αὐτῷ δόντα, ὥστε

τὴν πίστιν ὑμῶν καὶ ἐλπίδα εἶναι εἰς θεόν.

---

[1] ἀπροσωπολήμπτως, *impartially* (1).
[2] παροικία, ας, ἡ, *sojourning in a strange place*; the *foreign country* itself (2).
[3] ἀναστρέφω, active: *I overturn*; passive: *I behave, conduct myself, live* (9).
[4] φθαρτός, ή, όν, *perishable, subject to decay* (6).
[5] λυτρόω, *I redeem, ransom; set free, rescue* (3).
[6] μάταιος, αία, αιον, *empty, idle, fruitless, useless* (6).
[7] πατροπαράδοτος, ον, *handed down from one's fathers, inherited* (1).
[8] τίμιος, α, ον, *precious, valuable* (13).
[9] ἀμνός, οῦ, ὁ, *lamb* (4).
[10] ἄμωμος, ον, *unblemished, blameless* (8).
[11] ἄσπιλος, ον, *spotless, unstained, without blemish* (4).
[12] προγινώσκω, *I foreknow, know beforehand* (5).
[13] καταβολή, ῆς, ἡ, *foundation, beginning* (11).

---

(10)   1:17   ἐπικαλεῖσθε takes a double accusative in this context. Check out its
               meaning in the middle (Michaels, 60).

(11)   1:20   If the plural χρόνων is troublesome for you, check the lexicon for the
               exact meaning of χρόνος.

Chapter 12

ΠΡΟΣ ΤΙΜΟΘΕΟΝ Α΄ 4:6-16

No one should go through ministerial education without memorizing this passage. It is magnificent instruction for a young minister in a difficult church situation. That I have included fewer verses in this chapter is balanced by the need to do several word studies and to discuss the practical issues of ministry and ministerial education. Pay special attention to the aspect of the verbal forms. It will greatly help you see how Timothy was to act.

To my mind, one of the great tragedies of modern scholarship is that when it comes to the Pastorals, our time is consumed with critical discussions of authorship, ecclesiastical structures, and now the question of the role of women in church leadership. The Pastorals are so much more than these few issues, giving significant practical and theological insight to young ministers on how to deal with people, the role of Scripture in their ministry, and much more. Please spend time with all thirteen chapters. You may also want to translate Paul's discussion of the overwhelming power of God's kindness in our salvation (Titus 3:1-11), his encouragement to young Timothy in 2 Tim 1:3-14, the warning in 2 Tim 2:8-13, or his intensely personal good-bye in 2 Tim 4:6-22.

Commentary references are to William D. Mounce, *The Pastoral Epistles*, in Word Biblical Commentary (Word, 1996), which at this date is not quite ready for publication. In a later printing of the *Graded Reader* page numbers will be added.

Faith and Godliness (4:6-10)

4:6 Ταῦτα ὑποτιθέμενος[1] τοῖς ἀδελφοῖς καλὸς ἔσῃ διάκονος Χριστοῦ

Ἰησοῦ, ἐντρεφόμενος[2] τοῖς λόγοις τῆς <u>πίστεως</u> καὶ τῆς καλῆς <u>διδασκαλίας</u> ᾗ

---

[1] ὑποτίθημι, active: *I lay down*; middle: *I suggest, order, teach* (2).
[2] ἐντρέφω, *I bring up, rear; train* (1).

Exegetical Discussion

(1) 4:6 πίστις can be a technical term in the Pastorals for the Christian Faith. This is emphasized by the articular construction. Are the Pastorals the only place in Paul where πίστις is used this way? See Mounce on 1 Tim 1:2. To what does the articular τοῖς λόγοις τῆς πίστεως refer?

(2) 4:6 διδασκαλίας. Did you notice that διδασκαλίας is articular? Cf. 4:13 as well. This is a technical term in the Pastorals with a very special meaning. What is it?

παρηκολούθηκας·[1] **4:7** τοὺς δὲ βεβήλους[2] καὶ γραώδεις[3] μύθους[4] παραιτοῦ.[5]

γύμναζε[6] δὲ σεαυτὸν πρὸς εὐσέβειαν·[7] **4:8** ἡ γὰρ σωματικὴ[8] γυμνασία[9] πρὸς

ὀλίγον ἐστὶν ὠφέλιμος,[10] ἡ δὲ εὐσέβεια πρὸς πάντα ὠφέλιμός ἐστιν ἐπαγγελίαν

ἔχουσα ζωῆς τῆς νῦν καὶ τῆς μελλούσης. **4:9** πιστὸς ὁ λόγος καὶ πάσης

ἀποδοχῆς[11] ἄξιος· **4:10** εἰς τοῦτο γὰρ κοπιῶμεν καὶ ἀγωνιζόμεθα,[12] ὅτι

ἠλπίκαμεν ἐπὶ θεῷ ζῶντι, ὅς ἐστιν σωτὴρ πάντων ἀνθρώπων μάλιστα[13] πιστῶν.

---

[1] παρακολουθέω, *I follow, accompany; understand, follow faithfully* (4).
[2] βέβηλος, ον, *profane, godless* (5).
[3] γραώδης, ες, *characteristic of an old woman; silly, absurd* (1).
[4] μῦθος, ου, ὁ, *myth, fable* (5).
[5] παραιτέομαι, *I ask for, request; decline, reject, avoid* (12).
[6] γυμνάζω, *I train, exercise* (4).
[7] εὐσέβεια, ας, ἡ, *godliness, piety, religion* (15).
[8] σωματικός, ή, όν, *bodily* (2).
[9] γυμνασία, ας, ἡ, *training* (1).
[10] ὠφέλιμος, ον, *useful, beneficial, advantageous* (4).
[11] ἀποδοχή, ῆς, ἡ, *acceptance, approval* (2).
[12] ἀγωνίζομαι, *I engage in a contest, fight, struggle* (8).
[13] μάλιστα, *especially, particularly* (12).

---

(3) 4:7 εὐσέβεια is another technical term in the Pastorals. Do not be content with the simple lexicon definition. What does it actually mean in this context? See Mounce on 1 Tim 2:2.

(4) 4:8 ὀλίγον. Does ὀλίγον express time or amount?

(5) 4:9 πιστὸς ὁ λόγος is another technical phrase in the Pastorals, the "Faithful Sayings." See Mounce in *Form/Structure/Setting* on 1 Tim 1:12-17.

(6) 4:10 μάλιστα. What is the precise meaning of μάλιστα in this context? Do the Pastorals teach universalism? See Mounce.

Personal Exhortations to Timothy (4:11-16)

4:11 Παράγγελλε ταῦτα καὶ δίδασκε. **4:12** μηδείς σου τῆς <u>νεότητος</u>[1]

καταφρονείτω,[2] ἀλλὰ τύπος[3] γίνου τῶν πιστῶν ἐν λόγῳ, ἐν ἀναστροφῇ,[4] ἐν

ἀγάπῃ, ἐν πίστει, ἐν ἁγνείᾳ.[5] **4:13** ἕως ἔρχομαι πρόσεχε τῇ ἀναγνώσει,[6] τῇ

παρακλήσει, τῇ διδασκαλίᾳ. **4:14** μὴ ἀμέλει[7] τοῦ ἐν σοὶ χαρίσματος,[8] ὃ ἐδόθη

σοι διὰ προφητείας[9] μετὰ ἐπιθέσεως[10] τῶν χειρῶν τοῦ πρεσβυτερίου.[11]

4:15 ταῦτα μελέτα,[12] <u>ἐν τούτοις ἴσθι</u>, ἵνα σου ἡ προκοπὴ[13] φανερὰ[14] ᾖ πᾶσιν.

---

[1] νεότης, τητος, ἡ, *youth* (4).

[2] καταφρονέω, *I despise, scorn; disregard* (9). Followed by the genitive.

[3] τύπος, ου, ὁ, *visible impression, mark, trace; copy, image; form, pattern, example* (15).

[4] ἀναστροφή, ῆς, ἡ, *way of life, behavior* (13).

[5] ἁγνεία, ας, ἡ, *purity, chastity* (2).

[6] ἀνάγνωσις, εως, ἡ, *(public) reading* (3).

[7] ἀμελέω, *I neglect, am unconcerned* τινός *about someone* or *something* (4).

[8] χάρισμα, ατος, τό, *gift (freely and graciously given)* (17). It is used both of earthly goods given by God and of spiritual gifts.

[9] προφητεία, ας, ἡ, *prophecy; gift of prophecy; prophetic utterance* (19). On this event in Timothy's life see Mounce on 1 Tim 1:18.

[10] ἐπίθεσις, εως, ἡ, *laying on* (4).

[11] πρεσβυτέριον, ου, τό, *council of elders* (3).

[12] μελετάω, *I take care; meditate, practice, cultivate* (2).

[13] προκοπή, ῆς, ἡ, *progress, advancement* (3).

[14] φανερός, ά, όν, *visible, clear, evident* (18).

---

(7) 4:12   νεότης. It is an interesting word study to discover the range of ages νεότης covers. How old was Timothy? See Mounce.

(8) 4:13   V 13. Timothy is to center his ministry on three things, all of which are articular. What are they, and what is the significance of the articles? See Mounce.

(9) 4:15   ἐν τούτοις ἴσθι somewhat idiomatically expresses absorption in something. Donald Guthrie (*The Pastoral Epistles*, in The Tyndale New Testament Commentaries [Eerdmans, 1969]) comments, "The mind is to be immersed in these pursuits as the body in the air it breathes" (99).

4:16 ἔπεχε[1] σεαυτῷ καὶ τῇ διδασκαλίᾳ, ἐπίμενε[2] αὐτοῖς· τοῦτο γὰρ ποιῶν καὶ

σεαυτὸν σώσεις καὶ τοὺς ἀκούοντάς σου.

---

[1] ἐπέχω, transitive: *I hold fast*; intransitive: *I aim at* (5).
[2] ἐπιμένω, *I stay, remain*; *continue, persevere* (16).

Chapter 13

ΚΑΤΑ ΛΟΥΚΑΝ 23:26-49; 24:1-8

Luke writes with beautiful Greek style. It is not "easy" Greek but neither is it awkward. You will find that he likes to insert a modifier between an article and its substantive as in 1 Peter. We chose this passage because what is a New Testament graded reader if it does not include an account of the death and resurrection of Christ?

Starting with this chapter we will only help you with the most difficult forms and will hold the *Exegetical Discussion* to a minimum. By now you should be translating quite well, and when you are stuck you should know how to find the answer.

For a discussion of this passage you can read I. Howard Marshall, *The Gospel of Luke,* in The New International Greek Testament Commentary (Eerdmans, 1978).

The Crucifixion of Christ (23:26-49)

23:26 Καὶ ὡς ἀπήγαγον[1] αὐτόν, ἐπιλαβόμενοι[2] Σίμωνά <u>τινα</u>

Κυρηναῖον[3] ἐρχόμενον ἀπ᾽ ἀγροῦ ἐπέθηκαν αὐτῷ τὸν σταυρὸν φέρειν ὄπισθεν[4]

τοῦ Ἰησοῦ. **23:27** Ἠκολούθει δὲ αὐτῷ πολὺ πλῆθος τοῦ λαοῦ καὶ γυναικῶν αἳ

ἐκόπτοντο[5] καὶ ἐθρήνουν[6] αὐτόν. **23:28** στραφεὶς δὲ πρὸς αὐτὰς [ὁ] Ἰησοῦς

---

[1] ἀπάγω, *I lead away, bring before* (15).

[2] ἐπιλαμβάνομαι, *I take hold of, grasp* (19).

[3] Κυρηναῖος, ου, ὁ, *Cyrenian* (6).

[4] ὄπισθεν, *from behind* (7). A preposition taking the genitive.

[5] κόπτω, active: *I cut;* middle: *I beat (my breast as an act of mourning), mourn* (8).

[6] θρηνέω, *I lament, wail, mourn for* (4).

Exegetical Discussion

(1)   23:26   τινα. This is not a regular use of τινα but neither is it unusual. Be sure you understand it.

εἶπεν, Θυγατέρες Ἰερουσαλήμ, μὴ κλαίετε ἐπ' ἐμέ· πλὴν ἐφ' ἑαυτὰς κλαίετε καὶ

ἐπὶ τὰ τέκνα ὑμῶν, **23:29** ὅτι ἰδοὺ ἔρχονται ἡμέραι ἐν αἷς ἐροῦσιν, Μακάριαι

αἱ στεῖραι[1] καὶ αἱ κοιλίαι αἳ οὐκ ἐγέννησαν καὶ μαστοὶ[2] οἳ οὐκ ἔθρεψαν.[3]

23:30   τότε ἄρξονται **λέγειν τοῖς ὄρεσιν,**

                  Πέσετε ἐφ' ἡμᾶς,

             καὶ τοῖς βουνοῖς,[4]

             Καλύψατε[5] ἡμᾶς·

23:31 ὅτι εἰ ἐν τῷ ὑγρῷ[6] ξύλῳ ταῦτα ποιοῦσιν, ἐν τῷ ξηρῷ[7] τί γένηται;

          23:32 Ἤγοντο δὲ καὶ ἕτεροι κακοῦργοι[8] δύο σὺν αὐτῷ ἀναιρεθῆναι.

23:33 καὶ ὅτε ἦλθον ἐπὶ τὸν τόπον τὸν καλούμενον Κρανίον,[9] ἐκεῖ ἐσταύρωσαν

αὐτὸν καὶ τοὺς κακούργους, ὃν μὲν ἐκ δεξιῶν ὃν δὲ ἐξ ἀριστερῶν.[10] **23:34** ⟦ὁ δὲ

Ἰησοῦς ἔλεγεν, Πάτερ, ἄφες αὐτοῖς, οὐ γὰρ οἴδασιν τί ποιοῦσιν.⟧

---

[1] στεῖρα, ας, ἡ, *barren, sterile* (5). This noun is taken from the adjective στεῖρος. You can supply *woman* since the feminine form of the adjective is used.

[2] μαστός, οῦ, ὁ, *breast* (3).

[3] τρέφω, *I nourish, feed; rear, bring up* (9). τρέφω is from the root *θρεφ. The θ deaspirates to a τ because of the following φ. But when the φ is altered as it is here, the original θ returns. See *MBG*, v-1b(2).

[4] βουνός, οῦ, ὁ, *hill* (2).

[5] καλύπτω, *I cover, hide* (8).

[6] ὑγρός, ά, όν, *moist, pliant, green* when used of wood (1).

[7] ξηρός, ά, όν, *dry, dried up* (8).

[8] κακοῦργος, ον, generally used as a substantive: *criminal, evildoer* (4).

[9] κρανίον, ου, τό, *skull* (4).

[10] ἀριστερός, ά, όν, *left* (4).

διαμεριζόμενοι¹ δὲ τὰ ἱμάτια αὐτοῦ ἔβαλον κλήρους.² **23:35** καὶ εἱστήκει³ ὁ

λαὸς θεωρῶν. ἐξεμυκτήριζον⁴ δὲ καὶ οἱ ἄρχοντες λέγοντες, Ἄλλους ἔσωσεν,

σωσάτω ἑαυτόν, εἰ οὗτός ἐστιν ὁ Χριστὸς τοῦ θεοῦ ὁ ἐκλεκτός.

23:36 ἐνέπαιξαν⁵ δὲ αὐτῷ καὶ οἱ στρατιῶται προσερχόμενοι, ὄξος⁶

προσφέροντες αὐτῷ **23:37** καὶ λέγοντες, Εἰ σὺ εἶ ὁ βασιλεὺς τῶν Ἰουδαίων,

σῶσον σεαυτόν. **23:38** ἦν δὲ καὶ ἐπιγραφὴ⁷ ἐπ᾽ αὐτῷ, Ὁ βασιλεὺς τῶν Ἰουδαίων

οὗτος.

---

1   διαμερίζω, *I divide, separate, distribute* (11).

2   κλῆρος, ου, ὁ, *lot; that which is assigned by the lot, portion, share* (11).

3   This is the first of two pluperfects in this passage. See *MBG* §45.6 and Luke 23:49.

4   ἐκμυκτηρίζω, *I ridicule, sneer* (2).

5   ἐμπαίζω, *I mock, ridicule* τινί; *deceive* (13). When a ν is followed by a labial (π, β, φ, and ψ too), the ν becomes a μ (ἐν + παίζω ‣ ἐμπαίζω). When the augment is inserted, the consonant cluster νπ no longer occurs so the change is not made. Cf. *MBG* §24.1.

6   ὄξος, ους, τό, *sour wine, wine vinegar* (6).

7   ἐπιγραφή, ῆς, ἡ, *inscription* (5).

---

(2)   23:33   ὅν. In the ὅν μέν ... ὅν δέ construction, the relative pronouns are singular but their antecedent κακούργους is plural. Luke evidently views the two singular concepts together as a plural. The relative pronouns are also functioning almost as if they were the article in the normal ὁ μέν ... ὁ δέ construction.

23:39 Εἷς δὲ τῶν κρεμασθέντων[1] κακούργων ἐβλασφήμει αὐτὸν λέγων,

Οὐχὶ σὺ εἶ ὁ Χριστός; σῶσον σεαυτὸν καὶ ἡμᾶς. **23:40** ἀποκριθεὶς δὲ ὁ ἕτερος

ἐπιτιμῶν αὐτῷ ἔφη, Οὐδὲ φοβῇ σὺ τὸν θεόν, ὅτι ἐν τῷ αὐτῷ κρίματι εἶ; **23:41** καὶ

ἡμεῖς μὲν δικαίως,[2] ἄξια γὰρ ὧν ἐπράξαμεν ἀπολαμβάνομεν·[3] οὗτος δὲ οὐδὲν

ἄτοπον[4] ἔπραξεν. **23:42** καὶ ἔλεγεν, Ἰησοῦ, μνήσθητί[5] μου ὅταν ἔλθῃς εἰς τὴν

βασιλείαν σου. **23:43** καὶ εἶπεν αὐτῷ, Ἀμήν σοι λέγω, σήμερον μετ᾽ ἐμοῦ ἔσῃ

ἐν τῷ παραδείσῳ.[6]

23:44 Καὶ ἦν ἤδη ὡσεὶ ὥρα ἕκτη[7] καὶ σκότος ἐγένετο ἐφ᾽ ὅλην τὴν γῆν

---

[1] κρεμάννυμι, *I hang, suspend* (7). When intransitive it is deponent.

[2] δικαίως, *justly* (5).

[3] ἀπολαμβάνω, *I receive; recover, get back* (10).

[4] ἄτοπος, ον, *out of place, improper, wrong* (4).

[5] θη is the tense formative and there is no augment.

[6] παράδεισος, ου, ὁ, *paradise* (3).

[7] ἕκτος, η, ον, *sixth* (14).

---

(3) 23:39 Οὐχί. The criminal's use of Οὐχί tells us several things that English cannot convey. 1. Οὐχί is a strengthened form of the negation. The criminal's term is quite strong. 2. Οὐχί, like οὐ, implies that the answer is "Yes." But a knowledge of Greek can never replace common sense! Do you really think that this criminal believed Jesus was the Christ? Probably not. More likely the form of speech shows a strong sense of biting sarcasm. οὐδέ in the next verse performs the same function.

(4) 23:41 ὧν. Why the genitive ὧν is used is a bit difficult to see. It "should" have been ἅ because it is the object of the verb ἐπράξαμεν in the relative clause. One probably must see an understood τουτῶν to go with ἄξια ("worthy of these things") and assume that the pronoun ὧν was attracted to the case of that understood word.

(5) 23:43 τῷ παραδείσῳ. Why do you think τῷ παραδείσῳ is articular?

ἕως ὥρας ἐνάτης[1] **23:45** τοῦ ἡλίου ἐκλιπόντος,[2] ἐσχίσθη[3] δὲ τὸ καταπέτασμα[4]

τοῦ ναοῦ μέσον. **23:46** καὶ φωνήσας φωνῇ μεγάλῃ ὁ Ἰησοῦς εἶπεν, Πάτερ, **εἰς**

χεῖράς σου παρατίθεμαι[5] **τὸ πνεῦμά μου**. τοῦτο δὲ εἰπὼν ἐξέπνευσεν.[6]

23:47 Ἰδὼν δὲ ὁ ἑκατοντάρχης τὸ γενόμενον ἐδόξαζεν τὸν θεὸν λέγων, Ὄντως[7]

ὁ ἄνθρωπος οὗτος <u>δίκαιος</u> ἦν. **23:48** καὶ πάντες οἱ συμπαραγενόμενοι[8] ὄχλοι

ἐπὶ τὴν θεωρίαν[9] ταύτην, θεωρήσαντες τὰ γενόμενα, τύπτοντες[10] τὰ στήθη[11]

ὑπέστρεφον. **23:49** εἰστήκεισαν δὲ πάντες οἱ γνωστοὶ[12] αὐτῷ ἀπὸ μακρόθεν[13]

καὶ γυναῖκες αἱ συνακολουθοῦσαι[14] αὐτῷ ἀπὸ τῆς Γαλιλαίας ὁρῶσαι ταῦτα.

* * * * *

---

[1] ἔνατος, η, ον, *ninth* (10).

[2] ἐκλείπω, *I grow dark* when used of the sun (4).

[3] σχίζω, *I divide, tear apart* (11).

[4] καταπέτασμα, ματος, τό, *curtain, veil* (6).

[5] παρατίθημι, active: *I set before;* middle: *I set, spread; give out, entrust* (19).

[6] ἐκπνέω, *I expire, breathe out,* euphemism for *I die* (3).

[7] ὄντως, *certainly, truly* (10). An adverb formed from the participle ὤν.

[8] συμπαραγίνομαι, *I come together* (1).

[9] θεωρία, ας, ἡ, *sight, spectacle* (1).

[10] τύπτω, *I strike, beat* (13).

[11] στῆθος, ους, τό, *chest, breast* (5).

[12] γνωστός, ή, όν, *known, intelligible;* as a noun, *acquaintance, friend* (15).

[13] μακρόθεν, *from far away, from a distance* (14).

[14] συνακολουθέω, *I follow* (3). Uses the dative of the person who is followed.

---

(6)   23:47   δίκαιος. It is an interesting exercise in synoptic criticism to see what
phrase Matthew (27:54) and Mark (15:39) use instead of δίκαιος.

The Resurrection of Christ (24:1-8)

24:1 τῇ δὲ μιᾷ[1] τῶν σαββάτων ὄρθρου[2] βαθέως[3] ἐπὶ τὸ μνῆμα[4] <u>ἦλθον</u>

φέρουσαι ἃ ἡτοίμασαν ἀρώματα.[5] **24:2** εὗρον δὲ τὸν λίθον ἀποκεκυλισμένον[6]

ἀπὸ τοῦ μνημείου, **24:3** εἰσελθοῦσαι δὲ οὐχ εὗρον τὸ σῶμα τοῦ κυρίου Ἰησοῦ.

24:4 καὶ ἐγένετο ἐν τῷ ἀπορεῖσθαι[7] αὐτὰς περὶ τούτου καὶ ἰδοὺ ἄνδρες δύο

ἐπέστησαν <u>αὐταῖς</u> ἐν ἐσθῆτι[8] ἀστραπτούσῃ.[9] **24:5** ἐμφόβων[10] δὲ γενομένων

αὐτῶν καὶ κλινουσῶν[11] τὰ πρόσωπα εἰς τὴν γῆν εἶπαν πρὸς αὐτάς, Τί ζητεῖτε

τὸν ζῶντα μετὰ τῶν νεκρῶν· **24:6** οὐκ ἔστιν ὧδε, ἀλλὰ ἠγέρθη. μνήσθητε ὡς

---

[1]   Do not assume εἷς always means "one."

[2]   ὄρθρος, ου, ὁ, *dawn, early morning* (2).

[3]   βαθύς, εῖα, ύ, *deep* (4). With ὄρθρος it is an idiom meaning *very early in the morning.*

[4]   μνῆμα, ματος, τό, *grave, tomb* (8).

[5]   ἄρωμα, ματος, τό, *spice, perfume* (4).

[6]   ἀποκυλίω, *I roll away* (4).

[7]   ἀπορέω, usually in the middle: *I am at a loss, in doubt* (6).

[8]   ἐσθής, ῆτος, ἡ, *clothing* (8).

[9]   ἀστράπτω, *I flash, gleam* (2).

[10] ἔμφοβος, ον, *afraid, startled, terrified* (5).

[11] κλίνω, trans: *I incline, bend, bow, lay (down)*; passive: *I lean, fall (over)*; intrans: *I decline, am far spent* (7).

---

(7)   24:1   ἦλθον. How do we know that it was the women who came?

(8)   24:4   αὐταῖς. The preceding verb is a compound formed with ἐπί. In such constructions we often find the object of the verb governed by that preposition. ἐφίστημι takes the dative of the person.

ἐλάλησεν ὑμῖν ἔτι ὢν ἐν τῇ Γαλιλαίᾳ **24:7** λέγων τὸν υἱὸν τοῦ ἀνθρώπου ὅτι

δεῖ παραδοθῆναι εἰς χεῖρας ἀνθρώπων ἁμαρτωλῶν καὶ σταυρωθῆναι καὶ τῇ

τρίτῃ ἡμέρᾳ ἀναστῆναι. **24:8** καὶ ἐμνήσθησαν τῶν <u>ῥημάτων</u> αὐτοῦ.

---

(9)   24:8   ῥημάτων. What is the difference between λόγος and ῥῆμα? They make
interesting word study comparisons.

Chapter 14

ΠΡΟΣ ΕΦΕΣΙΟΥΣ 1:1-14

Ephesians 1 is a great chapter to translate. The structure is intricate and the theology is wonderful. Vv. 3-14 form a single sentence in Greek, although most English translations insert several periods (vv. 6, 10, 12). You must therefore concentrate on the overall structure of the passage. It is a perfect passage to phrase, and we strongly encourage you to do so. Traditionally vv 3-14 have been broken down into three paragraphs. What are they?

Two points in particular deserve attention. Be specific in your translation of prepositions. Paul is using them in exact ways, and he sometimes shifts the meaning of the same preposition from verse to verse. Secondly, be sure to identify the antecedent of every relative pronoun, especially ᾧ. This will help you see the structure and the flow of the passage.

Salutation (1:1-2)

1:1 Παῦλος ἀπόστολος Χριστοῦ Ἰησοῦ διὰ θελήματος θεοῦ τοῖς ἁγίοις τοῖς οὖσιν [ἐν Ἐφέσῳ[1]] καὶ πιστοῖς ἐν Χριστῷ Ἰησοῦ, **1:2** χάρις ὑμῖν καὶ εἰρήνη <u>ἀπὸ</u> θεοῦ πατρὸς ἡμῶν καὶ κυρίου Ἰησοῦ Χριστοῦ.

---

[1] Ἔφεσος, ου, ἡ, *Ephesus* (16).

Exegetical Discussion

(1) 1:2 ἀπό. The following is an extremely significant exegetical and theological point. You may want to ask your teacher to spend some time on this issue.

In the debate over whether the New Testament ever calls Jesus "God," most discussions concentrate on verses such as Romans 9:5, Titus 2:13, and John 10:30. But there are many other subtle ways in which we can see the authors' view of Jesus. One is Paul's use of prepositions in the salutations in his letters.

Blessing on God (1:3-14)

1:3 Εὐλογητὸς[1] ὁ θεὸς καὶ πατὴρ τοῦ κυρίου ἡμῶν Ἰησοῦ Χριστοῦ, ὁ

εὐλογήσας ἡμᾶς ἐν πάσῃ εὐλογίᾳ[2] πνευματικῇ ἐν τοῖς ἐπουρανίοις[3] ἐν Χριστῷ,

1:4 καθὼς ἐξελέξατο ἡμᾶς ἐν αὐτῷ πρὸ καταβολῆς[4] κόσμου εἶναι ἡμᾶς ἁγίους

καὶ ἀμώμους[5] κατενώπιον[6] αὐτοῦ <u>ἐν ἀγάπῃ</u>, **1:5** <u>προορίσας</u>[7] ἡμᾶς εἰς

υἱοθεσίαν[8] διὰ Ἰησοῦ Χριστοῦ εἰς αὐτόν, κατὰ τὴν εὐδοκίαν[9] τοῦ θελήματος

αὐτοῦ, **1:6** εἰς ἔπαινον[10] δόξης τῆς χάριτος αὐτοῦ ἧς ἐχαρίτωσεν[11] ἡμᾶς ἐν τῷ

---

[1] εὐλογητός, ή, όν, *blessed, praised* (8).

[2] εὐλογία, ας, ἡ, *blessing, praise* (16).

[3] ἐπουράνιος, ον, *heavenly* (19).

[4] καταβολή, ῆς, ἡ, *foundation* (11).

[5] ἄμωμος, ον, *blameless, unblemished* (8).

[6] κατενώπιον, *before, in the presence of* (3). It is an adverb used as an improper preposition with the genitive.

[7] προορίζω, *I predestine, decide beforehand* (6).

[8] υἱοθεσία, ας, ἡ, *adoption* (5).

[9] εὐδοκία, ας, ἡ, *goodwill, favor, wish* (9).

[10] ἔπαινος, ου, ὁ, *praise, approval; that which is worthy of praise* (11).

[11] χαριτόω, *I bestow favor upon, bless* (2).

The grammatical rule is that when you have the "preposition–noun–καί–noun" type construction, if the author views the two nouns as separate the preposition *must* be repeated with the second noun. But if the author views the two nouns as essentially one unit, then the preposition is *not* repeated.

This does not mean that the author views the two nouns–in this case "God" and "Jesus"–as absolutely identical. It means that he views them as a single unit.

(2)   1:4   ἐν ἀγάπῃ. Does ἐν ἀγάπῃ look back at the preceding verse, in which case it is our love (NRSV), or does it look forward to v 5, in which case it is God's love (NIV)?

(3)   1:5   προορίσας. Following προορίσας we find five prepositional phrases. Which ones modify προορίσας? Phrasing will help you decide.

ἠγαπημένῳ. **1:7** ἐν ᾧ ἔχομεν τὴν ἀπολύτρωσιν[1] διὰ τοῦ αἵματος αὐτοῦ, τὴν

ἄφεσιν[2] τῶν παραπτωμάτων,[3] κατὰ τὸ πλοῦτος τῆς χάριτος αὐτοῦ **1:8** ἧς

ἐπερίσσευσεν εἰς ἡμᾶς, ἐν πάσῃ σοφίᾳ καὶ φρονήσει,[4] **1:9** γνωρίσας ἡμῖν τὸ

μυστήριον τοῦ θελήματος αὐτοῦ, κατὰ τὴν εὐδοκίαν αὐτοῦ ἣν προέθετο[5] ἐν

αὐτῷ **1:10** εἰς οἰκονομίαν[6] τοῦ πληρώματος[7] τῶν καιρῶν, ἀνακεφαλαιώσα-

σθαι[8] τὰ πάντα ἐν τῷ Χριστῷ, τὰ ἐπὶ τοῖς οὐρανοῖς καὶ τὰ ἐπὶ τῆς γῆς ἐν αὐτῷ.

1:11 ἐν ᾧ καὶ ἐκληρώθημεν[9] προορισθέντες κατὰ πρόθεσιν[10] τοῦ τὰ πάντα

ἐνεργοῦντος κατὰ τὴν βουλὴν[11] τοῦ θελήματος αὐτοῦ **1:12** εἰς τὸ εἶναι ἡμᾶς εἰς

---

[1] ἀπολύτρωσις, εως, ἡ, *redemption* (10). What is the significance of it being articular?

[2] ἄφεσις, εως, ἡ, *forgiveness* (17).

[3] παράπτωμα, ματος, τό, *transgression, sin* (19).

[4] φρόνησις, εως, ἡ, *(frame of) mind; understanding, insight* (2).

[5] προτίθημι, active: *I set before;* middle: *I display publicly; plan, intend* (3). See the discussion at Romans 3:25.

[6] οἰκονομία, ας, ἡ, *arrangement, plan of salvation* (9).

[7] πλήρωμα, ματος, τό, *fullness, completion; that which fills; that which is full* (17).

[8] ἀνακεφαλαιόω, *I sum up* (2).

[9] κληρόω, active: *I appoint by lot;* middle: *I obtain by lot, receive* (1).

[10] πρόθεσις, εως, ἡ, *setting forth; purpose, plan* (12).

[11] βουλή, ῆς, ἡ, *purpose, decision* (12).

---

(4)   1:9   μυστήριον is a technical term that has a specific meaning in Paul's let-
               ters (cf. Eph 3:6). What is it, and how does knowing this affect your
               understanding of the verse?

ἔπαινον δόξης αὐτοῦ τοὺς προηλπικότας[1] ἐν τῷ Χριστῷ. **1:13** ἐν ᾧ καὶ ὑμεῖς

ἀκούσαντες τὸν λόγον τῆς ἀληθείας, τὸ εὐαγγέλιον τῆς σωτηρίας ὑμῶν, ἐν ᾧ

καὶ πιστεύσαντες ἐσφραγίσθητε[2] τῷ πνεύματι τῆς ἐπαγγελίας τῷ ἁγίῳ, **1:14** ὅ

ἐστιν ἀρραβὼν[3] τῆς κληρονομίας[4] ἡμῶν, εἰς ἀπολύτρωσιν τῆς περιποιήσεως,[5]

εἰς ἔπαινον τῆς δόξης αὐτοῦ.

---

[1] προελπίζω, *I hope before* (1).

[2] σφραγίζω, *I seal* (15).

[3] ἀρραβών, ῶνος, ὁ, *first installment, deposit, down payment, pledge* (3).

[4] κληρονομία, ας, ἡ, *inheritance; possession* (14).

[5] περιποίησις, εως, ἡ, *keeping safe, preserving; obtaining; possessing, possession* (5). To what/whom does it refer?

---

(5) 1:13 V 13. Work hard at seeing the structure of v 13. Identify the two parallel prepositional phrases. To what is εὐαγγέλιον grammatically and theologically tied?

(6) 1:14 ἀρραβών. The meaning of ἀρραβών has an interesting development into modern Greek. Although you cannot use its modern meaning to define what Paul means here, it does make an interesting illustration. It is the engagement ring!

Chapter 15

ΠΡΑΞΕΙΣ ΑΠΟΣΤΟΛΩΝ 2:22-42

The first paragraph is especially difficult. Do not become discouraged; it gets easier. Resist any temptation to think about the English. Force yourself to think through the Greek. This is a great passage to see how well you really know Greek. Be sure to read the *Exegetical Discussion* on Ἰησοῦν in 2:22. It is difficult currently to find a commentary that will help you with the Greek of this passage.

Peter's Speech (2:22-36)

2:22 Ἄνδρες Ἰσραηλῖται,[1] ἀκούσατε τοὺς λόγους τούτους· Ἰησοῦν τὸν

Ναζωραῖον,[2] ἄνδρα ἀποδεδειγμένον[3] ἀπὸ τοῦ θεοῦ εἰς ὑμᾶς δυνάμεσι καὶ

τέρασι[4] καὶ σημείοις οἷς ἐποίησεν δι᾽ αὐτοῦ ὁ θεὸς ἐν μέσῳ ὑμῶν καθὼς αὐτοὶ[5]

οἴδατε, **2:23** τοῦτον τῇ ὡρισμένῃ[6] βουλῇ[7] καὶ προγνώσει[8] τοῦ θεοῦ ἔκδοτον[9] διὰ

---

1 Ἰσραηλίτης, ου, ὁ, *Israelite* (9).
2 Ναζωραῖος, ου, ὁ, *Nazarene* (13).
3 ἀποδείκνυμι, *I proclaim, appoint; show forth, display* (4).
4 τέρας, ατος, τό, *wonder* (16).
5 αὐτοί is not functioning as a personal pronoun.
6 ὁρίζω, *I determine, appoint, fix; set limits to, define* (8).
7 βουλή, ῆς, ἡ, *purpose, counsel; decision* (12).
8 πρόγνωσις, εως, ἡ, *foreknowledge* (2)
9 ἔκδοτος, ον, *given up, delivered up* (1)

Exegetical Discussion

(1) 2:22 Ἰησοῦν. The key to recognizing the structure of the first paragraph is to see that the subject and main verb are at the end of v 23. You will also see that the direct object is repeated with a pronoun at the beginning of v 23, and there is another accusative modifying Ἰησοῦν later in v 23.

114

χειρὸς ἀνόμων[1] προσπήξαντες[2] ἀνείλατε,   **2:24** <u>ὃν</u> ὁ θεὸς ἀνέστησεν λύσας τὰς

ὠδῖνας[3] τοῦ θανάτου, καθότι[4] οὐκ ἦν δυνατὸν κρατεῖσθαι αὐτὸν ὑπ᾽ αὐτοῦ.

2:25 Δαυὶδ γὰρ λέγει εἰς αὐτόν,

> **Προορώμην[5]** τὸν κύριον ἐνώπιόν μου <u>διὰ παντός</u>,
>
> ὅτι ἐκ δεξιῶν μού ἐστιν ἵνα μὴ σαλευθῶ.[6]

2:26   διὰ τοῦτο ηὐφράνθη[7] ἡ καρδία μου καὶ ἠγαλλιάσατο[8] ἡ γλῶσσά μου,

> ἔτι δὲ καὶ ἡ σάρξ μου κατασκηνώσει[9] ἐπ᾽ ἐλπίδι,

2:27   ὅτι οὐκ ἐγκαταλείψεις[10] τὴν ψυχήν μου εἰς ᾅδην[11]

> οὐδὲ δώσεις τὸν ὅσιόν[12] σου ἰδεῖν διαφθοράν.[13]

---

[1] ἄνομος, ον, *lawless* (9).

[2] προσπήγνυμι, *I nail to, fix* or *fasten to* (1).

[3] ὠδίν, ῖνος, ἡ, *birth-pain* of the messianic woes (4).

[4] καθότι, *as, to the degree that; because* (6).

[5] προοράω, *I see previously; foresee*; middle: *I see before one, have before my eyes* (2).

[6] σαλεύω, active: *I shake, cause to move*; passive: *I am shaken* (15).

[7] εὐφραίνω, active: *I cheer, gladden*; passive: *I am glad, rejoice* (14).

[8] ἀγαλλιάω, *I exult, be glad* (11). It is usually deponent.

[9] κατασκηνόω, transitive: *I cause to dwell*; intransitive: *live, dwell* (4).

[10] ἐγκαταλείπω, *I leave (behind); forsake, abandon* (10).

[11] ᾅδης, ου, ὁ, *Hades* (10).

[12] ὅσιος, ία, ιον, *devout, pious, holy* (8).

[13] διαφθορά, ᾶς, ἡ, *destruction, corruption* (6).

---

(2)   2:23   βουλῇ. If βουλῇ καὶ προγνώσει are instrumental, does this mean that God made the Jews kill Jesus, and if so, why are they responsible for their actions? Or are they?

(3)   2:24   ὅν. What is the antecedent of ὅν?

(4)   2:25   διὰ παντός is listed in *BAGD* under διά as an idiom with an understood χρόνου (II.1.a, p. 179).

2:28   ἐγνώρισάς μοι ὁδοὺς ζωῆς,

πληρώσεις με εὐφροσύνης[1] μετὰ τοῦ προσώπου σου.

2:29 Ἄνδρες ἀδελφοί, ἐξὸν[2] εἰπεῖν μετὰ παρρησίας πρὸς ὑμᾶς περὶ τοῦ

πατριάρχου[3] Δαυίδ ὅτι καὶ ἐτελεύτησεν[4] καὶ ἐτάφη,[5] καὶ τὸ μνῆμα[6] αὐτοῦ ἔστιν

ἐν ἡμῖν ἄχρι τῆς ἡμέρας ταύτης. **2:30** προφήτης οὖν ὑπάρχων, καὶ εἰδὼς ὅτι

ὅρκῳ[7] **ὤμοσεν αὐτῷ** ὁ θεὸς **ἐκ καρποῦ τῆς ὀσφύος**[8] **αὐτοῦ καθίσαι ἐπὶ τὸν**

θρόνον αὐτοῦ, **2:31** προϊδὼν ἐλάλησεν περὶ τῆς ἀναστάσεως τοῦ Χριστοῦ ὅτι

οὔτε ἐγκατελείφθη εἰς ἅδην

οὔτε ἡ σὰρξ αὐτοῦ **εἶδεν διαφθοράν.**

2:32 τοῦτον τὸν Ἰησοῦν ἀνέστησεν ὁ θεός, οὗ πάντες ἡμεῖς ἐσμεν μάρτυρες·

2:33 τῇ δεξιᾷ οὖν τοῦ θεοῦ ὑψωθεὶς, τήν τε ἐπαγγελίαν τοῦ πνεύματος τοῦ

---

1   εὐφροσύνη, ης, ἡ, *joy, gladness, cheerfulness* (2).
2   ἐξὸν is the participle of ἔξεστιν and has the same basic meaning (*BAGD* §4).
3   πατριάρχης, ου, ὁ, *patriarch* (4).
4   τελευτάω, *I come to an end, die* (11).
5   θάπτω, *I bury* (11). See the footnote on τρέφω in Luke 23:29 regarding the form of this word.
6   μνῆμα, ματος, τό, *grave, tomb* (8).
7   ὅρκος, ου, ὁ, oath (10).
8   ὀσφῦς, ύος, ἡ, *waist, loins* (8). Refers both to where a belt is worn and to the location of the reproductive organs.

---

(5)   2:30   ἐκ is an awkward transition, but Peter is quoting Ps 132·11f and inserts the quotation without a smooth introduction.

ἁγίου λαβὼν παρὰ τοῦ πατρός, ἐξέχεεν[1] τοῦτο ὃ ὑμεῖς [καὶ] βλέπετε καὶ

ἀκούετε. **2:34** οὐ γὰρ Δαυὶδ ἀνέβη εἰς τοὺς οὐρανούς, λέγει δὲ αὐτός,

> **Εἶπεν [ὁ] κύριος τῷ κυρίῳ μου,**

> **Κάθου ἐκ δεξιῶν μου,**

2:35   **ἕως ἂν θῶ τοὺς ἐχθρούς σου ὑποπόδιον[2] τῶν ποδῶν σου.**

2:36 ἀσφαλῶς[3] οὖν γινωσκέτω πᾶς οἶκος Ἰσραὴλ ὅτι καὶ κύριον αὐτὸν καὶ

Χριστὸν ἐποίησεν ὁ θεός, τοῦτον τὸν Ἰησοῦν ὃν ὑμεῖς ἐσταυρώσατε.

Results of Peter's Speech (2:37-42)

2:37 Ἀκούσαντες δὲ κατενύγησαν[4] τὴν καρδίαν εἶπόν τε πρὸς τὸν

Πέτρον καὶ τοὺς λοιποὺς ἀποστόλους, Τί ποιήσωμεν, ἄνδρες ἀδελφοί;

2:38 Πέτρος δὲ πρὸς αὐτούς, Μετανοήσατε, [φησίν,] καὶ βαπτισθήτω ἕκαστος

ὑμῶν ἐπὶ τῷ ὀνόματι Ἰησοῦ Χριστοῦ εἰς ἄφεσιν[5] τῶν ἁμαρτιῶν ὑμῶν καὶ

λήμψεσθε τὴν δωρεὰν[6] τοῦ ἁγίου πνεύματος. **2:39** ὑμῖν γάρ ἐστιν ἡ ἐπαγγελία

καὶ τοῖς τέκνοις ὑμῶν καὶ πᾶσιν τοῖς εἰς μακράν,[7] ὅσους ἂν προσκαλέσηται

---

[1] ἐκχέω, *I pour out, shed* (16). The final ε does not contract (cf. *MBG*, cv-1a[7]).

[2] ὑποπόδιον, ου, τό, *footstool* (7).

[3] ἀσφαλῶς, *securely, beyond a doubt* (3).

[4] κατανύσσομαι, *I pierce, stab* (1). Its principal parts are "-, -, -, -, κατενύγην."

[5] ἄφεσις, ἀφέσεως, ἡ, *release; pardon, forgiveness* (17).

[6] δωρεά, ᾶς, ἡ, *gift* (11).

[7] μακράν, *far (away)* (10).

κύριος ὁ θεὸς ἡμῶν. **2:40** ἑτέροις τε λόγοις πλείοσιν διεμαρτύρατο[1] καὶ

παρεκάλει αὐτοὺς λέγων, Σώθητε ἀπὸ τῆς γενεᾶς τῆς σκολιᾶς[2] ταύτης. **2:41** οἱ

μὲν οὖν ἀποδεξάμενοι[3] τὸν λόγον αὐτοῦ ἐβαπτίσθησαν καὶ <u>προσετέθησαν</u>[4] ἐν

τῇ ἡμέρᾳ ἐκείνῃ ψυχαὶ ὡσεὶ τρισχίλιαι.[5] **2:42** ἦσαν δὲ προσκαρτεροῦντες[6] τῇ

διδαχῇ τῶν ἀποστόλων καὶ τῇ κοινωνίᾳ,[7] τῇ κλάσει[8] τοῦ ἄρτου καὶ ταῖς

προσευχαῖς.

---

[1] διαμαρτύρομαι, *I charge, warn; testify, bear witness* (15).
[2] σκολιός, ά, όν, *crooked, unscrupulous, dishonest* (4).
[3] ἀποδέχομαι, *I welcome* τινά; *recognize, praise* (7).
[4] προστίθημι, *I add, put to; provide, give, grant* (18).
[5] τρισχίλιοι, αι, α, *three thousand* (1).
[6] προσκαρτερέω, *I adhere to, persist in, am devoted to* (10).
[7] κοινωνία, ας, ἡ, *association, communion, fellowship; generosity; participation* (19).
[8] κλάσις, εως, ἡ, *breaking* (2).

---

(6)   2:41   προσετέθησαν. Why is προσετέθησαν passive?

Chapter 16

ΠΡΟΣ ΘΕΣΣΑΛΟΝΙΚΕΙΣ Β΄ 2:1-12

This passage may be short, but it is difficult. It is important that you concentrate on your phrasing, watching the construction of the verses and seeing what modifies what. Theologically, it is a fascinating passage and a good one for class discussion. Frankly, I had to suffer through this passage in second-year Greek, and so should you.

There are several good illustrations of articular infinitives, so be careful to identify the accusative functioning as the subject of the infinitive and review *BBG* §32.11 on the meaning of prepositions when used with infinitives. There are also several illustrations of why it is important to discover the *precise* meaning of a preposition. As always, be aware of the passive verbs and ask yourself why they are passive.

For a discussion of this passage you can read F. F. Bruce, *1 & 2 Thessalonians*, in Word Biblical Commentary (Word, 1982), or Charles A. Wanamaker, *Commentary on 1 & 2 Thessalonians*, in The New International Greek Testament Commentary (Eerdmans, 1990).

The Man of Lawlessness (2:1-12)

2:1 Ἐρωτῶμεν δὲ ὑμᾶς, ἀδελφοί, ὑπὲρ τῆς παρουσίας τοῦ κυρίου ἡμῶν

Ἰησοῦ Χριστοῦ καὶ ἡμῶν ἐπισυναγωγῆς[1] ἐπ᾽ αὐτὸν 2:2 εἰς τὸ μὴ ταχέως[2]

<u>σαλευθῆναι</u>[3] ὑμᾶς <u>ἀπὸ</u> τοῦ νοὸς μηδὲ θροεῖσθαι[4], μήτε διὰ πνεύματος μήτε διὰ

---

[1] ἐπισυναγωγή, ῆς, ἡ, *gathering, assembling* (2).

[2] ταχέως, *quickly, at once* (15). This is the positive form of the adverb.

[3] σαλεύω, *I shake* (15).

[4] θροέω, *I am inwardly disturbed* (3).

Exegetical Discussion

(1) 2:2 σαλευθῆναι. Because of the aspect of the aorist tense, it is sometimes used to describe a sudden action, as it does with σαλευθῆναι.

(2) 2:2 ἀπό. The basic meaning of ἀπό is *separation*. Sometimes it is easier to translate a passage using the basic meaning of a word rather than looking for one specific nuance in the lexicon. In this passage Paul is creating a picture of extreme inward disturbance, as if the readers were separated from their minds.

λόγου μήτε δι᾽ ἐπιστολῆς ὡς δι᾽ ἡμῶν, ὡς ὅτι ἐνέστηκεν[1] ἡ ἡμέρα τοῦ κυρίου·

2:3 μή τις ὑμᾶς ἐξαπατήσῃ[2] κατὰ μηδένα τρόπον.[3] ὅτι ἐὰν μὴ ἔλθῃ ἡ

ἀποστασία[4] πρῶτον καὶ ἀποκαλυφθῇ ὁ ἄνθρωπος τῆς ἀνομίας[5], ὁ υἱὸς τῆς

ἀπωλείας,[6] **2:4** ὁ ἀντικείμενος[7] καὶ ὑπεραιρόμενος[8] ἐπὶ πάντα λεγόμενον θεὸν

ἢ σέβασμα[9], ὥστε αὐτὸν εἰς τὸν ναὸν τοῦ θεοῦ καθίσαι ἀποδεικνύντα[10] ἑαυτὸν

---

[1] In past tenses ἐνίστημι means *I am present, have come; am imminent* (7).

[2] ἐξαπατάω, *I deceive, cheat* (6).

[3] τρόπος, ου, ὁ, *manner, way* (13).

[4] ἀποστασία, ας, ἡ, *apostasy, revolt, rebellion, abandonment* (2).

[5] ἀνομία, ας, ἡ, *lawlessness* (15).

[6] ἀπώλεια, ας, ἡ, *destruction, annihilation* (18).

[7] ἀντίκειμαι, *I resist, oppose* (8).

[8] ὑπεραίρω, *I rise up, exalt myself* (3). In our literature it is always middle, so some list the verb as ὑπεραίρομαι.

[9] σέβασμα, ατος, τό, *object of worship, sanctuary* (2).

[10] ἀποδείκνυμι, *I proclaim* (4). *BAGD* adds that it occurs with the double accusative (1 Cor 4:9) or with a ὅτι clause substituting for the second accusative.

---

(3) 2:3 ὅτι. We normally find ὅτι introducing a subordinate clause, i.e., not the main clause. The period after τρόπον makes translation of this passage awkward since there is no expressed main clause. "Don't let anyone deceive you in any way, for that day will not come ... (NIV)." "Let no one deceive you in any way; for that day will not come ... (NRSV)."

(4) 2:3 ἐάν. The ἐάν clause is the protasis of a conditional sentence (i.e., the *if* clause), but it does not have the apodosis (i.e., the *then* clause). It must be supplied from context. The NIV and NRSV insert, "that day will not come."

(5) **2:3** * ἡ. Notice the article before ἀποστασία. Paul is not speaking about just any rebellion, but *the* rebellion. This is called the **monadic article**. In related usage, the article is also used with abstract nouns to speak about a concrete, specific instance of an abstract concept. See Wallace. For example, the New Testament speaks of "the truth," i.e., the gospel (1 Tim 2:4). For it is by "the grace" that we are saved (Eph 2:8). Not by just any grace but by *the* grace, God's grace.

ὅτι ἔστιν θεός. **2:5** Οὐ μνημονεύετε ὅτι ἔτι ὤν[1] πρὸς ὑμᾶς ταῦτα ἔλεγον ὑμῖν;

2:6 καὶ νῦν τὸ κατέχον[2] οἴδατε εἰς τὸ ἀποκαλυφθῆναι αὐτὸν ἐν τῷ ἑαυτοῦ

καιρῷ. **2:7** τὸ γὰρ μυστήριον ἤδη ἐνεργεῖται τῆς ἀνομίας· μόνον ὁ κατέχων

ἄρτι[3] ἕως ἐκ μέσου γένηται. **2:8** καὶ τότε ἀποκαλυφθήσεται ὁ ἄνομος,[4] ὃν ὁ

κύριος [Ἰησοῦς] ἀνελεῖ τῷ πνεύματι τοῦ στόματος αὐτοῦ καὶ καταργήσει τῇ

ἐπιφανείᾳ[5] τῆς παρουσίας αὐτοῦ, **2:9** οὗ ἐστιν ἡ παρουσία κατ᾽ ἐνέργειαν[6] τοῦ

Σατανᾶ ἐν πάσῃ δυνάμει καὶ σημείοις καὶ τέρασιν[7] ψεύδους[8] **2:10** καὶ ἐν πάσῃ

ἀπάτῃ[9] ἀδικίας τοῖς ἀπολλυμένοις, ἀνθ᾽ ὧν[10] τὴν ἀγάπην τῆς ἀληθείας οὐκ

ἐδέξαντο εἰς τὸ σωθῆναι αὐτούς. **2:11** καὶ διὰ τοῦτο πέμπει αὐτοῖς ὁ θεὸς

ἐνέργειαν πλάνης[11] εἰς τὸ πιστεῦσαι αὐτοὺς τῷ ψεύδει, **2:12** ἵνα κριθῶσιν

πάντες οἱ μὴ πιστεύσαντες τῇ ἀληθείᾳ ἀλλὰ εὐδοκήσαντες τῇ ἀδικίᾳ.

---

[1] Check the breathing and accent. This is not a relative pronoun.

[2] κατέχω, *I hold back, detain, suppress, restrain* (17).

[3] Place a comma after ἄρτι and recognize that your translation of γένηται must be very "loose." You will also have to fill in several missing words.

[4] ἄνομος, ον, *lawless* (9).

[5] ἐπιφάνεια, ας, ἡ, *appearing, appearance, coming* (6).

[6] ἐνέργεια, ας, ἡ, *working, operation* (8).

[7] τέρας, ατος, τό, *an extraordinary occurrence, wonder* (16).

[8] ψεῦδος, ους, τό, *lie, falsehood* (10).

[9] ἀπάτη, ης, ἡ, *deception, deceit* (7).

[10] ἀνθ᾽ ὧν is an idiom meaning *because*.

[11] πλάνη, ης, ἡ, *error, deceit* (10).

Chapter 17

ΠΡΟΣ ΕΒΡΑΙΟΥΣ 5:11-6:12

Hebrews has never been called "easy," and yet once you know the rare vocabulary it is about as difficult as 1 Peter. This passage becomes easier to translate after 5:14. The author likes to separate the article from the word it is modifying with other modifiers. The article is also used as a pronoun in several key places. We will help you a little more than in the past several chapters.

You must think grammatically to translate this passage. What word modifies what word? To what is this clause linked? Phrasing will be essential, and you may want to make your phrasing slightly more grammatical. The previous verses discuss the high priesthood of Jesus. It is to this that the οὗ in v 11 refers.

Commentary references are to William L. Lane, *Hebrews 1-8,* in Word Biblical Commentary (Word, 1991). We will cite him since this passage is difficult.

Third Warning Passage (5:11-6:12)

5:11[1] Περὶ οὗ πολὺς ἡμῖν ὁ λόγος καὶ δυσερμήνευτος[2] λέγειν,[3] ἐπεὶ

νωθροὶ[4] γεγόνατε ταῖς ἀκοαῖς. **5:12** καὶ γὰρ ὀφείλοντες εἶναι διδάσκαλοι διὰ

τὸν χρόνον,[5] πάλιν χρείαν ἔχετε <u>τοῦ διδάσκειν</u> ὑμᾶς τινὰ[6] τὰ στοιχεῖα[7] τῆς

---

[1] The word order in this first verse is difficult. Maybe this restructuring will help: Περὶ οὗ ὁ λόγος πολὺς λέγειν ἡμῖν καὶ δυσερμήνευτος.

[2] δυσερμήνευτος, ον, *hard to explain* (1).

[3] λέγειν is complementary to the preceding adjective. See Lane, 130 *Note a,* and *BDF* §393.6.

[4] νωθρός, ά, όν, *lazy, sluggish* (2).

[5] διὰ τὸν χρόνον is an idiom. How would you discover what it means?

Right. Look up either διά or χρόνος in *BAGD.* You will find Hebrews 5:12 listed under διά, B II 1, with the meaning, *the reason why something happens, results, exists,* and from that derives the definition here *by this time.*

[6] τινά is the subject of the infinitive τοῦ δίδασκειν, which takes a double accusative.

[7] στοιχεῖον, ου, τό, *fundamental principles; elemental substances; heavenly bodies* (7).

ἀρχῆς τῶν λογίων[1] τοῦ θεοῦ καὶ γεγόνατε χρείαν[2] ἔχοντες γάλακτος[3] [καὶ] οὐ

στερεᾶς[4] τροφῆς.[5] **5:13** πᾶς γὰρ ὁ μετέχων[6] γάλακτος ἄπειρος[7] λόγου

δικαιοσύνης, νήπιος[8] γάρ ἐστιν· **5:14** <u>τελείων[9]</u> δέ ἐστιν ἡ στερεὰ τροφή,

τῶν[10] διὰ τὴν ἕξιν[11] τὰ αἰσθητήρια[12] γεγυμνασμένα[13] ἐχόντων <u>πρὸς</u>

διάκρισιν[14] καλοῦ τε καὶ κακοῦ.

---

[1] λόγιον, ου, τό, *saying* (4).

[2] This is a difficult construction. Notice that χρείαν cannot directly follow γεγόνατε in your translation. It is also unusual for a participle to follow γίνομαι. You may want to supply a noun.

[3] γάλα, γάλακτος, τό, *milk* (5).

[4] στερεός, ά, όν, *firm, hard, solid; steadfast, firm* of human character (4).

[5] τροφή, ῆς, ἡ, *nourishment, food* (16).

[6] μετέχω, *I share, participate* with the genitive of the thing *in* or *of something* (8).

[7] ἄπειρος, ον, *unacquainted with, unaccustomed to* (1). It can be followed by the genitive. ἄπειρος is not the same case as γάλακτος.

[8] νήπιος, ία, ιον, *infant, minor* (15).

[9] τέλειος, α, ον, *having attained the end* or *purpose, complete, perfect;* of persons: *full-grown, mature* (19).

[10] Find the word that τῶν is modifying.

[11] ἕξις, εως, ἡ, *exercise, practice; skill* (1). See Lane, 131 note h, for a discussion of how a noun can have an "active" sense (i.e., the noun seen as a process: *exercise*) or a "passive" sense (i.e., as a state: *condition, capacity*).

[12] αἰσθητήριον, ου, τό, *sense, faculty* (1).

[13] γυμνάζω, *I exercise, train* (4).

[14] διάκρισις, εως, ἡ, *distinguishing, differentiation; quarrel* (3).

Exegetical Discussion

(1)   5:12   τοῦ διδάσκειν is a genitive articular infinitive. Lane says it is epexegetical to χρείαν (131 *Note e*).

(2)   5:14   τελείων. Lane calls τελείων a genitive of relationship, meaning "belonging to," although Wallace reserves this category for familial relationships.

(3)   5:14   πρός. What is the precise meaning of πρός in this context? *BAGD* shows the accusative πρός can mean "of the goal aimed at or striven toward." Never be satisfied with the "usual" translation unless it fits the context. If not, check the lexicon for other options.

6:1 Διὸ ἀφέντες τὸν τῆς ἀρχῆς τοῦ Χριστοῦ λόγον ἐπὶ τὴν τελειότητα[1]

φερώμεθα, μὴ πάλιν θεμέλιον[2] καταβαλλόμενοι[3] μετανοίας ἀπὸ νεκρῶν ἔργων

καὶ πίστεως ἐπὶ θεόν, **6:2** βαπτισμῶν[4] διδαχῆς ἐπιθέσεώς[5] τε χειρῶν,

ἀναστάσεώς τε νεκρῶν καὶ κρίματος αἰωνίου. **6:3** καὶ τοῦτο ποιήσομεν,

ἐάνπερ[6] ἐπιτρέπῃ[7] ὁ θεός.

6:4[8] Ἀδύνατον[9] γὰρ τοὺς ἅπαξ[10] φωτισθέντας,[11] γευσαμένους[12] τε τῆς

δωρεᾶς[13] τῆς ἐπουρανίου[14] καὶ μετόχους[15] γενηθέντας πνεύματος ἁγίου

6:5 καὶ καλὸν γευσαμένους θεοῦ ῥῆμα δυνάμεις τε μέλλοντος αἰῶνος **6:6** καὶ

---

[1]   τελειότης, ητος, ἡ, *perfection, completeness, maturity* (2). See Lane, 131 *Note l.*

[2]   θεμέλιος, ου, ὁ, *foundation* (15).

[3]   καταβάλλω, active and passive: *I throw down, strike down;* middle: *I found, lay* a foundation (2).

[4]   βαπτισμός, οῦ, ὁ, *dipping, washing, baptism* (4). Note that it is plural.

[5]   ἐπίθεσις, εως, ἡ, *laying on* (4).

[6]   ἐάνπερ, *if indeed, if only, supposing that* (3).

[7]   ἐπιτρέπω, *I allow, permit; order, instruct* (18). ἐπιτρέπῃ is not indicative.

[8]   Lane (132 *Note r*) discusses the structure of vv 4-6. It is not as not as easy as one might expect to determine the meaning of the following phrases. There are two possible interpretations, one that views these peoples' conversions as valid, and another that says they only appeared to become Christians. It makes for an interesting class discussion.

[9]   ἀδύνατος, ον, *powerless; impossible* (10).

[10]   ἅπαξ, *once (for all)* (14).

[11]   φωτίζω, *I give light to, illuminate; bring to light* (11).

[12]   γεύομαι, *I taste, partake of, enjoy; come to know* (15).

[13]   δωρεά, ᾶς, ἡ, *gift* (11).

[14]   ἐπουράνιος, ον, *heavenly* (19).

[15]   μέτοχος, ον, *sharing, participating* with the genitive of the person/thing (6).

παραπεσόντας,[1] πάλιν ἀνακαινίζειν[2] εἰς μετάνοιαν, ἀνασταυροῦντας[3] ἑαυτοῖς

τὸν υἱὸν τοῦ θεοῦ καὶ παραδειγματίζοντας.[4]

6:7 γῆ[5] γὰρ ἡ πιοῦσα τὸν ἐπ᾽ αὐτῆς ἐρχόμενον πολλάκις[6] ὑετὸν[7] καὶ

τίκτουσα[8] βοτάνην[9] εὔθετον[10] ἐκείνοις δι᾽ οὓς καὶ γεωργεῖται,[11]

μεταλαμβάνει[12] εὐλογίας[13] ἀπὸ τοῦ θεοῦ· **6:8** <u>ἐκφέρουσα</u>[14] δὲ ἀκάνθας[15] καὶ

τριβόλους,[16] ἀδόκιμος[17] καὶ κατάρας[18] ἐγγύς, ἧς τὸ τέλος εἰς καῦσιν.[19]

---

[1] παραπίπτω, *I fall beside, go astray, commit apostasy* (1). What kind of participle is it?

[2] ἀνακαινίζω, *I renew, restore* (1).

[3] ἀνασταυρόω, *I recrucify* (1).

[4] παραδειγματίζω, *I expose, make an example of, hold up to contempt* (1).

[5] Before getting to the main verb, the author inserts a series of phrases modifying γῆ.

[6] πολλάκις, *many times, often, frequently* (18).

[7] ὑετός, οῦ, ὁ, *rain* (5).

[8] τίκτω, *I bear, give birth (to)* (18).

[9] βοτάνη, ης, ἡ, *herb, plant* (1).

[10] εὔθετος, ον, *fit, suitable, usable* τινί *for something* (3).

[11] γεωργέω, *I cultivate* (1).

[12] μεταλαμβάνω, *I receive my share, share in, receive* with the genitive or accusative of the thing (7).

[13] εὐλογία, ας, ἡ, *praise; fine speaking; blessing; consecration* (16).

[14] ἐκφέρω, *I carry* or *bring out; lead* or *send (out)* (8).

[15] ἄκανθα, ης, ἡ, *thorn-plant* (14).

[16] τρίβολος, ου, ὁ, *thistle* (2).

[17] ἀδόκιμος, ον, *unqualified, worthless, base* (8).

[18] κατάρα, ας, ἡ, *curse* (6).

[19] καῦσις, εως, ἡ, *burning* (1).

---

(4)   **6:8** *   ἐκφέρουσα is a **conditional participle** and you can use the key word *if*.

6:9 Πεπείσμεθα δὲ περὶ ὑμῶν, ἀγαπητοί, τὰ κρείσσονα[1] καὶ[2] ἐχόμενα

σωτηρίας, εἰ καὶ[3] οὕτως λαλοῦμεν. **6:10** οὐ γὰρ ἄδικος[4] ὁ θεὸς ἐπιλαθέσθαι[5]

τοῦ ἔργου ὑμῶν καὶ τῆς ἀγάπης ἧς ἐνεδείξασθε[6] εἰς τὸ ὄνομα αὐτοῦ,

διακονήσαντες τοῖς ἁγίοις καὶ διακονοῦντες. **6:11** ἐπιθυμοῦμεν[7] δὲ ἕκαστον

ὑμῶν τὴν αὐτὴν ἐνδείκνυσθαι σπουδὴν[8] πρὸς τὴν πληροφορίαν[9] τῆς ἐλπίδος

ἄχρι τέλους, **6:12** ἵνα μὴ νωθροὶ γένησθε, μιμηταὶ[10] δὲ τῶν διὰ πίστεως καὶ

μακροθυμίας[11] κληρονομούντων[12] τὰς ἐπαγγελίας.

---

[1] κρείσσων, ον, *better, preferable, more prominent; more useful* (19). Also listed as κρείττων; see *MBG*, a-4b(1).

[2] καί ἐχόμενα σωτηρίας is probably epexegetical.

[3] Check *BAGD* under εἰ to see what εἰ καί mean together.

[4] ἄδικος, ον, *unjust* (12).

[5] ἐπιλανθάνομαι, *I forget, neglect,* with the genitive or accusative of the person/thing (8).

[6] ἐνδείκνυμι, in our literature always middle, *I show, demonstrate* (11).

[7] ἐπιθυμέω, *I desire, long for* with the genitive or accusative of the thing desired (16).

[8] σπουδή, ῆς, ἡ, *haste, speed; eagerness, diligence, zeal* (12).

[9] πληροφορία, ας, ἡ, *full assurance; certainty* (4).

[10] μιμητής, οῦ, ὁ, *imitator; follower* (6). It is followed by the genitive.

[11] μακροθυμία, ας, ἡ, *patience, endurance* (14).

[12] κληρονομέω, *I inherit; acquire, obtain* (18).

Chapter 18

ΑΠΟΚΑΛΥΨΙΣ ΙΩΑΝΝΟΥ 5

This is your final passage from the New Testament, so it is fitting that we end with the ending. There are passages in Revelation that are significantly unusual in terms of grammar, but chapter five is quite easy to read. Commentary references are to Robert H. Mounce, *The Book of Revelation,* in The New International Commentary on the New Testament (Eerdmans, 1977).

The Worthy Lamb (5:1-14)

5:1 Καὶ εἶδον ἐπὶ τὴν δεξιὰν τοῦ καθημένου ἐπὶ τοῦ θρόνου βιβλίον

γεγραμμένον ἔσωθεν[1] καὶ ὄπισθεν[2] <u>κατεσφραγισμένον</u>[3] σφραγῖσιν[4] ἑπτά.

5:2 καὶ εἶδον ἄγγελον ἰσχυρὸν <u>κηρύσσοντα</u> ἐν φωνῇ μεγάλῃ, Τίς ἄξιος <u>ἀνοῖξαι</u>

---

[1] ἔσωθεν, *inside, within* (12).

[2] ὄπισθεν, *from behind,* i.e., *on the back* (7).

[3] κατασφραγίζω, *I seal (up)* (1).

[4] σφραγίς, ῖδος, ἡ, *seal, signet* (16).

Exegetical Discussion

(1)   **5:1** * κατεσφραγισμένον. Normally we would expect a conjunction such as καί before κατεσφραγισμένον. Its omission is termed **asyndeton**.

(2)   5:2 κηρύσσοντα. What is the difference in meaning between κηρύσσω and εὐαγγελίζω? Is the angel preaching here? Probably not. κηρύσσω emphasizes the act of proclamation rather than the content of what is proclaimed. Cf. 1 Peter 3:19.

(3)   5:2 ἀνοῖξαι brings us to the significant issue of how to interpret apocalyptic literature. A strictly literal reading would suggest that the scroll is to be opened before the seals are removed since the writing is both inside and outside. Notice also the chronological order of the infinitives, ἀνοῖξαι and λῦσαι. Don't look for literary precision in a book written as an apocalypse. Like poetry, it requires imagination rather than logic.

τὸ βιβλίον καὶ λῦσαι τὰς σφραγῖδας αὐτοῦ; **5:3** καὶ οὐδεὶς ἐδύνατο ἐν τῷ

οὐρανῷ οὐδὲ ἐπὶ τῆς γῆς οὐδὲ ὑποκάτω[1] τῆς γῆς ἀνοῖξαι τὸ βιβλίον οὔτε βλέπειν

αὐτό. **5:4** καὶ <u>ἔκλαιον</u> πολύ, ὅτι οὐδεὶς ἄξιος εὑρέθη ἀνοῖξαι τὸ βιβλίον οὔτε

βλέπειν αὐτό. **5:5** καὶ εἷς ἐκ τῶν πρεσβυτέρων λέγει μοι, Μὴ κλαῖε, ἰδοὺ

ἐνίκησεν ὁ λέων[2] ὁ ἐκ τῆς φυλῆς Ἰούδα, ἡ ῥίζα[3] Δαυίδ, <u>ἀνοῖξαι</u> τὸ βιβλίον καὶ

τὰς ἑπτὰ σφραγῖδας αὐτοῦ.

5:6 Καὶ εἶδον ἐν μέσῳ τοῦ θρόνου καὶ τῶν τεσσάρων ζῴων καὶ ἐν μέσῳ

τῶν πρεσβυτέρων ἀρνίον ἑστηκὸς ὡς ἐσφαγμένον[4] <u>ἔχων</u> κέρατα[5] ἑπτὰ καὶ

---

[1] ὑποκάτω, *under, below* (11).

[2] λέων, οντος, ὁ, *lion* (9).

[3] ῥίζα, ης, ἡ, *root* (16).

[4] σφάζω, *I slaughter, butcher* (10). Its principal parts are σφάξω, ἔσφαξα, - ἔσφαγμαι, ἐσφάγην. Eight of the ten occurrences of σφάζω in the N.T. are in Revelation.

[5] κέρας, ατος, τό, *horn* (11).

---

(4) 5:4 ἔκλαιον. The imperfect ἔκλαιον can be taken as inceptive to describe the Seer's breaking into tears. Since ἔκλαιον is both first person singular and third person plural, how can you tell whether it was John or those mentioned in verse 3 who wept?

(5) 5:5 ἀνοῖξαι. Does ἀνοῖξαι indicate result or purpose? What would the difference be?

(6) 5:6 ἔχων. Did you notice that ἔχων (masculine singular) does not grammatically agree with ἀρνίον (neuter accusative). There are several ways to explain this.

1. It could be a grammatical irregularity. Some feel the Seer did not have a full working knowledge of Greek. If the Seer is to be identified with the author of the Gospel and epistles of John, then some postulate that John had help writing those but was alone on Patmos when he had his vision.

ὀφθαλμοὺς ἑπτὰ οἵ εἰσιν τὰ [ἑπτὰ] <u>πνεύματα</u> τοῦ θεοῦ ἀπεσταλμένοι εἰς πᾶσαν

τὴν γῆν. **5:7** καὶ ἦλθεν καὶ εἴληφεν ἐκ τῆς δεξιᾶς τοῦ καθημένου ἐπὶ τοῦ

θρόνου. **5:8** καὶ ὅτε ἔλαβεν τὸ βιβλίον, τὰ τέσσαρα ζῷα καὶ οἱ εἴκοσι[1] τέσσαρες

πρεσβύτεροι ἔπεσαν ἐνώπιον τοῦ ἀρνίου ἔχοντες ἕκαστος κιθάραν[2] καὶ φιάλας[3]

χρυσᾶς[4] γεμούσας[5] θυμιαμάτων,[6] <u>αἵ</u> εἰσιν αἱ προσευχαὶ τῶν ἁγίων, **5:9** καὶ

---

[1] εἴκοσι, *twenty* (11). It is indeclinable.

[2] κιθάρα, ας, ἡ, *harp* (4).

[3] φιάλη, ης, ἡ, *bowl*, specifically, a bowl used in offerings (12).

[4] χρυσοῦς, ῆ, οῦν, *golden*, that is, *made of* or *adorned with gold* (18).

[5] γέμω, *I am full* (11). Can take the genitive or accusative of the thing.

[6] θυμίαμα, ματος, τό, *incense (offering)*, *burning* (6).

---

2. Others (e.g., R. Mounce) argue that the disjuncted style is appropriate for an ecstatic apocalyptic vision.

3. The shift in gender can be explained by the fact that the lamb is Christ, and the Seer shifts to the masculine to make this clear. In fact, one wonders whether the Seer saw a lamb that was Christ, or saw Christ envisioned as a lamb. The shift in gender may be an indication of the later.

(7) 5:6   πνεύματα. In a desire to find the Trinity here, some understand πνεύματα as representing the Holy Spirit. Compare with Rev 1:4, 3:1, and 4:5. What do you think?

(8) 5:8   αἵ. The antecedent of αἵ is φιάλας. In apocalyptic literature "bowls" can be "prayers" without any problem. Allow these observations to determine your hermeneutical approach to Revelation.

ᾄδουσιν[1] ᾠδὴν[2] <u>καινὴν</u> λέγοντες,

    Ἄξιος εἶ λαβεῖν τὸ βιβλίον

       καὶ ἀνοῖξαι τὰς σφραγῖδας αὐτοῦ,

    ὅτι ἐσφάγης καὶ ἠγόρασας τῷ θεῷ ἐν τῷ <u>αἵματί</u> σου

       ἐκ πάσης φυλῆς καὶ γλώσσης καὶ λαοῦ καὶ ἔθνους

5:10   καὶ ἐποίησας αὐτοὺς τῷ θεῷ ἡμῶν βασιλείαν καὶ ἱερεῖς,

       καὶ βασιλεύσουσιν ἐπὶ τῆς γῆς.

   5:11 Καὶ εἶδον, καὶ ἤκουσα φωνὴν ἀγγέλων πολλῶν κύκλῳ[3] τοῦ θρόνου

καὶ τῶν ζῴων καὶ τῶν πρεσβυτέρων, καὶ ἦν ὁ ἀριθμὸς[4] αὐτῶν μυριάδες[5]

---

[1] ᾄδω, *I sing* with the song in the accusative (5). It is a contracted form of ἀείδω.

[2] ᾠδή, ῆς, ἡ, *song* (7).

[3] κύκλῳ, *(all) around* (8). κύκλῳ is an adverb formed from the dative of κύκλος, which does not occur in the New Testament. It can function as an improper preposition with the genitive.

[4] ἀριθμός, οῦ, ὁ, *number* (18).

[5] μυριάς, άδος, ἡ, *ten thousand; myriad* in the sense of an approximate number (8).

---

(9)   5:9   καινήν. The ᾠδὴν καινήν to the Lamb is a new song because the covenant established through his death is a new covenant. The song is καινή, "new in nature, different from the usual, impressive, better than the old, superior in value or attraction" (*TDNT* 3:447), rather than νέα, new in time or origin. Although this classical distinction between the two words for "new" is not true in every context (cf. Matt 9:17; Heb 9:15 vs 12:24), it appears to be so here. Throughout the N.T. "new" is usually understood eschatologically, so that the newness associated with the gospel is the newness of the coming age.

(10) **5:9** *   αἵματι is a good example of **metonymy**, by which a word related to the thing is used to represent it, instead of naming the thing itself. It was by the *death* of Christ, not his actual *blood*, that people are "purchased" for God.

μυριάδων καὶ χιλιάδες χιλιάδων   **5:12** λέγοντες φωνῇ μεγάλῃ,

Ἄξιόν ἐστιν τὸ ἀρνίον τὸ ἐσφαγμένον λαβεῖν τὴν δύναμιν καὶ

πλοῦτον καὶ σοφίαν καὶ ἰσχὺν[1] καὶ τιμὴν καὶ δόξαν καὶ

εὐλογίαν.[2]

5:13 καὶ πᾶν κτίσμα[3] ὃ ἐν τῷ οὐρανῷ καὶ ἐπὶ τῆς γῆς καὶ ὑποκάτω τῆς γῆς καὶ

ἐπὶ τῆς θαλάσσης καὶ τὰ ἐν αὐτοῖς πάντα ἤκουσα λέγοντας,

Τῷ καθημένῳ ἐπὶ τῷ θρόνῳ καὶ τῷ ἀρνίῳ ἡ εὐλογία καὶ ἡ τιμὴ

καὶ ἡ δόξα καὶ τὸ κράτος[4] εἰς τοὺς αἰῶνας τῶν αἰώνων.

5:14 καὶ τὰ τέσσαρα ζῷα ἔλεγον, Ἀμήν. καὶ οἱ πρεσβύτεροι ἔπεσαν καὶ

προσεκύνησαν.

---

[1] ἰσχύς, ύος, ἡ, *strength, power, might* (10).
[2] εὐλογία, ας, ἡ, *praise; fine speaking, flattery; blessing* (16).
[3] κτίσμα, ματος, τό, *creature, that which is created* (4).
[4] κράτος, ους, τό, *power, might; mighty deed; strength, intensity* (12).

---

(11) 5:14   ἔλεγον may be iterative. In that case the four living creatures cry "Amen" after each of the seven attributes of verse 12 and the four in verse 13.

Chapter 19

ΨΑΛΜΟΙ ΜΑ´

In these last two chapters you are pretty much on your own. The only vocabulary listed are the words that do not occur in *BAGD* regardless of their frequency. In English this is Psalm 42, and English does not start the versification with the title. In other words, Psalm 41:2 in the LXX is Psalm 42:1 in English. Definitions are based on *LSJ*.

41:1   Εἰς τὸ τέλος· εἰς σύνεσιν τοῖς υἱοῖς Κορέ.

41:2   Ὃν τρόπον ἐπιποθεῖ ἡ ἔλαφος[1] ἐπὶ τὰς πηγὰς τῶν ὑδάτων,

οὕτως ἐπιποθεῖ ἡ ψυχή μου πρὸς σέ, ὁ θεός.

41:3   ἐδίψησεν ἡ ψυχή μου πρὸς τὸν θεὸν τὸν ζῶντα·

πότε ἥξω καὶ ὀφθήσομαι τῷ προσώπῳ τοῦ θεοῦ;

41:4   ἐγενήθη μοι[2] τὰ δάκρυά μου ἄρτος ἡμέρας καὶ νυκτός,

ἐν τῷ λέγεσθαί μοι καθ᾽ ἑκάστην ἡμέραν, Ποῦ ἐστιν ὁ θεός σου;

---

[1]   ἔλαφος, ου, ὁ or ἡ, *deer.*

[2]   Some MSS do not have μοι here but insert ἐμοί after μου.

41:5 ταῦτα ἐμνήσθην

καὶ ἐξέχεα ἐπ᾽ ἐμὲ τὴν ψυχήν μου,

ὅτι διελεύσομαι[1] ἐν τόπῳ σκηνῆς θαυμαστῆς,

ἕως τοῦ οἴκου τοῦ θεοῦ,

ἐν φωνῇ ἀγαλλιάσεως καὶ ἐξομολογήσεως

ἤχου ἑορτάζοντος.

41:6 ἵνα τί[2] περίλυπος εἶ, ἡ ψυχή μου,[3]

καὶ ἵνα τί συνταράσσεις με;

ἔλπισον ἐπὶ τὸν θεόν,

ὅτι ἐξομολογήσομαι αὐτῷ,

σωτήριον τοῦ προσώπου μου ὁ θεός μου.

---

[1] The NIV translates the Hebrew word underlying διελεύσομαι as a **customary imperfect**, using the key word *used to*.

[2] Some MSS join these two words as ἱνατί.

[3] Rahlfs reads only ψυχή, both here and in v 12.

41:7   πρὸς ἐμαυτὸν ἡ ψυχή μου ἐταράχθη·

        διὰ τοῦτο μνησθήσομαί σου

        ἐκ γῆς Ἰορδάνου,

        καὶ Ερμωνιιμ,[1]

        ἀπὸ ὄρους μικροῦ.

41:8   ἄβυσσος ἄβυσσον ἐπικαλεῖται

        εἰς φωνὴν τῶν καταρρακτῶν[2] σου·

        πάντες οἱ μετεωρισμοί[3] σου καὶ τὰ κύματά σου

        ἐπ᾽ ἐμὲ διῆλθον.

---

[1] Ερμωνιιμ and the following μικροῦ are difficult to translate. It is not clear if they are referring to real places. Ερμωνιιμ is a transliteration of the Hebrew, which is the unusual plural of the word for "Hermon." There are Hebrew MSS that have the singular, and the Syriac is singular. It is possible that the author is making a play on words. ὄρους μικροῦ could just mean the small mountains, not one in particular, and the plural "Hermons" (as it were) could be emphasizing the contrast between the two.

Notice also that other MSS spell the word Ερμωνιειμ, and some modern texts provide a breathing and possibly an accent (Ἑρμωνιείμ). Elsewhere the mountain's name is spelled Ἀερμών, not always with breathing and accent. This variation is typical of foreign names brought into Greek.

[2] καταρράκτης, ου, ὁ, *waterfall, cataract.*

[3] μετεωρισμός, οῦ, ὁ, *wave, breaker.*

41:9   ἡμέρας ἐντελεῖται κύριος τὸ ἔλεος αὐτοῦ,

καὶ νυκτὸς ᾠδὴ παρ' ἐμοί,

προσευχὴ τῷ θεῷ τῆς ζωῆς μου.

41:10   ἐρῶ τῷ θεῷ Ἀντιλήμπτωρ[1] μου εἶ,

διὰ τί[2] μου ἐπελάθου;

ἵνα τί σκυθρωπάζων[3] πορεύομαι,

ἐν τῷ ἐκθλίβειν[4] τὸν ἐχθρόν μου;

41:11   ἐν τῷ καταθλάσαι[5] τὰ ὀστᾶ μου

ὠνείδισάν με οἱ θλίβοντές με,

ἐν τῷ λέγειν αὐτούς μοι καθ' ἑκάστην ἡμέραν,

Ποῦ ἐστιν ὁ θεός σου;

---

[1]   Ἀντιλήμπτωρ, τορος, ὁ, listed in *LSJ* as ἀντιλήπτωρ (without the μ), *helper, protector*, although most English translations use *rock*.

[2]   διὰ τί can also be written as one word, διατί.

[3]   Guess what this word means by looking at its cognate adjective.

[4]   ἐκθλίβω, *I squeeze much, am distressed greatly*.

[5]   καταθλάω, *I crush in pieces*.

41:12   ἵνα τί περίλυπος εἶ, ἡ ψυχή μου,

καὶ ἵνα τί συνταράσσεις με;

ἔλπισον ἐπὶ τὸν θεόν,

ὅτι ἐξομολογήσομαι αὐτῷ,

σωτήριον[1] τοῦ προσώπου μου[2] ὁ θεός μου.

---

[1]   Some MSS read ἡ σωτηρία.
[2]   Some MSS insert καί after μου.

Chapter 20

ΔΙΔΑΧΗ ΤΩΝ
ΔΩΔΕΚΑ ΑΠΟΣΤΟΛΩΝ
1:1-6; 7:1-4; 11:1-6

The following are not the most difficult passages from the Didache but they are interesting. The vocabulary is not difficult, and only one word does not occur in *BAGD*. Have fun.

Two Ways (1:1-6)

1:1 Ὁδοὶ δύο εἰσί, μία τῆς ζωῆς καὶ μία τοῦ θανάτου, διαφορὰ δὲ πολλὴ μεταξὺ τῶν δύο ὁδῶν.

1:2 Ἡ μὲν οὖν ὁδὸς τῆς ζωῆς ἐστιν αὕτη· πρῶτον ἀγαπήσεις τὸν θεὸν τὸν ποιήσαντά σε, δεύτερον τὸν πλησίον σου ὡς σεαυτόν· πάντα δὲ ὅσα ἐὰν θελήσῃς μὴ γίνεσθαί σοι, καὶ σὺ ἄλλῳ μὴ ποίει.

1:3 Τούτων δὲ τῶν λόγων ἡ διδαχή ἐστιν αὕτη· εὐλογεῖτε τοὺς καταρωμένους ὑμῖν καὶ προσεύχεσθε ὑπὲρ τῶν ἐχθρῶν ὑμῶν, νηστεύετε δὲ ὑπὲρ τῶν διωκόντων ὑμᾶς. ποία γὰρ χάρις ἐὰν ἀγαπᾶτε τοὺς ἀγαπῶντας ὑμᾶς; οὐχὶ καὶ τὰ ἔθνη τὸ αὐτὸ ποιοῦσιν; ὑμεῖς δὲ ἀγαπᾶτε τοὺς μισοῦντας ὑμᾶς καὶ οὐχ ἕξετε ἐχθρόν. **1:4** ἀπέχου τῶν σαρκικῶν καὶ σωματικῶν ἐπιθυμιῶν. ἐὰν τίς σοι δῷ ῥάπισμα εἰς τὴν δεξιὰν σιαγόνα, στρέψον αὐτῷ καὶ τὴν ἄλλην, καὶ ἔσῃ

τέλειος· ἐὰν ἀγγαρεύσῃ σέ τις μίλιον ἕν, ὕπαγε μετ᾽ αὐτοῦ δύο· ἐὰν ἄρῃ τις τὸ

ἱμάτιόν σου, δὸς αὐτῷ καὶ τὸν χιτῶνα· ἐὰν λάβῃ τις ἀπὸ σοῦ τὸ σόν, μὴ ἀπαίτει,

οὐδὲ γὰρ δύνασαι. **1:5** παντὶ τῷ αἰτοῦντί σε δίδου καὶ μὴ ἀπαίτει· πᾶσι γὰρ

θέλει δίδοσθαι ὁ πατὴρ ἐκ τῶν ἰδίων χαρισμάτων. μακάριος ὁ διδοὺς κατὰ τὴν

ἐντολήν· ἀθῷος γάρ ἐστιν. οὐαὶ τῷ λαμβάνοντι· εἰ μὲν γὰρ χρείαν ἔχων

λαμβάνει τις, ἀθῷος ἔσται· ὁ δὲ μὴ χρείαν ἔχων δώσει δίκην, ἱνατί ἔλαβε καὶ

εἰς τί· ἐν συνοχῇ δὲ γενόμενος ἐξετασθήσεται[1] περὶ ὧν ἔπραξε, καὶ οὐκ

ἐξελεύσεται ἐκεῖθεν, μέχρις οὗ ἀποδῷ τὸν ἔσχατον κοδράντην. **1:6** ἀλλὰ καὶ

περὶ τούτου δὲ εἴρηται· Ἱδρωσάτω ἡ ἐλεημοσύνη σου εἰς τὰς χεῖράς σου, μέχρις

ἂν γνῷς τίνι δῷς.

Baptism (7:1-4)

7:1 Περὶ δὲ τοῦ βαπτίσματος, οὕτω βαπτίσατε· ταῦτα πάντα

προειπόντες, βαπτίσατε εἰς τὸ ὄνομα τοῦ πατρὸς καὶ τοῦ υἱοῦ καὶ τοῦ ἁγίου

πνεύματος ἐν ὕδατι ζῶντι. **7:2** ἐὰν δὲ μὴ ἔχῃς ὕδωρ ζῶν, εἰς ἄλλο ὕδωρ

βάπτισον· εἰ δ᾽ οὐ δύνασαι ἐν ψυχρῷ, ἐν θερμῷ. **7:3** ἐὰν δὲ ἀμφότερα μὴ ἔχῃς,

---

[1] ἐκτάσσω, *I draw out, examine.*

ἔκχεον εἰς τὴν κεφαλὴν τρὶς ὕδωρ εἰς ὄνομα πατρὸς καὶ υἱοῦ καὶ ἁγίου

πνεύματος. **7:4** πρὸ δὲ τοῦ βαπτίσματος προνηστευσάτω ὁ βαπτίζων καὶ ὁ

βαπτιζόμενος καὶ εἴ τινες ἄλλοι δύνανται· κελεύεις δὲ νηστεῦσαι τὸν

βαπτιζόμενον πρὸ μιᾶς ἢ δύο.

Traveling Teachers (11:1-6)

11:1 Ὃς ἂν οὖν ἐλθὼν διδάξῃ ὑμᾶς ταῦτα πάντα τὰ προειρημένα,

δέξασθε αὐτόν. **11:2** ἐὰν δὲ αὐτὸς ὁ διδάσκων στραφεὶς διδάσκῃ ἄλλην διδαχὴν

εἰς τὸ καταλῦσαι, μὴ αὐτοῦ ἀκούσητε· εἰς δὲ τὸ προσθεῖναι δικαιοσύνην καὶ

γνῶσιν κυρίου, δέξασθε αὐτὸν ὡς κύριον. **11:3** Περὶ δὲ τῶν ἀποστόλων καὶ

προφητῶν, κατὰ τὸ δόγμα τοῦ εὐαγγελίου οὕτως[1] ποιήσατε. **11:4** πᾶς δὲ

ἀπόστολος ἐρχόμενος πρὸς ὑμᾶς δεχθήτω ὡς κύριος· **11:5** οὐ μενεῖ δὲ εἰ μὴ

ἡμέραν μίαν· ἐὰν δὲ ᾖ χρεία, καὶ τὴν ἄλλην· τρεῖς δὲ ἐὰν μείνῃ, ψευδοπροφήτης

ἐστίν. **11:6** ἐξερχόμενος δὲ ὁ ἀπόστολος μηδὲν λαμβανέτω εἰ μὴ ἄρτον, ἕως οὗ

αὐλισθῇ· ἐὰν δὲ ἀργύριον αἰτῇ, ψευδοπροφήτης ἐστί.

---

[1]   Some MSS have the simple οὕτω.

Appendix A: Partial Summary of

Greek Grammar Beyond the Basics:
An Exegetical Syntax of the New Testament

Daniel B. Wallace

I cannot thank my friend Dan Wallace enough for allowing me to include my summary of his *Greek Grammar Beyond the Basics* in the *Reader*. I felt that it was necessary to have brief grammar notes included in the *Reader*, but it was essential that the notes tie into a larger grammar.

I have included his categories that are discussed in the *Exegetical Discussion* section of the *Graded Reader* and a few others. This means that I have omitted many of his categories, his approximately one hundred charts, all of his detailed discussions, and especially his many exegetical discussions of key biblical passages (which is one of the most valuable and unique features of his text). For example, I reduced his discussion of the genitive from thirty-two categories and sixty-four pages to twenty categories and five and one-half pages. Rarely have I altered Wallace's wording. This summary was done a few months before Wallace's full grammar was published, so there may be a few differences from his published text. See Wallace for his guidelines for the form of the Greek text he uses in the illustrations (i.e., he follows his own punctuation and capitalization scheme, and he differs from the UBS text periodically).

Following many of the category names are alternate names enclosed in parentheses. There may also be "key words" ("glosses") at the end of the name enclosed in square brackets (cf. *BBG* §7.4). When you learn a new category from the *Exegetical Discussion*, you may want to write the verse reference next to the category in this summary for further reference.

The Nominative Case

The nominative is the case of specific designation. The Greeks referred to it as the "naming case," for it often names the main topic of the sentence. The main topic in a sentence *semantically* is, of course, similar to the *syntactical* subject, but the two are not always identical. Hence, the most common use of the nominative case is as subject.

A. Primary Uses of the Nominative

1. Subject

The substantive in the nominative case is frequently the subject of a finite verb. The verb may be explicitly stated. But the subject may also be implied, "embedded," as it were, in the verb (e.g., ἔρχεται means "*he* comes").

John 3:16   ἠγάπησεν **ὁ θεὸς** τὸν κόσμον
                 God loved the world

2. Predicate Nominative

The predicate nominative is *approximately* the same as the subject and is joined to it by an equative verb, whether stated or implied. The verbs used for this "equation" are, most frequently, εἰμί, γίνομαι, and ὑπάρχω.

Matt 3:17   οὗτός ἐστιν ὁ **υἱός** μου ὁ ἀγαπητός
                 This is my beloved **Son**.

John 4:24   **πνεῦμα** ὁ θεός
                 God is **spirit**.

3. Nominative in Simple Apposition

The nominative case (as well as the other cases) can be an appositive to another substantive in the same case. An appositional construction involves (1) two adjacent substantives (2) in the same case, (3) which refer to the same person or thing, (4) and have the same syntactical relation to the rest of the clause.

Matt 3:1   παραγίνεται Ἰωάννης **ὁ βαπτιστὴς** κηρύσσων
                 John **the Baptist** came preaching.

B. Grammatically Independent Uses of the Nominative

All independent nominatives follow this general rule: The substantive in the nominative case is grammatically unrelated to the rest of the sentence.

4. Nominative Absolute

The nominative absolute is the use of the nominative case in introductory material, which is not to be construed as a sentence. A nominative absolute does not occur in a sentence, but only in titles, salutations, and other introductory phrases.

Matt 1:1   **Βίβλος** γενέσεως Ἰησοῦ Χριστοῦ
                 The book of the genealogy of Jesus Christ.

Rom 1:7   **χάρις** ὑμῖν καὶ **εἰρήνη** ἀπὸ θεοῦ πατρὸς ἡμῶν καὶ κυρίου Ἰησοῦ Χριστοῦ.
                 Grace to you and **peace** from God our Father and the Lord Jesus Christ.

5. *Nominativus Pendens (Pendent Nominative)*

This nominative substantive is the logical rather than syntactical subject at the beginning of a sentence, followed by a sentence in which this subject is now replaced by a pronoun in the case required by the syntax.

Rev 3:12   **ὁ νικῶν** ποιήσω *αὐτὸν* στῦλον
                 The one who overcomes: I will make *him* a pillar.

6. *Parenthetic Nominative*

A parenthetic nominative is actually the subject in a clause inside a sentence that may or may not have a different subject. It is the subject of an explanatory clause **within** another clause.

John 1:6   ἐγένετο ἄνθρωπος ἀπεσταλμένος παρὰ θεοῦ, **ὄνομα** αὐτῷ Ἰωάννης.
                 There came a man sent from God (his **name** was John).

7. *Nominative for Vocative (Nominative of Address)*

A substantive in the nominative is used in the place of the vocative case to designate the addressee.

John 17:25   **πατὴρ**[1] δίκαιε, καὶ ὁ κόσμος σε οὐκ ἔγνω
                 Righteous **Father**, even the world has not known you.

Mark 9:19   Ὦ **γενεὰ** ἄπιστος, ἕως πότε πρὸς ὑμᾶς ἔσομαι;
                 O unfaithful **generation**! How long will I be with you?

8. *Nominative of Exclamation*

The nominative substantive is used in an exclamation without any grammatical connection to the rest of the sentence.

Rom 7:24   ταλαίπωρος ἐγὼ **ἄνθρωπος**
                 [O] wretched **man** [that] I am!

C. Nominatives in Place of Oblique Cases

9. *Nominative of Appellation*

A title appears in the nominative and functions as though it were a proper name. Another case would normally be more appropriate, but the nominative is used because of the special character of the individual described. The key is that the nominative is *treated* as a proper name, which is expected to be in another case.

John 13:13   ὑμεῖς φωνεῖτέ με **ὁ διδάσκαλος** καὶ **ὁ κύριος**
                 You call me **Teacher** and **Lord**.

---

[1]   The UBS text reads πάτερ, which is a true vocative.

The Vocative Case

The vocative is the case used for addressing someone or, on occasion, for uttering exclamations. A substantive in the vocative is used in direct address to designate the addressee. It technically has no syntactical relation to the main clause.

1. *Simple Address*

This is the use of the vocative *without* ὦ preceding it. For the most part, no special significance is to be attached to the use of the vocative in such instances. (In many instances, however, there will obviously be great emotion in the utterance. In such cases, the context will be determinative.)

Matt 9:22   ὁ Ἰησοῦς ... εἶπεν, Θάρσει, **θύγατερ**· ἡ πίστις σου σέσωκέν σε.
             Jesus said, "Take heart, **daughter**! Your faith has saved you."

Luke 4:23   πάντως ἐρεῖτέ μοι τὴν παραβολὴν ταύτην· **Ἰατρέ**, θεράπευσον σεαυτόν·
             No doubt you will quote to me this proverb: "**Physician**, heal yourself."

2. *Emphatic (Emotional) Address*

This is the use of the vocative *with* ὦ preceding it. Here the presence of the particle ὦ is used in contexts where deep emotion is to be found.

Matt 15:28   ὁ Ἰησοῦς εἶπεν αὐτῇ, **Ὦ γύναι**, μεγάλη σου ἡ πίστις
             Jesus said to her, "**O woman**, great is your faith!"

Jas 2:20   θέλεις δὲ γνῶναι, **ὦ ἄνθρωπε κενέ**, ὅτι ἡ πίστις χωρὶς τῶν ἔργων ἀργή ἐστιν;
             Do you want to learn, **O empty man**, that faith without works is worthless?

The Genitive Case

In the eight-case system, the genitive defines, describes, qualifies, restricts, limits. In this respect it is similar to an adjective, but is more emphatic. Under the five-case system, the genitive case may be defined as *the case of qualification (or limitation as to kind) and (occasionally) separation*. The genitive is the most exegetically significant case to understand for exegesis and it must be mastered. We have had to omit large portions of Wallace's discussions and all of the exegetical examples. Be sure to read his full grammar on the genitive.

A. Adjectival Genitive

This broad category really touches the heart of the genitive. If the genitive is primarily descriptive, then it is largely similar to the adjective in functions. "The chief thing to remember is that the Genitive often practically does the duty of an adjective, distinguishing two otherwise similar things" (Moule, 38). However, although the genitive is primarily adjectival in force, it is more emphatic than a simple adjective would be.

1. *Descriptive Genitive [characterized by, described by]*

The genitive substantive describes the head noun in a loose manner. The nature of the collocation of the two nouns in this construction is usually quite ambiguous. This is the "catch-all" genitive, the "drip pan" genitive, the "black hole" of genitive categories that tries to suck many a genitive into its grasp!

Rom 13:12   ἐνδυσώμεθα τὰ ὅπλα **τοῦ φωτός**
              Let us put on the armor **of light**.

2. *Possessive Genitive [belonging to, possessed by]*

The substantive in the genitive possesses the thing to which it stands related. That is, in some sense the head noun is owned by the genitive noun. Such ownership at times can be broadly defined and need not imply the literal (and sometimes harsh) idea of possession of physical property. Instead of the word *of* replace it with *belonging to* or *possessed by*.

Matt 26:51   τὸν δοῦλον **τοῦ ἀρχιερέως**
              the slave **of the high priest**

John 20:28   Θωμᾶς εἶπεν αὐτῷ, ὁ κύριός **μου** καὶ ὁ θεός **μου**
              Thomas said to him, "**My** Lord and **my** God."

3. *Genitive of Relationship*

The substantive in the genitive indicates a *familial* relationship, typically the progenitor of the person named by the head noun.

Matt 20:20   ἡ μήτηρ **τῶν υἱῶν Ζεβεδαίου**
              the mother **of the sons of Zebedee**

John 21:15   Σίμων **Ἰωάννου**
              Simon, [son] **of John**

4. *Partitive (Wholative) Genitive [which is a part of]*

The substantive in the genitive denotes *the whole of which* the head noun is a part. This is a phenomenological use of the genitive that requires the head noun to have a lexical nuance indicating *portion*. For example, "some of the Pharisees," "one of you," "a tenth of the city," "the branch of the tree," "a piece of pie."

Luke 19:8   τὰ ἡμίσιά μου **τῶν ὑπαρχόντων**
              half **of** my **possessions**

Rom 11:17   τινες **τῶν κλάδων**
              some **of the branches**

5. *Attributive Genitive (Hebrew Genitive, Genitive of Quality)*

The genitive substantive specifies an attribute or innate quality of the head substantive. If the noun in the genitive can be converted into an attributive adjective, modifying the noun to which the genitive stands related, then the genitive is likely an attributive genitive.

Luke 18:6   ὁ κριτὴς **τῆς ἀδικίας**
              judge **of unrighteousness** (= **unrighteous** judge)

Rom 6:6   τὸ σῶμα **τῆς ἁμαρτίας**
              body **of sin** (= **sinful** body)

6. *Attributed Genitive*

This is just the opposite, semantically, of the attributive genitive. The head noun, rather than the genitive, is functioning (in sense) as an attributive adjective. If it is possible to convert the noun to which the genitive stands related into a mere adjective, then the genitive is a good candidate for this category. One simple way to do this conversion is to omit the *of* in translation between the head noun and genitive, and change the head noun into its corresponding adjective. Thus "newness *of* life" becomes "new life."

Rom 6:4   ἵνα ... οὕτως καὶ ἡμεῖς ἐν καινότητι **ζωῆς** περιπατήσωμεν

so that ... thus also we should walk in newness **of life**.

Eph 1:19   καὶ τί τὸ ὑπερβάλλον μέγεθος **τῆς δυνάμεως** αὐτοῦ

and what is the surpassing greatness **of** his **power** (= his surpassingly great **power**)

7. *Genitive of Material [made out of, consisting of]*

The genitive substantive specifies the material out of which the head noun is made.

Mark 2:21   ἐπίβλημα **ῥάκους** ἀγνάφου

a patch [made out] **of** unshrunk **cloth**

Rev 18:12   γόμον **χρυσοῦ** καὶ **ἀργύρου** καὶ **λίθου** τιμίου

cargo **of gold** and **silver** and precious **stone**

8. *Genitive of Content [full of, containing]*

The genitive substantive specifies the contents of the word to which it is related. This word may be either a noun, adjective, or verb.

John 21:8   τὸ δίκτυον **τῶν ἰχθύων**

the net **full of fish**

Luke 2:40   τὸ δὲ παιδίον ηὔξανεν καὶ ἐκραταιοῦτο πληρούμενον **σοφίας**[1]

Now the child continued to grow and become strong, (being) filled **with wisdom** (or full **of wisdom**)

9. *Genitive in Simple Apposition*

Comments relating to both "Genitive in Simple Apposition" and "Genitive of Apposition."

The substantive in the genitive case refers to the same thing as the substantive to which it is related. The equation, however, is not exact.

By "appositional genitive" we mean *both* kinds of apposition (simple and gen. of apposition). Insert *which is, namely,* or *who is* between the head noun and the genitive noun. If this makes sense, an appositional genitive is likely.

Both categories fit the *which is* formula, so another test needs to be used to distinguish the two. If the word *of* can be used before the genitive in question, then it is a genitive of apposition. If it cannot, then it is simple apposition related to another genitive.

---

[1]   The UBS text reads σοφίᾳ.

Genitive in Simple Apposition

In simple apposition, both nouns are in the genitive case and the appositive does *not* name a specific example that falls within the category named by the noun to which it is related. Rather, it simply gives a different designation that either clarifies who is the one named or shows a different relation to the rest of the clause than what the first noun by itself could display.

Matt 2:11   εἶδον τὸ παιδίον μετὰ Μαρίας **τῆς μητρὸς** αὐτοῦ
They saw the child with Mary, his **mother**.

Eph 1:2   χάρις ὑμῖν καὶ εἰρήνη ἀπὸ θεοῦ **πατρὸς** ἡμῶν
Grace to you and peace from God our **Father**.

10. Genitive of Apposition (Epexegetical Genitive, Genitive of Definition) [which is, that is, namely, who is]

See the opening comments in the previous category.

In the genitive of apposition, the head noun will: (1) state a large category, (2) be ambiguous, or (3) be metaphorical in its meaning, while the genitive names a concrete or specific example that either falls *within* that category, clarifies its ambiguity, or brings the metaphor down to earth.

Luke 22:1   ἡ ἑορτὴ **τῶν ἀζύμων**
the feast **of unleavened bread**

John 2:21   ἔλεγεν περὶ τοῦ ναοῦ **τοῦ σώματος** αὐτοῦ
He was speaking concerning the temple **of** his **body** (= the temple, **which is** his **body**).

11. Genitive of Subordination [over]

The genitive substantive specifies that which is subordinated to or under the dominion of the head noun.

Matt 9:34   τῷ ἄρχοντι **τῶν δαιμονίων**
the ruler **over the demons**

B. Ablatival Genitive

The ablatival genitive basically involves the notion of separation. This idea can be static (i.e., in a separated state) or progressive (movement away from, so as to become separated). The emphasis may be on either the state resulting from the separation or the cause of separation (in the latter, origin or source is emphasized). For the most part, the ablatival genitive is being replaced in Koine Greek by ἐκ or ἀπό with the genitive.

12. Genitive of Separation [out of, away from, from]

The genitive substantive is that from which the *verb* or sometimes the head noun is separated. Thus the genitive is used to indicate the point of departure.

Matt 10:14   ἐκτινάξατε τὸν κονιορτὸν **τῶν ποδῶν** ὑμῶν
Shake the dust **from** your **feet**.

Eph 2:12   ἀπηλλοτριωμένοι **τῆς πολιτείας** τοῦ Ἰσραήλ
having been alienated **from the commonwealth** of Israel

13. Genitive of Comparison [than]

The genitive substantive, almost always after a comparative adjective (e.g., πλείων, μείζων), is used to indicate comparison. The genitive, then, is the standard against which the comparison is made.

Matt 6:25　　οὐχὶ ἡ ψυχὴ πλεῖόν ἐστιν **τῆς τροφῆς**;
　　　　　　　Is not your life worth more **than food**?

John 14:28　ὁ πατὴρ μείζων **μού** ἐστιν
　　　　　　　The Father is greater **than I [am]**.

C. Verbal Genitive (Genitive Related to a Verbal Noun)

The subjective, objective, and plenary genitives are used with head nouns that involve a verbal idea. That is, the head noun has a verb as a cognate (e.g., βασιλεύς has βασιλεύω as cognate).

14. Subjective Genitive

The genitive substantive functions semantically as the *subject* of the verbal idea implicit in the head noun. If a subjective genitive is suspected, attempt to convert the verbal noun to which the genitive is related into a verbal form and turn the genitive into its subject. Thus, for example, "the revelation of Jesus Christ" in Gal 1:12 becomes "[What/the fact that] Jesus Christ reveals."

Matt 24:27　οὕτως ἔσται ἡ παρουσία **τοῦ υἱοῦ** τοῦ ἀνθρώπου
　　　　　　　So will the coming **of the Son** of Man be (= So shall it be when the **Son** of Man comes).

Rom 8:35　　τίς ἡμᾶς χωρίσει ἀπὸ τῆς ἀγάπης **τοῦ Χριστοῦ**;
　　　　　　　Who will separate us from the love of **Christ** (= Who will separate us from **Christ's** love for us)?

15. Objective Genitive

The genitive substantive functions semantically as the *direct object* of the verbal idea implicit in the head noun. When an objective genitive is suspected, attempt to convert the verbal noun to which the genitive is related into a verbal form and turn the genitive into its direct object. Thus, for example, "a demonstration of his righteousness" in Rom 3:25 becomes "demonstrating his righteousness." A simpler and less fool-proof method is to supply for the word *of* the words *for*, *about*, *concerning*, *toward*, or sometimes *against*.

Matt 12:31　ἡ δὲ **τοῦ πνεύματος** βλασφημία οὐκ ἀφεθήσεται
　　　　　　　But the blasphemy **of the Spirit** will not be forgiven (= blasphemy **against the Spirit**" or "blaspheming the Spirit).

Luke 11:42　οὐαὶ ὑμῖν τοῖς Φαρισαίοις, ὅτι ... παρέρχεσθε τὴν κρίσιν καὶ τὴν ἀγάπην **τοῦ θεοῦ**
　　　　　　　Woe to you Pharisees! For ... you have neglected justice and love **that you have for God!**

16. Plenary Genitive

The noun in the genitive is *both* subjective and objective. In most cases, the subjective produces the objective notion. Simply apply the "keys" used for the subjective and objective genitives. If *both* ideas seem to fit in a given passage, *and do not contradict but rather complement one another*, then there is a good possibility that the genitive in question is a plenary genitive.

2 Cor 5:14   ἡ γὰρ ἀγάπη **τοῦ Χριστοῦ** συνέχει ἡμᾶς
for the love **of Christ** constrains us

Rom 5:5   ἡ ἀγάπη **τοῦ θεοῦ** ἐκκέχυται ἐν ταῖς καρδίαις ἡμῶν διὰ πνεύματος ἁγίου τοῦ δοθέντος ἡμῖν
The love **of God** has been poured out within our hearts through the Holy Spirit who was given to us.

D. Adverbial Genitive

This is the use of the genitive that is similar in force to an adverb. As well, often this use of the genitive has the force of a prepositional phrase. Thus the genitive will normally be related to a verb or adjective rather than a noun. (Even in instances where it is dependent on a noun, there is usually an implicit verbal idea in the noun.)

17. Genitive of Time (within which, during which)

The genitive substantive indicates the *kind* of time, or time *within which* the word to which it stands related takes place. The easiest way to remember the genitive of time (as opposed to the dat. and acc. of time) is to relate the genitive back to its basal significance. The genitive is the case of quality, attribute, description, or *kind*. Thus, the genitive of time indicates the *kind* of time.

John 3:2   ἦλθεν πρὸς αὐτὸν **νυκτός**
He came to him **during the night**.

1 Thess 2:9   **νυκτὸς** καὶ **ἡμέρας** ἐργαζόμενοι
working **night** and **day**

18. Genitive of Association [in association with]

The genitive substantive indicates the one with whom the noun to which it stands related is associated.

Matt 23:30   οὐκ ἂν ἤμεθα **αὐτῶν** κοινωνοὶ ἐν τῷ αἵματι τῶν προφητῶν
We would not have shared **with them** in the blood of the prophets.

Rom 8:17   εἰ δὲ τέκνα, καὶ κληρονόμοι· κληρονόμοι μὲν θεοῦ, συγκληρονόμοι δὲ **Χριστοῦ**
Now if we are children, [we are] also heirs: on the one hand, heirs of God, on the other hand, fellow heirs **with Christ**.

E. After Certain Words

There are some uses of the genitive that do not neatly fit into any of the above categories. Or, if they do fit into one of the above categories, they are related to a word other than a noun.

19. Genitive After Certain Verbs (as a Direct Object)

Certain verbs take a genitive substantive as direct object. These verbs commonly correspond in meaning to some other function of the genitive, e.g., separation, partitive, source, etc. The predominant uses can be grouped into four types of verbs: *sensation, emotion/volition, sharing, ruling.*

Mark 5:41   κρατήσας **τῆς χειρὸς** τοῦ παιδίου λέγει αὐτῇ, Ταλιθα κουμ
Touching **the hand** of the little girl, he said to her, "Talitha cum."

20. Genitive After Certain Adjectives (and Adverbs)

Certain adjectives (such as ἄξιος, "worthy [of]") and adverbs normally take a genitive "object." In many instances the adjective/adverb is an embedded transitive verb, thus taking an objective genitive (e.g., "he is deserving of X" means "he deserves X") or involving a partitive idea.

Matt 26:66   ἔνοχος **θανάτου** ἐστίν
              He is deserving **of death**.

The Dative Case

The true dative is used to designate the person more remotely concerned. It is the case of *personal interest*, pointing out the person *to* or *for* whom something is done. Since the dative, instrumental, and locative share the same form, we will consider them as *one* case ("case" being defined as a matter of form rather than function within the five-case system). The *instrumental* idea involves *means* and generally answers the question, "How?" The *locative* notion involves *place* and answers the question, "Where?" Thus, a broad view of the dative case suggests that it answers one of three questions: To/for whom? How? or Where?

A. Pure Dative Uses

The subgroups here are specific uses built on the root idea of *personal interest* and *reference/respect*.

1. Dative of Indirect Object [to, for]

The dative substantive is that *to* or *for* which the action of a verb is performed. The indirect object will *only occur with a transitive verb*. When the transitive verb is in the *active* voice, the indirect object receives the direct object ("the boy hit the ball *to me*"); when the verb is in the *passive* voice, the indirect object receives the subject of the verb ("the ball was hit *to me*"). The keys are (1) the verb must be transitive, and (2) if the dative can be translated with *to* or *for* it is most likely indirect object.

John 4:10   καὶ ἔδωκεν ἄν **σοι** ὕδωρ ζῶν
             and he would have given **to you** living water

Luke 1:13   ἡ γυνή σου Ἐλισάβετ γεννήσει υἱόν **σοι**, καὶ καλέσεις τὸ ὄνομα αὐτοῦ Ἰωάννην.
             Your wife Elizabeth will bear a son **to you**, and you will call his name John.

2. Dative of Interest [for the benefit of, in the interest of / to the disadvantage of, against]

The dative substantive indicates the person (or, rarely, thing) interested in the verbal action. The dative of advantage (*commodi*) has a *to* or *for* idea, while the dative of disadvantage (*incommodi*) has an *against* idea.

Matt 23:31   μαρτυρεῖτε **ἑαυτοῖς**
             You testify **against yourselves**

1 Cor 6:13   τὰ βρώματα **τῇ κοιλίᾳ**
             food is **for** [the benefit of] **the stomach**

3. *Dative of Reference/Respect [with reference to]*

The dative substantive is that in reference to which something is presented as true. An author will use this dative to qualify a statement that would otherwise typically not be true.

Rom 6:2   οἵτινες ἀπεθάνομεν **τῇ ἁμαρτίᾳ**, πῶς ἔτι ζήσομεν ἐν αὐτῇ;
                How shall we who died [with reference] **to sin** still live in it?

Rom 6:11   λογίζεσθε ἑαυτοὺς εἶναι νεκροὺς μὲν **τῇ ἁμαρτίᾳ**, ζῶντας δὲ **τῷ θεῷ**
                Consider yourselves to be dead **to sin**, but alive **to God**.

4. *Dative in Simple Apposition*

Though not technically a syntactical category, the dative case (as well as the other cases) can be an appositive to another substantive in the *same* case. An appositional construction involves two adjacent substantives that refer to the same person or thing and have the same syntactical relation to the rest of the clause. The first dative substantive can belong to *any* dative category and the second is merely a clarification of who or what is mentioned. Thus, the appositive "piggy-backs" on the first dative's use, as it were.

Matt 27:2   παρέδωκαν Πιλάτῳ **τῷ ἡγεμόνι**
                They handed [him] over to Pilate, **the governor**.

Luke 1:47   ἠγαλλίασεν τὸ πνεῦμά μου ἐπὶ τῷ θεῷ **τῷ σωτῆρί** μου
                My spirit rejoices in God my **Savior**.

B. Local Dative Uses

The subgroups here are specific uses built on the root idea of *position*, whether spatial, nonphysical, or temporal.

5. *Dative of Sphere [in the sphere of]*

The dative substantive indicates the sphere or realm in which the word to which it is related takes place or exists. Normally this word is a verb, but not always.

Acts 16:5   αἱ ... ἐκκλησίαι ἐστερεοῦντο **τῇ πίστει**
                The churches grew **in faith**.

Matt 5:8   μακάριοι οἱ καθαροὶ **τῇ καρδίᾳ**
                Blessed are the pure **in heart**.

6. *Dative of Time (when)*

The noun in the dative indicates the *time when* the action of the main verb is accomplished. The dative routinely denotes *point of time*, answering the question "When?" In the eight-case system, this would be the locative of time. Though common enough, this usage is being increasingly replaced in Koine Greek with ἐν + the dative.

Matt 17:23   **τῇ τρίτῃ ἡμέρᾳ** ἐγερθήσεται
                [At a point in time] **on the third day** he will be raised.

Matt 24:20   προσεύχεσθε δὲ ἵνα μὴ γένηται ἡ φυγὴ ὑμῶν χειμῶνος μηδὲ **σαββάτῳ**
                But pray that your flight will not be during the winter nor **on the sabbath**.

C. Instrumental Dative Uses

The subgroups here are specific uses built on the root idea of *means*, although some loosely fit under this umbrella.

7. *Dative of Association (Accompaniment, Comitative) [in association with]*

The dative substantive indicates the person or thing one associates with or accompanies.

Acts 9:7   οἱ δὲ ἄνδρες οἱ συνοδεύοντες **αὐτῷ**
            the men who were traveling **with him**

2 Cor 6:14   μὴ γίνεσθε ἑτεροζυγοῦντες **ἀπίστοις**
            Do not become unequally yoked [in association] **with unbelievers**.

8. *Dative of Manner (Adverbial Dative) [with, in (answering "How?")]*

The dative substantive denotes the manner in which the action of the verb is accomplished. Like many adverbs, this use of the dative answers the question "How?" The manner can be an accompanying action, attitude, emotion, or circumstance. Hence, such a dative noun routinely has an abstract quality. This usage is being supplanted by ἐν + dative (or μετά + gen.) in Koine Greek.

John 7:26   **παρρησίᾳ** λαλεῖ
            He speaks **with boldness** (= boldly).

1 Cor 10:30 εἰ ἐγὼ **χάριτι** μετέχω
            if I partake [of the food] **with thanksgiving** (= thankfully)

9. *Dative of Means/Instrument [by, by means of, with]*

The dative substantive is used to indicate the means or instrument by which the verbal action is accomplished.

Matt 8:16   ἐξέβαλεν τὰ πνεύματα **λόγῳ**
            He cast out the spirits **by** [means of] **a word**.

John 11:2   ἐκμάξασα τοὺς πόδας αὐτοῦ **ταῖς θριξὶν** αὐτῆς
            She wiped his feet **with** her **hair**.

10. *Dative of Measure/Degree of Difference [by]*

The dative substantive, when following or preceding a comparative adjective or adverb, may be used to indicate the extent to which the comparison is true or the degree of difference that exists in the comparison.

Rom 5:8-9   ἔτι ἁμαρτωλῶν ὄντων ἡμῶν Χριστὸς ὑπὲρ ἡμῶν ἀπέθανεν. (9) **πολλῷ** οὖν μᾶλλον
            δικαιωθέντες νῦν ἐν τῷ αἵματι αὐτοῦ σωθησόμεθα δι᾽ αὐτοῦ ἀπὸ τῆς ὀργῆς.
            While we were yet sinners, Christ died for us. **Much** more [literally, "more **by**
            much"], then, since we have now been justified by his blood, we will be saved from
            the [coming] wrath through him.

Phil 2:12   ὑπηκούσατε ... **πολλῷ** μᾶλλον ἐν τῇ ἀπουσίᾳ μου
            you obeyed ... **much** more in my absence

11. Dative of Cause [because of]

The dative substantive indicates the cause or basis of the action of the verb.

Luke 15:17 Πόσοι μίσθιοι τοῦ πατρός μου περισσεύονται ἄρτων, ἐγὼ δὲ **λιμῷ** ὧδε ἀπόλλυμαι;
How many of my father's hirelings are overflowing in bread, but I am perishing here **because of a famine**?

Rom 4:20 οὐ διεκρίθη **τῇ ἀπιστίᾳ**
He did not waver **because of unbelief**.

D. The Uses of the Dative After Certain Words

There are some uses of the dative that do not neatly fit into any of the above categories.

12. Dative Direct Object

A number of verbs take the dative as their direct object. Also, it should be noted that such datives are usually related to verbs implying personal relation. Thus the meanings of the verbs correspond in meaning to the basic idea of the pure dative.

Heb 1:6 καὶ προσκυνησάτωσαν **αὐτῷ** πάντες ἄγγελοι θεοῦ.
And let all the angels of God worship **him**.

13. Dative After Certain Nouns

A few nouns take datives after them. Again, the notion of personal interest is almost always seen. This category is not particularly common. These nouns are *verbal* nouns (i.e., they are cognate to a verb, such as ὀφειλέτης [ὀφείλω], ὑπάντησις [ὑπαντάω]). Furthermore, frequently that noun finds its counterpart in one of the verbs taking a dative direct object: διακονία-διακονέω, εὐχαριστία-εὐχαριστέω, etc.

Matt 8:34 πᾶσα ἡ πόλις ἐξῆλθεν εἰς ὑπάντησιν **τῷ Ἰησοῦ**
All the city came out for a meeting **with Jesus**.

1 Cor 16:15 διακονίαν **τοῖς ἁγίοις**
service **to the saints**

14. Dative After Certain Adjectives

A few adjectives are followed by the dative case. Once again, when the idea of personal interest appears, the dative is naturally used.

Matt 13:31 ὁμοία ἐστὶν ἡ βασιλεία τῶν οὐρανῶν **κόκκῳ** σινάπεως
The kingdom of heaven is like a mustard **seed**.

Rom 1:30 **γονεῦσιν** ἀπειθεῖς
disobedient **to parents**

The Accusative Case

The accusative is used to limit the action of a verb as to extent, direction, or goal. "The accusative measures an idea as to its content, scope, direction" (Robertson, 468).

A. Substantival Uses of the Accusative

1. Accusative Direct Object

The accusative substantive indicates the immediate object of the action of a transitive verb. It receives the action of the verb. In this way it limits the verbal action.

Matt 5:46   ἐὰν ἀγαπήσητε *τοὺς ἀγαπῶντας* **ὑμᾶς**
               if you love *those who love* **you**

Mark 2:17   οὐκ ἦλθον καλέσαι **δικαίους** ἀλλὰ **ἁμαρτωλούς**
               I did not come to call **the righteous** but **sinners**.

2. Double Accusative

There are two types of double accusative constructions—i.e., constructions in which a verb takes two accusatives. Because the semantics are different, it is important to distinguish them.

a. Double Accusative of the Person and Thing

Certain verbs take two direct objects, one a person and the other a thing. The thing is the nearer object; the person is the more remote object. Another way to put this is that the person is the object *affected*, while the thing is the object *effected*.

John 14:26   ἐκεῖνος **ὑμᾶς** διδάξει **πάντα**
               He will teach **you all things**.

Matt 27:31   ἐξέδυσαν **αὐτὸν τὴν χλαμύδα** καὶ ἐνέδυσαν **αὐτὸν τὰ ἱμάτια** αὐτοῦ
               They stripped **him of** [his] **robe** and put his own **garments on him**.

b. Double Accusative of Object-Complement

An object-complement double accusative is a construction in which one accusative substantive is the direct object of the verb and the other accusative (either noun, adjective, participle, or infinitive) complements the object in that it predicates something about it. The complement may be substantival or adjectival. This usage occurs only with certain kinds of verbs.

Matt 22:43   Δαυὶδ ἐν πνεύματι καλεῖ **αὐτὸν κύριον**
               David in the Spirit calls **him**[obj] **Lord**[comp].

Matt 4:19   ποιήσω **ὑμᾶς ἁλιεῖς** ἀνθρώπων
               I will make **you**[obj] **fishers**[comp] of men.

3. Predicate Accusative

The accusative substantive (or adjective) stands in predicate relation to another accusative substantive. The two will be joined by an equative verb, either an infinitive or participle.

Luke 4:41   ᾔδεισαν **τὸν Χριστὸν** αὐτὸν εἶναι
               They knew that he was **the Christ**.

> Eph 2:1   ὑμᾶς ὄντας **νεκροὺς** τοῖς παραπτώμασιν
>   although you were **dead** in [your] trespasses

4. *Accusative Subject of the Infinitive*

The accusative substantive frequently functions semantically as the subject of the infinitive. Though older grammars insist that technically this is an accusative of respect, from a descriptive and functional perspective, it is better to treat it as subject.

> Matt 22:3   ἀπέστειλεν **τοὺς δούλους** αὐτοῦ καλέσαι τοὺς κεκλημένους
>   He sent his **servants** to call those who had been invited.

> Heb 5:12   χρείαν ἔχετε τοῦ διδάσκειν ὑμᾶς **τινά**
>   You need **someone** to teach you.

5. *Accusative in Simple Apposition*

Though not technically a syntactical category, the accusative case (as well as the other cases) can be an appositive to another substantive in the *same* case. An appositional construction involves two adjacent substantives that refer to the same person or thing and have the same syntactical relation to the rest of the clause. The first accusative substantive can belong to *any* accusative category, and the second is merely a clarification of who or what is mentioned. Thus, the appositive "piggy-backs" on the first accusative's use, as it were.

> Mark 1:16   Ἀνδρέαν **τὸν ἀδελφὸν** Σίμωνος
>   Andrew **the brother** of Simon

> Acts 16:31   πίστευσον ἐπὶ τὸν κύριον **Ἰησοῦν** καὶ σωθήσῃ σύ
>   Believe in the Lord **Jesus** and you will be saved.

B. Adverbial Uses of the Accusative

6. *Adverbial Accusative (Accusative of Manner)*

The accusative substantive functions semantically like an adverb in that it *qualifies* the action of the verb rather than indicating *quantity* or *extent* of the verbal action. It frequently acts like an adverb of manner, though not always.

> Matt 10:8   **δωρεὰν** ἐλάβετε, **δωρεὰν** δότε
>   You received **freely, freely** give.

> Matt 6:33   ζητεῖτε δὲ **πρῶτον** τὴν βασιλείαν τοῦ θεοῦ
>   but seek **first** the kingdom of God

7. *Accusative of Measure (Extent of Time or Space) [for the extent of, for the duration of]*

The accusative substantive indicates the extent of the verbal action. This can either be how far (extent of space) or for how long (extent of time).

> Luke 2:44   νομίσαντες δὲ αὐτὸν εἶναι ἐν τῇ συνοδίᾳ ἦλθον ἡμέρας **ὁδὸν**
>   but assuming that he was in the group, they went a day's **journey**

> Matt 20:6   τί ὧδε ἑστήκατε **ὅλην τὴν ἡμέραν** ἀργοί;
>   Why have you been standing here idle **the whole day**?

8. *Accusative of Respect or (General) Reference [with reference to, or concerning]*

The accusative substantive restricts the reference of the verbal action. It indicates *with reference to what* the verbal action is represented as true.

Matt 27:57	ἄνθρωπος πλούσιος ἀπὸ Ἁριμαθαίας, **τοὔνομα** Ἰωσήφ
	a rich man from Arimathea, Joseph **by name**
John 6:10	ἀνέπεσαν οὖν οἱ ἄνδρες **τὸν ἀριθμὸν** ὡς πεντακισχίλιοι
	Then the men sat down–**with reference to number** about 5000.

The Article

Understanding the article is essential for biblical exegesis, and our summary here is especially shortened. Be sure to see Wallace's full grammar on the article, especially his discussion of "Colwell's Rule" and "Granville Sharp's Rule," and his discussion of the absence of the article. Some of the following categories overlap.

A. As a Pronoun ([partially] Independent Use)

The article is not a true pronoun in Koine Greek, even though it derived from the demonstrative. But in many instances it can function semantically in the place of a pronoun.

1. Personal Pronoun [he, she, it]

The article is often used in the place of a *third* person personal pronoun in the nominative case. It is only used this way with the μὲν ... δέ construction or with δέ alone. (Thus, ὁ μὲν ... ὁ δέ or simply ὁ δέ.)

John 4:32	**ὁ** δὲ εἶπεν αὐτοῖς
	But **he** said to them

2. Relative Pronoun [who, which]

Sometimes the article is equivalent to a relative pronoun in *force*. This is especially true when it is repeated after a noun before a phrase (e.g., a gen. phrase).

1 Cor 1:18	ὁ λόγος **ὁ** τοῦ σταυροῦ
	the word **that is** of the cross
Luke 7:32	ὅμοιοί εἰσιν παιδίοις **τοῖς** ἐν ἀγορᾷ καθημένοις
	They are like children **who** [are] sitting in the marketplace.

3. Possessive Pronoun [his, her]

The article is sometimes used in contexts in which possession is implied. The article itself does not involve possession, but this notion can be inferred from the presence of the article alone in certain contexts.

Eph 5:25	οἱ ἄνδρες, ἀγαπᾶτε **τὰς** γυναῖκας
	Husbands, love **your** wives.

B. With Substantives (Dependent or Modifying Use)

[Wallace classifies all of the following categories except the last as subcategories of the "individualizing article."] The individualizing article particularizes, distinguishing otherwise similar objects; the generic (or categorical) article is used to distinguish one category of individuals from another.

4. Simple Identification

The article is frequently used to distinguish one individual from another.

Luke 4:20   πτύξας τὸ βιβλίον ἀποδοὺς **τῷ** ὑπηρέτῃ ἐκάθισεν
He closed the book and gave it back to **the** attendant and sat down.

5. Anaphoric (Previous Reference)

The anaphoric article is the article denoting previous reference. The first mention of the substantive is usually anarthrous because it is merely being introduced. But subsequent mentions of it use the article, for the article is now pointing back to *the* substantive previously mentioned.

John 4:40, 43 ἔμεινεν ἐκεῖ δύο ἡμέρας ... μετὰ δὲ **τὰς** δύο ἡμέρας ...
He stayed there two days ... after **the** two days ...

2 Tim 4:2   κήρυξον **τὸν** λόγον
Preach **the** word! (see 2 Tim 3:16)

6. Deictic ("Pointing" Article)

The article is occasionally used to point out an object or person which/who is present at the moment of speaking. It typically has a demonstrative force.

Matt 14:15   προσῆλθον αὐτῷ οἱ μαθηταὶ λέγοντες· ἔρημός ἐστιν **ὁ** τόπος
The disciples came to him, saying, "**This** place is deserted."

7. Par Excellence

The article is frequently used to point out a substantive that is, in a sense, "in a class by itself." It is the only one deserving of the name. For example, if in late January someone were to say to you, "Did you see the game?" you might reply, "Which game?" They might then reply, "*The* game! The only game worth watching! The *BIG* game! You know, the Super Bowl!" This is the article used in a *par excellence* way.

John 1:21   ὁ προφήτης εἶ σύ;
Are you **the** prophet?

8. Monadic ("One of a Kind" or "Unique" Article)

The article is frequently used to identify monadic or one-of-a-kind nouns, such as "*the* devil," "*the* sun," "*the* Christ."

John 1:29   ἴδε ὁ ἀμνὸς τοῦ θεοῦ ὁ αἴρων τὴν ἁμαρτίαν τοῦ κόσμου.
Behold **the** lamb of God who takes away the sin of the world!

9. Well-Known ("Celebrity" Article)

The article points out an object that is well known, but for reasons *other* than the above categories (i.e., not anaphoric, deictic, *par excellence*, or monadic). Thus it refers to a well-known object that has not been mentioned in the preceding context (anaphoric), nor is considered to be the best of its class (*par excellence*), nor is one of a kind (monadic).

Jas 1:1   ταῖς δώδεκα φυλαῖς ταῖς ἐν **τῇ** διασπορᾷ
           to the twelve tribes that are in **the** dispersion

10. Abstract (the Article with Abstract Nouns)

Abstract nouns by their very nature focus on a quality. However, when such a noun is articular, that quality is "tightened up," as it were, defined more closely, distinguished from other notions.

Matt 7:23   οἱ ἐργαζόμενοι **τὴν** ἀνομίαν
            the workers of lawlessness

John 4:22   **ἡ** σωτηρία ἐκ τῶν Ἰουδαίων ἐστίν
            Salvation is from the Jews.

11. Generic (Categorical) Article [as a class]

While the *individualizing* article distinguishes or identifies a particular object belonging to a larger class, the *generic* article distinguishes one class from another. This is somewhat less frequent than the individualizing article (though it still occurs hundreds of times in the NT). It categorizes rather than particularizes.

Matt 18:17   ἔστω σοι ὥσπερ **ὁ** ἐθνικὸς καὶ **ὁ** τελώνης
             Let him be [with reference] to you as **the** Gentile [as a class] and **the** tax-collector [as a class].

C. As a Substantiver

The article can turn almost any part of speech into a noun: adverbs, adjectives, prepositional phrases, particles, infinitives, participles, and even finite verbs. As well, the article can turn a phrase into a nominal entity. This incredible flexibility is part of the genius of the Greek article.

Matt 8:28   ἐλθόντος αὐτοῦ εἰς **τὸ** πέραν
             when he came to **the** other side

Matt 5:5   μακάριοι **οἱ** πραεῖς, ὅτι αὐτοὶ κληρονομήσουσιν τὴν γῆν
             Blessed are **the** meek, for they shall inherit the earth.

Luke 7:19   σὺ εἶ **ὁ** ἐρχόμενος;
             Are you **the** one who is to come?

Mark 10:40   **τὸ** δὲ καθίσαι ἐκ δεξιῶν μου ἢ ἐξ εὐωνύμων οὐκ ἔστιν ἐμὸν δοῦναι
             but to sit at my right hand or my left hand is not mine to give

Matt 10:3   Ἰάκωβος **ὁ** τοῦ Ἀλφαίου
             James, **the** [son] of Alphaeus

Acts 11:2   **οἱ** ἐκ περιτομῆς
             those of the circumcision [party]

1 Cor 14:16 πῶς ἐρεῖ **τὸ** ἀμήν;
             How will he say **the** "Amen"?

D. As a Function Marker

When the article is used as a grammatical function marker, it may or may not also bear a semantic force. But even when it does bear such a force, the grammatical (structural) use is usually prominent.

12. To Denote Adjectival Positions

Especially when the article is used to denote the second attributive position would we say that it has almost no semantic meaning.

Mark 8:38 ὅταν ἔλθῃ ἐν τῇ δόξῃ τοῦ πατρὸς αὐτοῦ μετὰ **τῶν** ἀγγέλων **τῶν** ἁγίων
whenever he comes in his Father's glory with **the** holy angels

13. With Possessive Pronouns

Almost invariably the article is used when a possessive pronoun is attached to the noun.

Mark 1:41 ἐκτείνας **τὴν** χεῖρα αὐτοῦ
stretching out his hand

14. In Genitive Phrases

In genitive phrases both the head noun and the genitive noun normally have or lack the article ("Apollonius' canon").

Mark 1:15 ἤγγικεν **ἡ** βασιλεία **τοῦ** θεοῦ
The kingdom of God is near.

15. With Indeclinable Nouns

The article is used with indeclinable nouns to show the case of the noun.

Luke 1:68 εὐλογητὸς κύριος ὁ θεὸς **τοῦ** Ἰσραήλ
Blessed is the Lord God of Israel.

16. With Participles

The article before participles functions both as a substantiver and as a function marker. The presence of the article indicates a substantival (or adjectival) function for the participle. Of course, the participle can also often be substantival or adjectival without the article, though there is the greater possibility of ambiguity in such instances.

Luke 6:21 μακάριοι **οἱ** κλαίοντες νῦν
Blessed are **those** who weep now.

17. With Demonstratives

The article is used with the demonstratives in predicate position to indicate attributive function.

Matt 16:18 ἐπὶ ταύτῃ **τῇ** πέτρᾳ οἰκοδομήσω μου τὴν ἐκκλησίαν
On this rock I will build my church.

18. With Nominative Nouns

Normally a subject will have the article (unless it is a pronoun or proper name).

Luke 11:7   ἡ θύρα κέκλεισται
The door is shut.

19. To Distinguish Subject from Predicate Nominative and Object from Complement

Generally speaking, the subject will be distinguished from the predicate nominative by having the article.

Matt 12:8   κύριος ἐστιν τοῦ σαββάτου **ὁ** υἱὸς τοῦ ἀνθρώπου
The Son of Man is lord of the Sabbath.

E. Absence of the Article

It is not necessary for a noun to have the article in order for it to be definite. But conversely, a noun *cannot* be *in*definite when it has the article. Thus it *may* be definite without the article, and it *must* be definite with the article. When a substantive is anarthrous, it may have one of three forces: indefinite, qualitative, or definite. [Be sure to read Wallace on the significance of the absence of the article and study his many exegetically significant examples. The following is significantly shortened.]

20. Indefinite

An indefinite noun refers to one member of a class, without specifying which member. For example, in John 4:7 we have "**A** woman from Samaria." The anarthrous γυνή is indefinite, telling us nothing about this particular woman.

21. Qualitative

A qualitative noun places the stress on quality, nature, or essence. It does not merely indicate membership in a class of which there are other members (such as an indefinite noun), nor does it stress individual identity (such as a definite noun). It is akin to a generic noun in that it focuses on the *kind.* Further, like a generic, *it emphasizes class traits.* Yet, unlike generic nouns, a qualitative noun often has in view one individual rather than the class as a whole.

1 John 4:8   ὁ θεὸς **ἀγάπη** ἐστίν
God is **love.**

22. Definite

A definite noun lays the stress on individual identity. It has in view membership in a class, but this particular member is already marked out by the author. [Wallace lists many examples.]

Luke 5:8   **Σίμων Πέτρος** προσέπεσεν τοῖς γόνασιν Ἰησοῦ
Simon Peter fell at the feet **of Jesus.**

Voice

Voice is that property of the verb that indicates how the subject is related to the action (or state) expressed by the verb. In general, the voice of the verb may indicate that the subject is *doing* the action (active), *receiving* the action (passive), or both *doing and receiving* (at least the results of) the action (middle).

A. Active Voice

In general it can be said that in the active voice the subject *performs, produces,* or *experiences the action* or exists in the *state* expressed by the verb.

1. Simple Active

The subject *performs* or *experiences* the action. The verb may be transitive or intransitive. This is the normal or routine use, by far the most common.

Mark 4:2   **ἐδίδασκεν** αὐτοὺς ἐν παραβολαῖς πολλά
He **was teaching** them many things in parables.

2. Causative (Ergative) Active [cause]

The subject is not directly involved in the action, but may be said to be the ultimate source or cause of it. That cause may be volitional, but is not necessarily so. For the simple verb, sometimes the gloss *cause to* can be used before the verb and its object; in such cases it is sometimes best to convert the verb to a passive (e.g., *he causes him to be baptized*).

Matt 5:45   τὸν ἥλιον αὐτοῦ **ἀνατέλλει** ἐπὶ πονηροὺς καὶ ἀγαθοὺς καὶ **βρέχει** ἐπὶ δικαίους καὶ ἀδίκους
He **causes** his sun **to rise** on [both] evil and good [people], and he **causes it to rain** on [both] the righteous and unrighteous.

3. Stative Active

The subject exists in the state indicated by the verb. This kind of active includes both equative verbs (copulas) and verbs that are *translated* with an adjective in the predicate (e.g., πλουτέω–"I am rich").

Luke 16:23   **ὑπάρχων** ἐν βασάνοις
[the rich man] **existing** in a state of torment

John 1:1   Ἐν ἀρχῇ **ἦν** ὁ λόγος
In the beginning **was** the Word.

4. Reflexive Active

The subject acts upon himself or herself. In such cases naturally the *reflexive pronoun* is employed as the direct object (e.g., ἑαυτόν), while the corresponding reflexive middle omits the pronoun.

Mark 15:30   **σῶσον** σεαυτόν
Save yourself!

1 Tim 4:7   **γύμναζε** σεαυτὸν πρὸς εὐσέβειαν
Train yourself toward godliness!

B. Middle Voice

Defining the function of the middle voice is not an easy task because it encompasses a large and amorphous group of nuances. But in general, in the middle voice the subject *performs* or *experiences the action* expressed by the verb in such a way that *emphasizes the subject's participation*. It may be said that the subject acts *with a vested interest*. "The middle calls special attention to the subject ... the subject is acting in relation to himself somehow" (Robertson, 804).

The difference between the active and middle is one of emphasis. The active voice emphasizes the *action* of the verb; the middle emphasizes the *actor* [subject] of the verb. For many middle voices (especially the indirect middle), putting the subject in *italics* would communicate this emphasis.

1. Direct (Reflexive, Direct Reflexive) Middle

With the direct middle, the subject acts *on* himself or herself. The genius of the middle can most clearly be seen by this use. But because of its very subtlety, nonnative speakers tended to replace this with more familiar forms. In the NT, the direct middle is quite rare, used almost exclusively with certain verbs whose lexical nuance included a reflexive notion (such as putting on clothes), or in a set idiom that had become fixed in the language.

Matt 27:5   ἀπήγξατο
              He hanged himself.

2. Indirect (Indirect Reflexive, Benefactive, Intensive, Dynamic) Middle

The subject acts *for* (or sometimes *by*) himself or herself, or in his or her *own interest*. This is a common use of the middle in the NT; apart from the deponent middle, it is the most common. This usage is closest to the general definition of the middle suggested by many grammarians.

Acts 5:2   καὶ **ἐνοσφίσατο** ἀπὸ τῆς τιμῆς
              And he **kept back** [some] of the price [**for himself**].

Matt 27:24   ὁ Πιλᾶτος ... **ἀπενίψατο** τὰς χεῖρας ... λέγων· ἀθῷός εἰμι ἀπὸ τοῦ αἵματος τούτου
              Pilate **washed** his **hands** saying, "I am innocent of this man's blood."

3. Causative Middle

The subject *has* something done *for* or *to* himself or herself. As well, the subject may be the *source* behind an action done in his/her behalf. This usage, though rare, involves some exegetically important texts.

Luke 11:38   ὁ Φαρισαῖος ἰδὼν ἐθαύμασεν ὅτι οὐ πρῶτον **ἐβαπτίσατο**[1] πρὸ τοῦ ἀρίστου
              When the Pharisee saw this, he was amazed because [Jesus] did not first **have himself washed** before the meal.

4. Permissive Middle

The subject *allows* something to be done *for* or *to* himself or herself. This usage, though rare, involves some exegetically important texts.

Luke 2:4-5   Ἀνέβη Ἰωσὴφ ἀπὸ τῆς Γαλιλαίας ... (5) **ἀπογράψασθαι** σὺν Μαριάμ
              Joseph went up from Galilee ... (5) **to be enrolled** with Mary.

---

[1] The UBS text reads ἐβαπτίσθη.

Acts 22:16   ἀναστὰς **βάπτισαι** καὶ **ἀπόλουσαι** τὰς ἁμαρτίας σου
Rise, **have yourself baptized** and **allow** your sins **to be washed away**.

5. Deponent Middle

A deponent middle verb is one that has no active form for a particular principal part in Hellenistic Greek, and one whose force in that principal part is evidently active. See Wallace for his list of true deponents.

C. Passive Voice

In general it can be said that in the passive voice the subject *is acted upon* or *receives the action* expressed by the verb. No volition—nor even necessarily awareness of the action—is implied on the part of the subject. That is, the subject may or may not be aware, its volition may or may not be involved. But these things are not stressed when the passive is used.

[Wallace breaks his discussion of the passive voice into "Passive constructions" (with and without expressed agency, and the passive with an accusative object) and three "Passive uses," two of which are listed below.]

1. Simple Passive

The most common use of the passive voice is to indicate that the subject receives the action. No implication is made about cognition, volition, or cause on the part of the subject. This usage occurs both with and without an expressed agent.

Mark 4:6   ὅτε ἀνέτειλεν ὁ ἥλιος **ἐκαυματίσθη**
When the sun rose, **it was scorched**.

Acts 1:5   ὑμεῖς ἐν πνεύματι **βαπτισθήσεσθε** ἁγίῳ
You **will be baptized** with the Holy Spirit.

2. Deponent Passive

A verb that has no active *form* may be active in meaning though passive in form. Two of the most common deponent passives are ἐγενήθην and ἀπεκρίθην.

Mood

In general, *mood* is the feature of the verb that presents the verbal action or state with reference to its *actuality* or *potentiality*. *Voice* indicates *how* the subject *relates* to the *action* or state of the verb; *tense* is used primarily to portray the *kind* of action. There are four moods in Greek: indicative, subjunctive, optative, and imperative. See further qualifications in Wallace.

A. The Indicative Mood

The indicative mood is, in general, the mood of assertion, or *presentation of certainty*. It is not correct to say that it is the mood of certainty or reality. This belongs to the *presentation* (i.e., the indicative may *present* something as being certain or real, though the speaker might not believe it).

1. Declarative Indicative

The indicative is routinely used to present an assertion as a non-contingent (or unqualified) statement. This is by far its most common use.

Mark 4:3   ἐξῆλθεν ὁ σπείρων σπεῖραι
              The sower **went out** to sow.

John 1:1   Ἐν ἀρχῇ ἦν ὁ λόγος
              In the beginning **was** the Word.

2. Interrogative Indicative

The indicative can be used in a question. The question *expects an assertion* to be made; it expects a declarative indicative in the answer. (This contrasts with the subjunctive, which asks a question of moral "oughtness" or obligation, or asks whether something is possible.)

Matt 27:11   σὺ εἶ ὁ βασιλεὺς τῶν Ἰουδαίων;
              Are you the king of the Jews?

John 1:38   λέγει αὐτοῖς, Τί ζητεῖτε; οἱ δὲ εἶπαν αὐτῷ, Ῥαββί, ... ποῦ μένεις;
              He said to them, "What **do you seek**?" And they said to him, "Rabbi, ... where **are you staying**?"

3. Conditional Indicative

This is the use of the indicative in the protasis of conditional sentences. The conditional element is made explicit with the particle εἰ. The first class condition indicates *the assumption of truth for the sake of argument*, while the second class condition indicates *the assumption of an untruth for the sake of argument*.

Matt 12:27   εἰ ἐγὼ ἐν Βεελζεβοὺλ ἐκβάλλω τὰ δαιμόνια, οἱ υἱοὶ ὑμῶν ἐν τίνι ἐκβάλλουσιν;
              If I **cast out** demons by Beelzebul, by whom do your sons cast them out?

John 5:46   εἰ ἐπιστεύετε Μωϋσεῖ, ἐπιστεύετε ἂν ἐμοί
              If **you believed** Moses, you would believe me.

4. Potential Indicative

The indicative is used with verbs of obligation, wish, or desire, followed by an infinitive. The nature of the verb root, rather than the indicative, is what makes it look like a potential mood in its semantic force.

Luke 11:42   ταῦτα ἔδει ποιῆσαι
              It was necessary [for you] to have done these things.

1 Cor 11:7   ἀνὴρ οὐκ ὀφείλει κατακαλύπτεσθαι τὴν κεφαλήν
              A man **should** not cover his head.

5. Cohortative (Command, Volitive) Indicative

The *future* indicative is sometimes used for a command, almost always in OT quotations (because of a literal translation of the Hebrew). However, it was used even in classical Greek, though infrequently.

Matt 19:18   οὐ φονεύσεις, οὐ μοιχεύσεις, οὐ κλέψεις, οὐ ψευδομαρτυρήσεις
              You shall not **murder, you shall** not **commit adultery, you shall** not **steal, you shall** not **bear false witness**.

B. The Subjunctive Mood

The subjunctive is the most common of the oblique moods in the NT. In general, the subjunctive can be said to *represent the verbal action (or state) as uncertain but probable*. It is not correct to call this the mood of uncertainty because the optative also presents the verb as uncertain. Rather, it is better to call it the mood of *probability* so as to distinguish it from the optative. Still, this is an overly simplistic definition in light of its usage in the NT.

[Wallace breaks the discussion down into the use of the subjunctive in independent (categories 1-4) and dependent (categories 5-10) clauses.]

1. *Hortatory (Volitive) Subjunctive [let us]*

The subjunctive is commonly used to exhort or command oneself and one's associates. This use of the subjunctive is used "to urge some one to unite with the speaker in a course of action upon which he has already decided" (Chamberlain, 83). Since there is no first person imperative, the hortatory subjunctive is used to do roughly the same task. Thus this use of the subjunctive is an exhortation in the *first person plural*. The typical translation, rather than *we should ...*, is *let us ....*

Mark 4:35   καὶ λέγει αὐτοῖς, ... **Διέλθωμεν** εἰς τὸ πέραν

              And he said to them, ... "**Let us go** to the other side."

2. *Deliberative (Dubitative) Subjunctive*

The deliberative subjunctive asks either a *real* or *rhetorical* question. The semantics of the two are often quite different. Both imply some *doubt* about the response, but the *real* question is usually in the *cognitive* area (such as "How can we ... ?" in which the inquiry is about the means), while the *rhetorical* question is *volitive* (e.g., "Should we ... ?" in which the question has to do with moral obligation). Both are fairly common with first person verbs, though second and third person verbs can be found. The future indicative is also used in deliberative questions, though the subjunctive is more common.

Matt 6:31   μὴ μεριμνήσητε λέγοντες· τί **φάγωμεν**; ἤ· τί **πίωμεν**; ἤ· τί **περιβαλώμεθα**;

              Do not be anxious, saying, "What **should we eat**?" or "What **should we drink**?" or "What **should we wear**?"

Mark 8:37   τί **δοῖ** ἄνθρωπος ἀντάλλαγμα τῆς ψυχῆς αὐτοῦ;

              What **can** a person **give** in exchange for his life?

3. *Emphatic Negation Subjunctive*

Emphatic negation is indicated by οὐ μή plus the aorist subjunctive or, less frequently, οὐ μή plus the future indicative. This is the strongest way to negate something in Greek. One might think that the negative with the subjunctive could not be as strong as the negative with the indicative. However, while οὐ + the indicative denies a *certainty*, οὐ μή + the subjunctive denies a *potentiality*. οὐ μή rules out even the idea as being a possibility.

Matt 24:35   οἱ λόγοι μου *οὐ μὴ* **παρέλθωσιν**

              My words **will** *not at all* **pass away**.

John 10:28   δίδωμι αὐτοῖς ζωὴν αἰώνιον καὶ *οὐ μὴ* **ἀπόλωνται** εἰς τὸν αἰῶνα

              I give them eternal life, and **they will** *not at all* **perish**.

4. *Prohibitive Subjunctive*

This is the use of the subjunctive in a prohibition—that is, a negative command. It is used to forbid the occurrence of an action. The structure is usually μή + aorist subjunctive, typically in the second person. Its force is equivalent to an imperative after μή; hence, it should be translated *Do not* rather than *You should not*.

Matt 1:20   μὴ **φοβηθῇς** παραλαβεῖν Μαρίαν τὴν γυναῖκά σου
             Do *not* **be afraid** to take Mary as your wife.

5. *Subjunctive in Conditional Sentences*

This is the use of the subjunctive in the protasis of conditional sentences. The conditional element is made explicit by the particle ἐάν. Both the particle and the subjunctive give the condition a sense of contingency.

Matt 4:9   ταῦτά σοι πάντα δώσω, *ἐὰν* πεσὼν **προσκυνήσῃς** μοι
             I will give you all these things, *if* **you will** fall down and **worship** me

Mark 5:28   ἔλεγεν ὅτι *ἐὰν* **ἅψωμαι** κἂν τῶν ἱματίων αὐτοῦ σωθήσομαι
             She was saying [to herself], "*If* only **I touch** his garments, I will be healed."

6. *Ἵνα + the Subjunctive*

The single most common category of the subjunctive in the NT is after ἵνα, comprising about one third of all subjunctive instances. There are seven basic uses included in this construction: purpose, result, purpose-result, substantival, epexegetical, complementary, and command.

a. *Purpose*

Matt 12:10   ἐπηρώτησαν αὐτὸν λέγοντες· εἰ ἔξεστιν τοῖς σάββασιν θεραπεῦσαι; *ἵνα* **κατηγορήσωσιν** αὐτοῦ
             They questioned him, saying, "Is it lawful to heal on the Sabbath?" *in order that* **they might accuse** him.

b. *Result*

John 9:2   ῥαββί, τίς ἥμαρτεν, οὗτος ἢ οἱ γονεῖς αὐτοῦ, *ἵνα* τυφλὸς **γεννηθῇ**;
             Rabbi, who sinned, this man or his parents, *with the result that* **he should be born** blind?

c. *Substantival*

Matt 18:6   συμφέρει αὐτῷ *ἵνα* **κρεμασθῇ** μύλος ὀνικὸς περὶ τὸν τράχηλον αὐτοῦ ...
             [*that* a millstone **should be tied** around his neck] is better for him ...

d. *Epexegetical*

Luke 7:6   οὐ ἱκανός εἰμι *ἵνα* ὑπὸ τὴν στέγην μου **εἰσέλθῃς**
             I am not worthy [*that* **you should enter** under my roof].

e. *Complementary*

Matt 26:4   συνεβουλεύσαντο *ἵνα* τὸν Ἰησοῦν δόλῳ **κρατήσωσιν** καὶ **ἀποκτείνωσιν**
             They counseled together [**to arrest** Jesus in a sly way and **to kill** (him)].

7. Subjunctive with Verbs of Fearing, Etc.

Μή plus the subjunctive can be used after verbs of *fearing, warning, watching out for*, etc. Not unusual in the better writers (Paul, Luke, Hebrews), this construction serves as a warning or suggests caution or anxiety.

Luke 21:8   βλέπετε *μὴ* **πλανηθῆτε**
                Watch out *that* **you are** *not* **deceived**.

1 Cor 8:9   βλέπετε *μή πως* ἡ ἐξουσία ὑμῶν αὕτη πρόσκομμα **γένηται** τοῖς ἀσθενέσιν
                Take care *lest* somehow this liberty of yours **should become** a stumbling block to the weak.

8. Subjunctive in Indirect Questions

The subjunctive is sometimes used in indirect questions. In such a usage, it follows the main verb, but appears awkward, even unconnected, in the sentence structure. Because of this, the subjunctive (and its accompanying interrogative particle) needs to be smoothed out in translation.

Matt 15:32   ἤδη ἡμέραι τρεῖς προσμένουσίν μοι καὶ οὐκ ἔχουσιν τί **φάγωσιν**
                They have already been with me for three days and they do not have anything **to eat**.

Luke 9:58   ὁ υἱὸς τοῦ ἀνθρώπου οὐκ ἔχει ποῦ τὴν κεφαλὴν **κλίνῃ**
                The Son of Man has no place where **he could lay** his head.

9. Subjunctive in Indefinite Relative Clause

The subjunctive is frequently used after ὅστις (ἄν/ἐάν) or ὅς (δ᾽) ἄν. The construction normally indicates a generic (or sometimes an uncertain) subject; hence, the particle of contingency and the need for a subjunctive. The construction is roughly the *equivalent of a third class or fifth class condition*. The difference is that in indefinite relative clauses the element of contingency is not that of time but of person. Hence, the subjunctive is often translated like an indicative, since the potential element belongs to the subject rather than the verb.

Mark 3:29   ὃς δ᾽ ἂν **βλασφημήσῃ** εἰς τὸ πνεῦμα τὸ ἅγιον, οὐκ ἔχει ἄφεσιν εἰς τὸν αἰῶνα
                Whoever **blasphemes** against the Holy Spirit never has forgiveness.

John 4:14   ὃς δ᾽ ἂν **πίῃ** ἐκ τοῦ ὕδατος οὗ ἐγὼ δώσω αὐτῷ, οὐ μὴ διψήσει εἰς τὸν αἰῶνα
                Whoever **drinks** of the water that I will give him will never thirst again.

10. Subjunctive in Indefinite Temporal Clause

The subjunctive is frequently used after a temporal adverb (or improper preposition) meaning *until* (e.g., ἕως, ἄχρι, μέχρι). It indicates a future contingency from the perspective of the time of the main verb.

Matt 5:26   οὐ μὴ ἐξέλθῃς ἐκεῖθεν, ἕως ἂν **ἀποδῷς** τὸν ἔσχατον κοδράντην
                You will not at all leave from there *until* **you have paid back** the last cent.

John 13:38   οὐ μὴ ἀλέκτωρ φωνήσῃ ἕως οὗ **ἀρνήσῃ** με τρίς
                The cock will not at all crow *until* **you have denied** me three times.

C. The Optative Mood

There are less than 70 optatives in the entire NT. In general, it can be said that the optative is the mood used when a speaker wishes to portray an action as *possible*. It usually addresses cognition, but may be used to appeal to the volition. Along with the subjunctive and imperative, the optative is one of the potential or oblique moods.

1. Voluntative Optative (Optative of Obtainable Wish, Volitive Optative)

This is the use of the optative in an independent clause to express an *obtainable wish* or a *prayer*. It is frequently an appeal to the *will*, in particular when used in prayers.

Rom 3:3-4   εἰ ἠπίστησάν τινες, μὴ ἡ ἀπιστία αὐτῶν τὴν πίστιν τοῦ θεοῦ καταργήσει; (4) μὴ **γένοιτο**· γινέσθω δὲ ὁ θεὸς ἀληθής, πᾶς δὲ ἄνθρωπος ψεύστης

If some did not believe, their unbelief will not nullify the faithfulness of God, will it? (4) **May it** never **be**! But let God be [found] true, and every man [be found] a liar!

2. Potential Optative

This use of the optative occurs with the particle ἄν in the apodosis of an incomplete fourth class condition. It is used to indicate a consequence in the future of an unlikely condition. There are no complete fourth class conditions in the NT. The protasis (which also uses the optative) needs to be supplied. The idea is *If he **could do** something, he **would** do this*. Only a handful of examples occur in the NT, all in Luke's writings.

Luke 1:62   ἐνένευον τῷ πατρὶ αὐτοῦ τὸ τί ἄν **θέλοι** καλεῖσθαι αὐτό

They were making signs to his father as to what **he would want** to call him.

Acts 17:18   τινες ἔλεγον· τί ἄν **θέλοι** ὁ σπερμολόγος οὗτος λέγειν;

Some [of the philosophers] were saying, "What **would** this babbler **say**?"

D. The Imperative Mood

The imperative mood is the mood of *intention*. It is the mood furthest removed from certainty. Ontologically, as one of the potential or oblique moods, the imperative moves in the realm of *volition* (involving the imposition of one's will upon another) and *possibility*.

1. Command

The imperative is most commonly used for commands, outnumbering prohibitive imperatives about five to one. The basic force of the imperative of command involves somewhat different nuances with each tense. With the *aorist*, the force generally is to *command the action as a whole*, without focusing on duration, repetition, etc. In keeping with its aspectual force, the aorist puts forth a *summary command*. With the *present*, the force generally is to *command the action as an ongoing process*. This is in keeping with the present's aspect, which portrays an *internal* perspective.

Mark 2:14   **ἀκολούθει** μοι
Follow me!

Mark 6:37   **δότε** αὐτοῖς ὑμεῖς φαγεῖν
Give them [something] to eat

2. *Prohibition*

The imperative is commonly used to forbid an action. It is simply a negative command. μή (or a cognate) is used before the imperative to turn the command into a prohibition.

Matt 6:3   *μὴ* **γνώτω** ἡ ἀριστερά σου τί ποιεῖ ἡ δεξιά σου
               Do *not* **let** your left hand **know** what your right hand is doing.

3. *Request (Entreaty, Polite Command)*

The imperative is often used to express a request. This is normally seen when the speaker is addressing a superior. Imperatives (almost always in the aorist tense) directed toward God in prayers fit this category. The request can be a positive one or a negative one (*please, do not ...*); in such cases the particle μή precedes the verb.

Matt 6:10-11   **ἐλθέτω** ἡ βασιλεία σου· **γενηθήτω** τὸ θέλημά σου ... τὸν ἄρτον ἡμῶν τὸν ἐπιούσιον **δὸς** ἡμῖν σήμερον
                  Let your kingdom **come**, **let** your will **be done** ... **give** us today our daily bread.

Luke 11:1   κύριε, **δίδαξον** ἡμᾶς προσεύχεσθαι
               Lord, **teach** us [how] to pray.

4. *Permissive Imperative (Imperative of Toleration)*

The imperative is rarely used to connote permission or, better, *toleration*. This usage does not normally imply that some deed is optional or approved. It often views the act as a *fait accompli*. In such instances, the mood could almost be called "an imperative of resignation."

Matt 8:31-32   εἰ ἐκβάλλεις ἡμᾶς, ἀπόστειλον ἡμᾶς εἰς τὴν ἀγέλην τῶν χοίρων. (32) καὶ εἶπεν αὐτοῖς· **ὑπάγετε**.
                  "If you cast us out, send us into the herd of swine." (32) And he said to them, "**Go!**"

1 Cor 7:15   εἰ ὁ ἄπιστος χωρίζεται, **χωριζέσθω**
               If the unbeliever departs, **let him depart**.

5. *As a Stereotyped Greeting*

Sometimes the imperative is used in a stereotyped manner in which it has suppressed its original injunctive force. The imperative is reduced to an exclamation. This occurs especially in greetings.

Luke 1:28   **χαῖρε**, κεχαριτωμένη, ὁ κύριος μετὰ σοῦ
               Greetings, favored [lady]! The Lord is with you.

John 19:3   **χαῖρε** ὁ βασιλεὺς τῶν Ἰουδαίων
               Hail, king of the Jews!

The Tenses

In general, *tense* in Greek involves two elements: *aspect* (kind of action, [sometimes called *Aktionsart*, though a difference does need to be made between the two]) and *time*. Aspect is the primary value of tense in Greek and time is secondary, if involved at all. In other words, *tense is that feature of the verb that indicates the speaker's presentation of the verbal action (or state) with reference to its aspect and, under certain conditions, its time.* [See Wallace's discussion of the significance of tense, aspect, and time, and also his discussion of the difference between portrayal and reality.]

The Present Tense

With reference to *aspect,* the present tense is internal (that is, it portrays the action from the inside of the event, without special regard for beginning or end), but it makes no comment as to fulfillment (or completion). The present tense's portrayal of an event "focuses on its development or progress and sees the occurrence in regard to its internal make-up, without beginning or end in view" (Fanning, 102). It is sometimes called progressive: It "basically represents an activity as in process (or in progress)" (McKay, 225).

With reference to *time,* the present indicative is usually present time, but it may be other than or broader than the present time (e.g., historical present, gnomic present).

The specific uses of the present tense can be categorized into three large groups: narrow-band presents, broad-band presents, and special uses. "Narrow band" means that the action is portrayed as occurring over a relatively short interval; "broad band" means that the action is portrayed as occurring over a longer interval; "special uses" include instances that do not fit into the other two categories, especially those involving a time frame that is other than the present.

A. Narrow-Band Presents

The action is portrayed as being in progress, or as occurring. In the indicative mood, it is portrayed as occurring in the present time ("right now"), that is, at the time of speaking.

1. Instantaneous (Aoristic, Punctiliar) Present

The present tense may be used to indicate that an action is completed at the moment of speaking. This occurs only in the indicative.

Mark 2:5   ὁ Ἰησοῦς ... λέγει τῷ παραλυτικῷ· τέκνον, **ἀφίενταί** σου αἱ ἁμαρτίαι.
             Jesus ... said to the paralytic, "Child, your sins **are forgiven.**"

2. Progressive (Descriptive) Present

The present tense may be used to describe a scene in progress, especially in narrative literature.

Matt 25:8   αἱ λαμπάδες ἡμῶν **σβέννυνται**
             Our lamps **are** [right now] **going out.**

B. Broad-Band Presents

The following four categories of the present tense include those that are used to indicate an event or occurrence taking place over a long interval, or an extended sequence of events.

3. Extending-from-Past Present (Present of Past Action Still in Progress)

The present tense may be used to describe an action that, begun in the past, continues in the present. The emphasis is on the present time.

Luke 15:29   τοσαῦτα ἔτη **δουλεύω** σοι
             I have served you for these many years.

4. Iterative Present

The present tense may be used to describe an event that *repeatedly* happens.

Matt 7:7   Αἰτεῖτε ... ζητεῖτε ... κρούετε
                 Ask ... **seek** ... **knock.**

5. Customary (Habitual, General) Present

The customary present is used to signal either (1) an action that *regularly occurs* or (2) an *ongoing state*. The action is usually *iterative*, or repeated, but not without interruption.

Luke 18:12   **νηστεύω** δὶς τοῦ σαββάτου
                 I [customarily] **fast** twice a week.

6. Gnomic Present

The present tense may be used to make a statement of a general, timeless fact. "It does not say that something *is* happening, but that something *does* happen" (Williams, 27). The action or state continues without time limits.

2 Cor 9:7   ἱλαρὸν γὰρ δότην **ἀγαπᾷ** ὁ θεός
                 God **loves** [as a general, timeless fact] a cheerful giver.

C. Special Uses of the Present Tense

7. Historical (Dramatic) Present

The historical present is used fairly frequently in narrative literature to portray a past event *vividly*, as though the reader were in the midst of the scene as it unfolds. [This category is frequently misunderstood; see Wallace for his discussions of exegetically significant examples.]

Matt 26:40   **ἔρχεται** πρὸς τοὺς μαθητὰς καὶ **εὑρίσκει** αὐτοὺς καθεύδοντας, καὶ **λέγει** ...
                 He came to his disciples and **found** them sleeping, and **he said** ...

8. Futuristic Present

The present tense may be used to describe a future event, though it typically adds the connotations of immediacy and certainty. Most instances involve verbs whose *lexical* meaning involves anticipation (such as ἔρχομαι, -βαίνω, πορεύομαι, etc.).

a. Completely Futuristic

The present tense may describe an event that is *wholly* subsequent to the time of speaking, as if it were present.

John 4:25   Μεσσίας **ἔρχεται**
                 Messiah **is coming.**

b. Mostly Futuristic (Ingressive-Futuristic)

The present tense may describe an event *begun* in the present time but completed in the future.

Mark 10:33   **ἀναβαίνομεν** εἰς Ἱεροσόλυμα
                 I am going up to Jerusalem.

9. Present Retained in Indirect Discourse

Generally speaking, the *tense* of the Greek verb in indirect discourse is *retained* from the direct discourse. This category is frequently confused with the historical present with dire exegetical consequences; see Wallace.

John 5:13   ὁ δὲ ἰαθεὶς οὐκ ᾔδει τίς **ἐστιν**
             Now the man who had been healed did not know who he **was**.

The Imperfect Tense

Like the present tense, the imperfect displays an internal aspect. That is, it portrays the action from within the event, without regard for beginning or end. This contrasts with the aorist, which portrays the action in summary fashion. For the most part, the aorist takes a snapshot of the action while the imperfect (like the present) takes a motion picture, portraying the action as it unfolds. As such, the imperfect is often incomplete and focuses on the process of the action.

A. Narrow-Band Imperfects

The action is portrayed as being in progress, or as occurring in the past time (since all imperfects are in the indicative).

1. Progressive (Descriptive) Imperfect [continually]

The imperfect is often used to describe an action or state that is in progress in past time from the viewpoint of the speaker.

Mark 9:31   **ἐδίδασκεν** τοὺς μαθητὰς αὐτοῦ καὶ **ἔλεγεν** αὐτοῖς
             He was teaching his disciples and **was saying** to them

2. Ingressive (Inchoative, Inceptive) Imperfect [began doing]

The imperfect may be used to stress the beginning of an action.

Matt 5:2   καὶ ἀνοίξας τὸ στόμα αὐτοῦ **ἐδίδασκεν** αὐτούς
             And when he opened his mouth, **he began teaching** them.

B. Broad-Band Imperfects

Like the present tense, several imperfects involve a time-frame that is fairly broadly conceived.

3. Iterative Imperfect [kept on]

The imperfect is sometimes used for repeated action in past time. It is similar to the customary imperfect, but it is not something that regularly recurs.

John 19:3   **ἔλεγον**, Χαῖρε
             They kept on saying, "Hail!"

4. Customary (Habitual, General) Imperfect [used to]

The imperfect is used to indicate a *regularly* recurring activity in past time (habitual), or a *state* that continues for some time (general).

Luke 2:41   Καὶ **ἐπορεύοντο** οἱ γονεῖς αὐτοῦ κατ᾽ ἔτος εἰς Ἱερουσαλήμ
                 And his parents **used to go** [or **customarily went**] into Jerusalem each year.

C. Special Uses of the Imperfect

5. Conative (Voluntative, Tendential) Imperfect [wanted to, could almost]

This use of the imperfect tense occasionally portrays the action as something that was *desired (voluntative), attempted (conative)*, or at the point of *almost doing* something (*tendential*).

Matt 3:14   ὁ δὲ Ἰωάννης **διεκώλυεν** αὐτόν
                 but John **was trying to prevent** him

6. Imperfect Retained in Indirect Discourse

Like the present, the imperfect can be retained from the direct discourse in the indirect.

John 2:22   ἐμνήσθησαν οἱ μαθηταὶ αὐτοῦ ὅτι τοῦτο **ἔλεγεν**
                 His disciples remembered that **he had said** this.

The Future Tense

With reference to aspect, the future seems to offer an external portrayal, something of a temporal counterpart to the aorist indicative. The external portrayal "presents an occurrence in summary, viewed as a whole from the outside, without regard for the internal make-up of the occurrence" (Fanning, 97). With reference to time, the future tense is always future from the speaker's presentation (or, when in a participial form, in relation to the time of the main verb).

1. Predictive Future

The future tense will often indicate that something will take place or come to pass.

Acts 1:11   οὗτος ὁ Ἰησοῦς ... **ἐλεύσεται**
                 This Jesus ... **will come**.

2. Imperatival Future

The future indicative is sometimes used for a command, almost always in OT quotations (because of a literal translation of the Hebrew). However, it was used, even in classical Greek, though sparingly.

Matt 22:37   **ἀγαπήσεις** κύριον τὸν θεόν σου
                  You shall love the Lord your God.

3. Deliberative Future

The deliberative future asks a question that implies some doubt about the response. The question, asked in the first person singular or plural, is generally either cognitive or volitional. Cognitive questions ask, "How will we?" while volitional questions ask, "Should we?" Thus, the force of such questions is one of "oughtness"–that is, possibility, desirability, or necessity.

Rom 6:2   πῶς ἔτι **ζήσομεν** ἐν αὐτῇ;
           How then **shall we** still **live** in it?

4. Gnomic Future

The future is very rarely used to indicate the likelihood that a *generic* event will take place. The idea is not that a particular event is in view, but that such events are true to life.

Rom 5:7   μόλις γὰρ ὑπὲρ δικαίου τις **ἀποθανεῖται**·
           Scarcely for a righteous man **will** one **die**.

The Aorist Tense

The aorist tense "presents an occurrence in summary, viewed as a whole from the outside, without regard for the internal make-up of the occurrence" (Fanning, 97). It may be helpful to think of the aorist as taking a snapshot of the action while the imperfect (like the present) takes a motion picture, portraying the action as it unfolds. In the indicative, the aorist usually indicates past time with reference to the time of speaking (thus, "absolute time"). Aorist participles usually suggest antecedent time to that of the main verb (i.e., past time in a relative sense).

1. Constative (Complexive, Punctiliar, Comprehensive, Global) Aorist

The aorist normally views the action *as a whole,* taking no interest in the internal workings of the action. It describes the action as bare fact.

Rev 20:4   **ἐβασίλευσαν** μετὰ τοῦ Χριστοῦ χίλια ἔτη.
            They **reigned** with Christ for a thousand years.

2. Ingressive (Inceptive, Inchoative) Aorist [began to]

The aorist tense is often used to stress the beginning of an action or the entrance into a state. Unlike the ingressive imperfect, there is no implication that the action continues. This is simply left unstated.

Matt 22:7   ὁ δὲ βασιλεὺς **ὠργίσθη**
             Now the king **became angry**.

3. Consummative (Culminative, Ecbatic, Effective) Aorist

The aorist is often used to stress the cessation of an act or state. Certain verbs, by their very *lexical* nature, almost require this usage. For example, "he died" is hardly going to be an ingressive idea. The context also assists in this usage at times: It implies that an act was already in progress and the aorist then brings the action to a conclusion.

John 1:42   **ἤγαγεν** αὐτὸν πρὸς τὸν Ἰησοῦν.
             He **brought** him to Jesus.

4. *Gnomic Aorist*

The aorist indicative is occasionally used to present a timeless, general fact. When it does so, it does not refer to a particular event that *did* happen, but to a generic event that *does* happen. Normally, it is translated like a simple present tense.

1 Pet 1:24   ἐξηράνθη ὁ χόρτος, καὶ τὸ ἄνθος ἐξέπεσεν
The grass **withers** and the flower **falls off**.

5. *Epistolary Aorist*

This is the use of the aorist in the epistles in which the author self-consciously describes his letter from the time frame of the audience.

Phil 2:28   ἔπεμψα αὐτόν
I have sent him.

6. *Proleptic (Futuristic) Aorist*

The aorist *indicative* can be used to describe an event that is not yet past as though it were already completed in order to stress the certainty of the event.

Rom 8:30   οὓς δὲ ἐδικαίωσεν, τούτους καὶ ἐδόξασεν.
whom he justified, these **he** also **glorified**.

7. *Immediate Past (Dramatic) Aorist [just now]*

The aorist tense can be used of an event that happened rather recently. Its force can usually be brought out with something like "just now," as in "just now I told you."

Matt 26:65   ἴδε νῦν ἠκούσατε τὴν βλασφημίαν
Behold, **just** now **you heard** his blasphemy.

The Perfect and Pluperfect Tenses

The perfect and pluperfect tenses are identical in aspect though different in time. Thus both speak of an event accomplished in the past (in the indicative mood) with results existing afterwards–the perfect speaking of existing results in the present, the pluperfect speaking of existing results in the past.

A. The Perfect Tense

The force of the perfect indicative is simply that it describes an event that, completed in the past, has results existing in the present time (i.e., in relation to the time of the speaker).

1. *Intensive (Resultative) Perfect*

The perfect may be used to emphasize the *results* or *present state* produced by a past action. The English present often is the best translation for such a perfect.

Mark 6:14   Ἰωάννης ὁ βαπτίζων ἐγήγερται ἐκ νεκρῶν
John the baptizer **is risen** from the dead.

2. *Extensive (Consummative) Perfect*

The perfect may be used to emphasize the *completed action* of a past action or process from which a present state emerges. It should normally be translated in English as a present perfect.

John 1:34   **ἑώρακα** καὶ **μεμαρτύρηκα** ὅτι οὗτός ἐστιν ὁ υἱὸς τοῦ θεοῦ.
I have seen and **I have testified** that this is the Son of God.

3. *Perfect with a Present Force*

Certain verbs occur frequently (or exclusively) in the perfect tense without the usual aspectual significance, especially with stative perfect verbs. They have come to be used just like present tense verbs. Οἶδα is the most commonly used verb in this category, but other verbs also are used this way: ἕστηκα, πέποιθα, μέμνημαι, κέκραγα.

John 1:26   μέσος ὑμῶν **ἕστηκεν** ὃν ὑμεῖς οὐκ **οἴδατε**
In your midst **stands** one whom **you do** not **know**.

B. The Pluperfect Tense

As was stated above, for the most part, the perfect and pluperfect are identical in aspect though different in time. The force of the pluperfect tense is that it describes an event that, completed in the past, has results that exist in the past as well (in relation to the time of speaking). *The pluperfect makes no comment about the results existing up to the time of speaking.* Such results may exist at the time of speaking, or they may not; the pluperfect contributes nothing either way.

1. *Intensive (Resultative) Pluperfect*

This use of the pluperfect places the emphasis on the existing results. Its force can be brought out by translating it as a simple past tense.

Luke 4:29   ἤγαγον αὐτὸν ἕως ὀφρύος τοῦ ὄρους ἐφ᾽ οὗ ἡ πόλις **ᾠκοδόμητο** αὐτῶν
They led him to the brow of the hill on which their city **was built**.

2. *Extensive (Consummative) Pluperfect*

The pluperfect may be used to emphasize the completion of an action in past time, without focusing on the existing results. It is usually best translated as a past perfect ("had" + perfect passive participle).

John 4:8   οἱ γὰρ μαθηταὶ αὐτοῦ **ἀπεληλύθεισαν** εἰς τὴν πόλιν
For his disciples **had gone** into the city.

The Infinitive

The infinitive is an indeclinable verbal noun. As such it participates in some of the features of the verb and some of the noun. Like a *verb*, the infinitive has tense and voice, but not person or mood. Its number is always singular. Like the oblique moods (i.e., nonindicative moods), the infinitive is normally negatived by μή rather than οὐ. Like a *noun*, the infinitive can have many of the case functions that an ordinary noun can have. Although technically infinitives do not have gender, frequently the neuter singular article is attached to them. [See Wallace for a discussion of the various structures used with the different semantic categories of the infinitive.]

A. Adverbial Uses

1. Purpose [to, in order to, for the purpose of]

The infinitive is used to indicate the purpose or goal of the action or state of its controlling verb. It answers the question "Why?" in that it looks ahead to the anticipated and intended result.

Matt 5:17   μὴ νομίσητε ὅτι ἦλθον **καταλῦσαι** τὸν νόμον

Do not think that I came **to destroy** the law.

2. Result [so that, so as to, with the result that]

The infinitive of result indicates the outcome produced by the controlling verb. In this respect it is similar to the infinitive of purpose, but the former puts an emphasis on intention while the latter places the emphasis on effect. A number of instances are difficult to distinguish, leaving room for exegetical discussion. As a general guideline, however, if in doubt, label a given infinitive as purpose (it occurs almost four times as often as result).

Luke 5:7   ἔπλησαν ἀμφότερα τὰ πλοῖα **ὥστε βυθίζεσθαι** αὐτά

They filled both the boats **so that they began to sink**.

3. Time

This use of the infinitive indicates a temporal relationship between its action and the action of the controlling verb. It answers the question "When?" Many grammars confuse the categories "Antecedent time" and "Subsequent time"; see Wallace for a discussion.

a. Antecedent time [after]

The action of the infinitive of antecedent time occurs *before* the action of the controlling verb. Its structure is μετὰ τό + the infinitive and should be translated *after* plus an appropriate *finite* verb.

Matt 26:32   **μετὰ** δὲ **τὸ ἐγερθῆναί** με προάξω ὑμᾶς εἰς τὴν Γαλιλαίαν.

And **after** I **have been raised**, I will go before you into Galilee.

b. Contemporaneous time [while, as, when]

The action of the infinitive of contemporaneous time occurs *simultaneously* with the action of the controlling verb. Its structure is ἐν τῷ + the infinitive. It should be translated *while* (for present infinitives) or *as, when* (for aorist infinitives) plus an appropriate *finite* verb.

Matt 13:4   **ἐν τῷ σπείρειν** αὐτὸν ἃ μὲν ἔπεσεν παρὰ τὴν ὁδόν

While he **was sowing**, some fell on the road.

c. Subsequent time [before]

The action of the infinitive of subsequent time occurs *after* the action of the controlling verb. Its structure is πρὸ τοῦ, πρίν, or πρὶν ἤ + the infinitive. It should be translated *before* plus an appropriate *finite* verb.

John 1:48   **πρὸ τοῦ** σε Φίλιππον **φωνῆσαι** ὄντα ὑπὸ τὴν συκῆν εἶδόν σε.

Before Philip **called** you, while you were under the fig tree, I saw you.

4. Cause

The causal infinitive indicates the reason for the action of the controlling verb. In this respect, it answers the question "Why?" Unlike the infinitive of purpose, however, the causal infinitive gives a *retrospective* answer (i.e., it looks back to the ground or reason), while the purpose infinitive gives *prospective* answer (looking forward to the intended result).

John 2:24   Ἰησοῦς οὐκ ἐπίστευεν αὐτὸν αὐτοῖς **διὰ τὸ** αὐτὸν **γινώσκειν** πάντας

Jesus was not entrusting himself to them **because** he **knew** all men.

5. Means [by ... doing]

The infinitive of means describes the way in which the action of the controlling verb is accomplished. In some respects this could be called an "epexegetical infinitive" (but we are reserving that term exclusively for substantival infinitives). It answers the question "How?"

Acts 3:26   ὁ θεὸς ... ἀπέστειλεν αὐτὸν εὐλογοῦντα ὑμᾶς **ἐν τῷ ἀποστρέφειν** ἕκαστον ἀπὸ τῶν πονηριῶν ὑμῶν.

God ... sent him to bless you **by turning** each [one of you] from your wicked ways.

6. Complementary (Supplementary)

The infinitive is frequently used with "helper" verbs to complete their thought. Such verbs rarely occur without the infinitive.

Phil 1:12   **γινώσκειν** δὲ ὑμᾶς *βούλομαι,* ἀδελφοί, ὅτι τὰ κατ' ἐμέ ...

Now *I want* you **to know**, brothers, that my circumstances ...

Mark 2:19   ὅσον χρόνον ἔχουσιν τὸν νυμφίον μετ' αὐτῶν οὐ *δύνανται* **νηστεύειν**.

As long as they have the bridegroom with them *they can*not **fast**.

B. Substantival Uses

7. Subject

An infinitive or an infinitive phrase sometimes functions as the subject of a finite verb. This category includes instances where the infinitive occurs with *impersonal verbs* such as δεῖ, ἔξεστιν, δοκεῖ, etc.

Phil 1:21   ἐμοὶ γὰρ **τὸ ζῆν** Χριστὸς καὶ **τὸ ἀποθανεῖν** κέρδος.

For to me, **to live** is Christ and **to die** is gain.

8. Direct Object

An infinitive or an infinitive phrase sometimes functions as the direct object of a finite verb.

2 Cor 8:11   νυνὶ δὲ καὶ **τὸ ποιῆσαι** ἐπιτελέσατε

But now also complete **the doing** [of it].

9. Indirect Discourse

This is the use of the infinitive (or infinitive phrase) after a verb of *perception* or *communication*. The controlling verb introduces the indirect discourse, of which the infinitive is the main verb.

Mark 12:18   Σαδδουκαῖοι ... οἵτινες λέγουσιν ἀνάστασιν μὴ **εἶναι**
               Sadducees ... who say **there is** no resurrection

Eph 4:21-22   ἐν αὐτῷ ἐδιδάχθητε ... (22) **ἀποθέσθαι** ὑμᾶς ... τὸν παλαιὸν ἄνθρωπον
               you have been taught in him ... that you **have put off** the old man

10. Appositional [namely]

Like any other substantive, the substantival infinitive may stand in apposition to a noun, pronoun, or substantival adjective.

Jas 1:27   θρησκεία καθαρὰ ... αὕτη ἐστίν, **ἐπισκέπτεσθαι** ὀρφανοὺς καὶ χήρας
         Pure religion ... is this, **namely, to visit** orphans and widows.

11. Epexegetical

The epexegetical infinitive clarifies, explains, or qualifies a noun or adjective. This use of the infinitive is usually bound by certain lexical features of the noun or adjective. That is, they normally are words indicating ability, authority, desire, freedom, hope, need, obligation, or readiness.

John 4:32   Ἐγὼ βρῶσιν ἔχω **φαγεῖν** ἣν ὑμεῖς οὐκ οἴδατε
         I have food **to eat** of which you are not aware.

The Participle

The participle is a *declinable verbal adjective*. It derives from its verbal nature tense and voice; from its adjectival nature, gender, number and case. Like the infinitive, the participle's *verbal* nature is normally seen in a dependent manner. That is, it is normally adverbial (in a broad sense) rather than functioning independently as a verb. Its *adjectival* side comes out just as strongly as a dependent or modifying adjective. [Exegesis requires that you master the participle. Be sure to read Wallace for his fuller discussions and especially his exegetical examples.]

A. Adjectival Participles

This category involves both the dependent and independent adjectival participles (i.e., both the adjectival proper and substantival). For a structural clue, the student should note the article. If it stands before a participle and functions as a modifying article (normal use), then that participle *must* be adjectival. If the participle does *not* have the article, it *may* be adjectival.

1. Adjectival Proper (Dependent)

The participle may function like an adjective and either modify a substantive (attributive) or assert something about it (predicate).

John 4:11   τὸ ὕδωρ τὸ **ζῶν**
         the **living** water

Heb 4:12   **Ζῶν** γὰρ ὁ λόγος τοῦ θεοῦ
         For the word of God is **living**.

2. *Substantival (Independent)*

This is the independent use of the adjectival participle (i.e., not related to a noun). It functions in the place of a substantive.

1 Tim 6:15   ὁ βασιλεὺς τῶν **βασιλευόντων** καὶ κύριος τῶν **κυριευόντων**
the king of those **who are reigning** and lord of those **who are lording it (over)** [others]

B. Verbal Participles

The first four categories are dependent verbal participles, example seven is an independent verbal participle, and the genitive absolute is the last example.

3. *Adverbial (Circumstantial)*

The adverbial or circumstantial participle is grammatically subordinated to its controlling verb (usually the main verb of the clause). Like an ordinary adverb, the participle modifies the verb, answering the question *When?* (temporal), *How?* (means, manner), *Why?* (purpose, cause), etc.

a. Temporal [after, when]

In relation to its controlling verb, the temporal participle answers the question *When?* Three kinds of time are in view: antecedent, contemporaneous, and subsequent. The antecedent participle should be translated *after doing, after he did,* etc. The contemporaneous participle should normally be translated *while doing.* And the subsequent participle should be translated *before doing, before he does,* etc.

Matt 4:2   **νηστεύσας** ... ὕστερον ἐπείνασεν
After he fasted ... he then became hungry.

Phil 1:3-4   Εὐχαριστῶ ... (4) τὴν δέησιν **ποιούμενος**
I am thankful ... **when I pray.**

b. Manner

The participle indicates the manner in which the action of the finite verb is carried out.

Matt 19:22   ἀπῆλθεν **λυπούμενος**
He went away **grieving.**

c. Means [by means of]

This participle indicates the means by which the action of a finite verb is accomplished. This means may be physical or mental.

Matt 27:4   ἥμαρτον **παραδοὺς** αἷμα ἀθῷον
I have sinned **by betraying** innocent blood.

d. Cause [because]

The causal participle indicates the *cause* or *reason* or *ground* of the action of the finite verb.

Matt 1:19   Ἰωσὴφ ... δίκαιος **ὢν**
Joseph ... **because he was** a righteous man

e. Condition [if]

This participle *implies* a condition on which the fulfillment of the idea indicated by the main verb depends.

Gal 6:9   θερίσομεν μὴ **ἐκλυόμενοι**
We shall reap **if we do not lose heart**.

f. Concession [although]

The concessive participle implies that the state or action of the *main verb* is true *in spite of* the state or action of the participle.

Eph 2:1   Καὶ ὑμᾶς **ὄντας** νεκρούς
And **although** you **were** dead

g. Purpose (Telic) [in order to]

The participle of purpose indicates the purpose of the action of the finite verb. Unlike other participles, a simple "-ing" flavor will miss the point. Almost always this can (and usually should) be translated like an English infinitive.

Matt 27:49   εἰ ἔρχεται Ἠλίας **σώσων** αὐτόν
if Elijah is going to come **to save** (= **with the purpose of saving**) him

h. Result [with the result of]

The participle of result is used to indicate the actual outcome or result of the action of the main verb. It is similar to the participle of purpose in that it views the *end* of the action of the main verb, but it is dissimilar in that the participle of purpose also indicates or emphasizes intention or design, while result emphasizes what the action of the main verb actually accomplishes.

Eph 2:15   ἵνα τοὺς δύο κτίσῃ ἐν αὐτῷ εἰς ἕνα καινὸν ἄνθρωπον **ποιῶν** εἰρήνην
in order that he might create in himself the two into one new man, [**with the result of**] **making** peace

4. Attendant Circumstance

The attendant circumstance participle is used to communicate an action that, in some sense, is coordinate with the finite verb. In this respect it is not dependent, for it is translated like a verb. Yet it is still dependent *semantically*, because it cannot exist without the main verb. It is translated as a finite verb connected to the main verb by "and." (It is not translated "*and* + finite verb" but "finite verb + *and*." This is a largely misundersdtood category. Many include the participle of result; see Wallace.)

Matt 9:13   **πορευθέντες** δὲ μάθετε τί ἐστιν ...
Now **go and** learn what this means ...

5. Periphrastic

An anarthrous participle can be used with a verb of being (such as εἰμί or ὑπάρχω) to form a finite verbal idea. This participle is called periphrastic because it is a *round-about* way of saying what could be expressed by a single verb. As such, it more naturally corresponds to English: ἦν ἐσθίων means *he was eating*, just as ἤσθιεν does.

Col 1:6   καθὼς καὶ ἐν παντὶ τῷ κόσμῳ ἐστὶν **καρποφορούμενον**
just as in all the world it *is* **bearing fruit**

Mark 10:32	ἦσαν ... **ἀναβαίνοντες** ... καὶ ἦν **προάγων** αὐτοὺς ὁ Ἰησοῦς
	They were **going up** ... and Jesus *was* **going before** them.

Mark 13:25	καὶ οἱ ἀστέρες ἔσονται ... **πίπτοντες**
	And the stars *will be* **falling**.

2 Cor 4:3	εἰ δὲ καὶ ἔστιν **κεκαλυμμένον** τὸ εὐαγγέλιον ἡμῶν
	But even if our gospel *is* **veiled** [or *has become* **veiled**]

Acts 21:29	ἦσαν γὰρ **προεωρακότες** Τρόφιμον
	for they *had* **previously seen** Trophimus

6. *Redundant (Pleonastic)*

A verb of saying (or sometimes thinking) can be used with a participle with basically the same meaning (as in ἀποκριθεὶς εἶπεν). Because such an idiom is foreign to English, many modern translations simply render the controlling verb.

Luke 12:17	διελογίζετο ἐν ἑαυτῷ **λέγων**
	he was thinking within himself, **saying**

7. *Independent Verbal Participle as an Imperative (Imperatival)*

Occasionally, though rarely, participles can function as though they were finite verbs and are not dependent on any verb in the context for their mood. The participle as an imperative is a case in point; this use of the participle is not attached to any verb in the context. But note this: "In general it may be said that no participle should be explained this way that can properly be connected with a finite verb" (Robertson, 1134).

Rom 12:9	**ἀποστυγοῦντες** τὸ πονηρόν, **κολλώμενοι** τῷ ἀγαθῷ
	Hate the evil! **Cleave** to the good!

8. *Genitive Absolute*

In defining the genitive absolute participial construction, we can define it *structurally* or define it *semantically*.

Structurally, the genitive absolute consists of the following: (1) A noun or pronoun in the genitive case (though this is sometimes absent); (2) a genitive *anarthrous* participle (always); (3) the entire construction at the front of a sentence (usually).

Semantically, there are three items to notice once the structure has been identified: (1) This construction will usually be unconnected with the rest of the sentence (i.e., its subject, the genitive noun or pronoun, will be different from the subject of the main clause); (2) the participle will *always* be circumstantial (adverbial) or, at least, dependent-verbal (i.e., it cannot be an adjectival participle); (3) the participle will usually (about 90% of the time) be *temporal*, though it can on occasion express any of the adverbial ideas.

Matt 9:18	Ταῦτα αὐτοῦ **λαλοῦντος** ... ἄρχων εἷς ἐλθὼν προσεκύνει αὐτῷ
	While he was saying these things ... a certain ruler came and began worshiping him.

Rom 7:3	**ζῶντος** τοῦ ἀνδρὸς ... γένηται ἀνδρὶ ἑτέρῳ
	while her husband **is still alive** ... she becomes another man's [wife]

John 5:13	Ἰησοῦς ἐξένευσεν ὄχλου **ὄντος** ἐν τῷ τόπῳ
	Jesus departed **while** a crowd **was** in that place.

Appendix B:

Phrasing

We have discussed phrasing in the *Introduction* (pp. xv - xxii) and in the first phrasing exercise (p. 10). All we can do here is encourage you to do it. Please do not cheat yourself out of the joy of discovery. Try to do the phrasing on your own, and then double-check your work using my phrasing. Remember, you and I may differ. That's okay. I could be wrong, or we could see different emphases in the text.

1 John 1:1-2:2; 2:28-3:10

Prologue (1:1-4)

1:1   Ὃ ἦν ἀπ' ἀρχῆς,
       ὃ ἀκηκόαμεν,
       ὃ ἑωράκαμεν τοῖς ὀφθαλμοῖς ἡμῶν,
       ὃ ἐθεασάμεθα καὶ αἱ χεῖρες ἡμῶν ἐψηλάφησαν
       περὶ τοῦ λόγου τῆς ζωῆς -

1:2   καὶ
              ἡ ζωὴ ἐφανερώθη,
       καὶ
       ἑωράκαμεν καὶ
       μαρτυροῦμεν καὶ
       ἀπαγγέλλομεν   ὑμῖν τὴν ζωὴν τὴν αἰώνιον
                              ἥτις   ἦν πρὸς τὸν πατέρα
                                             καὶ
                                      ἐφανερώθη ἡμῖν -

1:3   ὃ ἑωράκαμεν
              καὶ
       ἀκηκόαμεν,
       ἀπαγγέλλομεν καὶ ὑμῖν,
              ἵνα καὶ ὑμεῖς κοινωνίαν ἔχητε
                              μεθ' ἡμῶν.
       καὶ ... δὲ
       ἡ κοινωνία ... ἡ ἡμετέρα
              μετὰ τοῦ πατρὸς
              καὶ
              μετὰ τοῦ υἱοῦ αὐτοῦ
              Ἰησοῦ Χριστοῦ.

1:4   καὶ
       ταῦτα γράφομεν ἡμεῖς,
              ἵνα ἡ χαρὰ ἡμῶν ᾖ πεπληρωμένη.

Walk in the Light (1:5-2:2)

1:5   Καὶ
ἔστιν αὕτη ἡ ἀγγελία
       ἣν ἀκηκόαμεν ἀπ᾽ αὐτοῦ
           καὶ
         ἀναγγέλλομεν ὑμῖν,

       ὅτι ὁ θεὸς φῶς ἐστιν
           καὶ
         σκοτία ἐν αὐτῷ οὐκ ἔστιν οὐδεμία.

1:6   Ἐὰν εἴπωμεν ὅτι κοινωνίαν ἔχομεν μετ᾽ αὐτοῦ
     καὶ
   ἐν τῷ σκότει περιπατῶμεν,
ψευδόμεθα
     καὶ
οὐ ποιοῦμεν τὴν ἀλήθειαν·

1:7   δὲ
   ἐὰν ... ἐν τῷ φωτὶ περιπατῶμεν ὡς αὐτός ἐστιν ἐν τῷ φωτί,
κοινωνίαν ἔχομεν μετ᾽ ἀλλήλων
     καὶ
τὸ αἷμα Ἰησοῦ τοῦ υἱοῦ αὐτοῦ καθαρίζει ἡμᾶς ἀπὸ πάσης ἁμαρτίας.

1:8   ἐὰν εἴπωμεν ὅτι ἁμαρτίαν οὐκ ἔχομεν,
ἑαυτοὺς πλανῶμεν
     καὶ
ἡ ἀλήθεια οὐκ ἔστιν ἐν ἡμῖν.

1:9   ἐὰν ὁμολογῶμεν τὰς ἁμαρτίας ἡμῶν,
πιστός ἐστιν καὶ δίκαιος,
      ἵνα ἀφῇ ἡμῖν τὰς ἁμαρτίας
        καὶ
       καθαρίσῃ ἡμᾶς ἀπὸ πάσης ἀδικίας.

1:10   ἐὰν εἴπωμεν ὅτι οὐχ ἡμαρτήκαμεν
ψεύστην ποιοῦμεν αὐτὸν
     καὶ
ὁ λόγος αὐτοῦ οὐκ ἔστιν ἐν ἡμῖν.

2:1   Τεκνία μου,
ταῦτα γράφω ὑμῖν ἵνα μὴ ἁμάρτητε.
     καὶ
   ἐάν τις ἁμάρτῃ,
παράκλητον ἔχομεν πρὸς τὸν πατέρα
   Ἰησοῦν Χριστὸν δίκαιον·

2:2   καὶ
         αὐτὸς ἱλασμός ἐστιν περὶ τῶν ἁμαρτιῶν ἡμῶν,
                 οὐ περὶ τῶν ἡμετέρων
                 δὲ μόνον ἀλλὰ καὶ
                 περὶ ὅλου τοῦ κόσμου.

The Children of God (2:28-3:3)

2:28   Καὶ νῦν, τεκνία, μένετε ἐν αὐτῷ,
                         ἵνα   ἐὰν φανερωθῇ
                                 σχῶμεν παρρησίαν
                                 καὶ
                         μὴ αἰσχυνθῶμεν ἀπ᾽ αὐτοῦ ἐν τῇ παρουσίᾳ αὐτοῦ.

2:29   ἐὰν εἰδῆτε ὅτι δίκαιός ἐστιν,
         γινώσκετε ὅτι καὶ πᾶς ὁ ποιῶν τὴν δικαιοσύνην ἐξ αὐτοῦ γεγέννηται

3:1   ἴδετε ποταπὴν ἀγάπην δέδωκεν ἡμῖν ὁ πατήρ,
                         ἵνα τέκνα θεοῦ κληθῶμεν,
             καὶ
         ἐσμέν.

         διὰ τοῦτο ὁ κόσμος οὐ γινώσκει ἡμᾶς,
                 ὅτι οὐκ ἔγνω αὐτόν.

3:2   Ἀγαπητοί,
         νῦν τέκνα θεοῦ ἐσμεν,
             καὶ
         οὔπω ἐφανερώθη τί ἐσόμεθα.
         οἴδαμεν ὅτι   ἐὰν φανερωθῇ,
                     ὅμοιοι αὐτῷ ἐσόμεθα,
                             ὅτι ὀψόμεθα αὐτὸν καθώς ἐστιν.

3:3   καὶ
         πᾶς ὁ ἔχων τὴν ἐλπίδα ταύτην ἐπ᾽ αὐτῷ ἁγνίζει ἑαυτόν,
                                 καθὼς ἐκεῖνος ἁγνός ἐστιν.

The Sinlessness of God's Children (3:4-10)

3:4   Πᾶς ὁ ποιῶν τὴν ἁμαρτίαν καὶ τὴν ἀνομίαν ποιεῖ,
           καὶ
     ἡ ἁμαρτία ἐστὶν ἡ ἀνομία.

3:5   καὶ
     οἴδατε ὅτι ἐκεῖνος ἐφανερώθη, ἵνα τὰς ἁμαρτίας ἄρῃ,
           καὶ
     ἁμαρτία ἐν αὐτῷ οὐκ ἔστιν.
3:6   πᾶς ὁ ἐν αὐτῷ μένων   οὐχ ἁμαρτάνει·
     πᾶς ὁ ἁμαρτάνων   οὐχ ἑώρακεν αὐτὸν
                       οὐδὲ ἔγνωκεν αὐτόν.

3:7   Τεκνία,
     μηδεὶς πλανάτω ὑμᾶς·

     ὁ ποιῶν τὴν δικαιοσύνην δίκαιός ἐστιν,
                       καθὼς ἐκεῖνος δίκαιός ἐστιν·
3:8   ὁ ποιῶν τὴν ἁμαρτίαν ἐκ τοῦ διαβόλου ἐστίν,
                        ὅτι ἀπ᾽ ἀρχῆς ὁ διάβολος ἁμαρτάνει.

     εἰς τοῦτο ἐφανερώθη ὁ υἱὸς τοῦ θεοῦ,
          ἵνα λύσῃ τὰ ἔργα τοῦ διαβόλου.

3:9   Πᾶς ὁ γεγεννημένος ἐκ τοῦ θεοῦ   ἁμαρτίαν οὐ ποιεῖ,
                           ὅτι σπέρμα αὐτοῦ ἐν αὐτῷ μένει,
                 καὶ
          οὐ δύναται ἁμαρτάνειν,
                 ὅτι ἐκ τοῦ θεοῦ γεγέννηται.

3:10   ἐν τούτῳ φανερά ἐστιν   τὰ τέκνα τοῦ θεοῦ
                         καὶ
                       τὰ τέκνα τοῦ διαβόλου·

         πᾶς ὁ μὴ ποιῶν   δικαιοσύνην   οὐκ ἔστιν ἐκ τοῦ θεοῦ,
         καὶ
         ὁ μὴ ἀγαπῶν   τὸν ἀδελφὸν αὐτοῦ.

John 15:1-27

Jesus, the True Vine; God the Father, the Vine-Dresser (15:1-4)

15:1   Ἐγώ εἰμι ἡ ἄμπελος ἡ ἀληθινὴ
         καὶ
     ὁ πατήρ μου ὁ γεωργός ἐστιν.

15:2   πᾶν κλῆμα ἐν ἐμοὶ μὴ φέρον καρπὸν αἴρει αὐτό,
         καὶ
     πᾶν τὸ καρπὸν φέρον καθαίρει αὐτὸ
                   ἵνα καρπὸν πλείονα φέρῃ.

15:3   ἤδη ὑμεῖς καθαροί ἐστε
             διὰ τὸν λόγον
                 ὃν λελάληκα ὑμῖν·

15:4   μείνατε   ἐν ἐμοί,
         κἀγὼ
     ...   ἐν ὑμῖν.

         καθὼς
     τὸ κλῆμα οὐ δύναται καρπὸν φέρειν ἀφ᾽ ἑαυτοῦ
                       ἐὰν μὴ μένῃ ἐν τῇ ἀμπέλῳ,
         οὕτως οὐδὲ
     ὑμεῖς
                 ἐὰν μὴ ἐν ἐμοὶ μένητε.

Jesus Is the Vine; We Are the Branches (15:5-11)

15:5   ἐγώ εἰμι ἡ ἄμπελος,
     ὑμεῖς τὰ κλήματα.

     ὁ μένων   ἐν ἐμοὶ
         κἀγὼ
     ...   ἐν αὐτῷ
     οὗτος φέρει καρπὸν πολύν,
             ὅτι χωρὶς ἐμοῦ οὐ δύνασθε ποιεῖν οὐδέν.

15:6   ἐὰν μή τις μένῃ ἐν ἐμοί,
    ἐβλήθη ἔξω ὡς τὸ κλῆμα
      καὶ
    ἐξηράνθη
      καὶ
    συνάγουσιν αὐτὰ
      καὶ
    εἰς τὸ πῦρ βάλλουσιν
      καὶ
    καίεται.

15:7   ἐὰν μείνητε ἐν ἐμοὶ
        καὶ
      τὰ ῥήματά μου ἐν ὑμῖν μείνῃ,

     ὃ ἐὰν θέλητε
    αἰτήσασθε,
      καὶ
    γενήσεται ὑμῖν.

15:8   ἐν τούτῳ
   ἐδοξάσθη ὁ πατήρ μου,
     ἵνα   καρπὸν πολὺν φέρητε
          καὶ
        γένησθε ἐμοὶ μαθηταί.

15:9   καθὼς
   ἠγάπησέν με ὁ πατήρ,
     κἀγὼ
   ὑμᾶς ἠγάπησα·

   μείνατε ἐν τῇ ἀγάπῃ τῇ ἐμῇ.

15:10 ἐὰν τὰς ἐντολάς μου τηρήσητε,
   μενεῖτε ἐν τῇ ἀγάπῃ μου,

     καθὼς
   ἐγὼ τὰς ἐντολὰς τοῦ πατρός μου τετήρηκα
     καὶ
   μένω αὐτοῦ ἐν τῇ ἀγάπῃ.

15:11 Ταῦτα λελάληκα ὑμῖν
      ἵνα   ἡ χαρὰ ἡ ἐμὴ ἐν ὑμῖν ᾖ
          καὶ
        ἡ χαρὰ ὑμῶν πληρωθῇ.

Love One Another (15:12-25)

15:12   αὕτη ἐστὶν ἡ ἐντολὴ ἡ ἐμή,
              ἵνα ἀγαπᾶτε ἀλλήλους
                    καθὼς ἠγάπησα ὑμᾶς.

15:13   μείζονα ταύτης ἀγάπην οὐδεὶς ἔχει,
                 ἵνα τις τὴν ψυχὴν αὐτοῦ θῇ ὑπὲρ τῶν φίλων αὐτοῦ.

15:14   ὑμεῖς φίλοι μού ἐστε
                 ἐὰν ποιῆτε ἃ ἐγὼ ἐντέλλομαι ὑμῖν.

15:15   οὐκέτι
         λέγω ὑμᾶς δούλους,
                 ὅτι ὁ δοῦλος οὐκ οἶδεν τί ποιεῖ αὐτοῦ ὁ κύριος·
              δὲ
         ὑμᾶς ... εἴρηκα φίλους,
                 ὅτι πάντα ἃ ἤκουσα παρὰ τοῦ πατρός μου ἐγνώρισα ὑμῖν.

15:16   οὐχ ὑμεῖς με ἐξελέξασθε,
              ἀλλ᾽
         ἐγὼ   ἐξελεξάμην ὑμᾶς
                    καὶ
              ἔθηκα ὑμᾶς

                 ἵνα   ὑμεῖς ὑπάγητε
                          καὶ
                          καρπὸν φέρητε
                          καὶ
                          ὁ καρπὸς ὑμῶν μένῃ,

                 ἵνα   ὅ τι ἂν αἰτήσητε τὸν πατέρα ἐν τῷ ὀνόματί μου δῷ ὑμῖν.

15:17   ταῦτα ἐντέλλομαι ὑμῖν,
              ἵνα ἀγαπᾶτε ἀλλήλους.

15:18   Εἰ ὁ κόσμος ὑμᾶς μισεῖ,
         γινώσκετε ὅτι ἐμὲ πρῶτον ὑμῶν μεμίσηκεν.

15:19   εἰ ἐκ τοῦ κόσμου ἦτε,
         ὁ κόσμος ἂν τὸ ἴδιον ἐφίλει·
              δέ
                 ὅτι ... ἐκ τοῦ κόσμου οὐκ ἐστέ,
                    ἀλλ᾽
                 ἐγὼ ἐξελεξάμην ὑμᾶς ἐκ τοῦ κόσμου,
         διὰ τοῦτο μισεῖ ὑμᾶς ὁ κόσμος.

15:20   μνημονεύετε τοῦ λόγου οὗ ἐγὼ εἶπον ὑμῖν,
                        Οὐκ ἔστιν δοῦλος μείζων τοῦ κυρίου αὐτοῦ.

            εἰ ἐμὲ ἐδίωξαν,
     καὶ ὑμᾶς διώξουσιν·
            εἰ τὸν λόγον μου ἐτήρησαν,
     καὶ τὸν ὑμέτερον τηρήσουσιν.

15:21   ἀλλὰ ταῦτα πάντα ποιήσουσιν εἰς ὑμᾶς
                        διὰ τὸ ὄνομά μου,
                        ὅτι οὐκ οἴδασιν τὸν πέμψαντά με.

15:22   εἰ μὴ ἦλθον καὶ ἐλάλησα αὐτοῖς,
     ἁμαρτίαν οὐκ εἴχοσαν·
            νῦν δὲ
     πρόφασιν οὐκ ἔχουσιν περὶ τῆς ἁμαρτίας αὐτῶν.

15:23   ὁ ἐμὲ μισῶν καὶ τὸν πατέρα μου μισεῖ.

15:24   εἰ τὰ ἔργα μὴ ἐποίησα ἐν αὐτοῖς
                        ἃ οὐδεὶς ἄλλος ἐποίησεν,
     ἁμαρτίαν οὐκ εἴχοσαν·
            νῦν δὲ καὶ
     ἑωράκασιν καὶ
     μεμισήκασιν   καὶ ἐμὲ καὶ
                        τὸν πατέρα μου.

15:25   ἀλλ᾿
            ἵνα πληρωθῇ   ὁ λόγος
                        ὁ ἐν τῷ νόμῳ αὐτῶν γεγραμμένος

            ὅτι **Ἐμίσησάν με δωρεάν.**

The Holy Spirit (15:26-27)

15:26   Ὅταν ἔλθῃ ὁ παράκλητος
                        ὃν ἐγὼ πέμψω ὑμῖν παρὰ τοῦ πατρός,
                        τὸ πνεῦμα τῆς ἀληθείας
                        ὃ παρὰ τοῦ πατρὸς ἐκπορεύεται,
     ἐκεῖνος μαρτυρήσει περὶ ἐμοῦ·
15:27   καὶ ... δὲ
     ὑμεῖς ... μαρτυρεῖτε,
            ὅτι ἀπ᾿ ἀρχῆς μετ᾿ ἐμοῦ ἐστε.

Mark 1:1-28

No phrasing supplied, since this passage is narrative.

Mark 8:27-9:8

Peter's Confession (8:27-9:1)

8:27   Καὶ
ἐξῆλθεν ὁ Ἰησοῦς καὶ οἱ μαθηταὶ αὐτοῦ εἰς τὰς κώμας Καισαρείας τῆς Φιλίππου·
      καὶ
ἐν τῇ ὁδῷ ἐπηρώτα τοὺς μαθητὰς αὐτοῦ λέγων αὐτοῖς,

Τίνα με λέγουσιν οἱ ἄνθρωποι εἶναι;

8:28   δὲ
οἱ ... εἶπαν αὐτῷ λέγοντες [ὅτι]   Ἰωάννην τὸν βαπτιστήν,
                      καὶ ἄλλοι,
              Ἠλίαν,
                  δὲ ἄλλοι
              ὅτι εἷς τῶν προφητῶν.

8:29   καὶ
αὐτὸς ἐπηρώτα αὐτούς,   Ὑμεῖς δὲ τίνα με λέγετε εἶναι;
ἀποκριθεὶς ὁ Πέτρος λέγει αὐτῷ,   Σὺ εἶ ὁ Χριστός.

8:30   καὶ
ἐπετίμησεν αὐτοῖς ἵνα μηδενὶ λέγωσιν περὶ αὐτοῦ.

8:31   Καὶ
ἤρξατο διδάσκειν αὐτοὺς ὅτι δεῖ   τὸν υἱὸν τοῦ ἀνθρώπου πολλὰ παθεῖν καὶ
                            ἀποδοκιμασθῆναι ὑπὸ   τῶν πρεσβυτέρων καὶ
                                            τῶν ἀρχιερέων καὶ
                                          τῶν γραμματέων καὶ
                            ἀποκτανθῆναι καὶ
                            μετὰ τρεῖς ἡμέρας ἀναστῆναι·

8:32   καὶ
παρρησίᾳ τὸν λόγον ἐλάλει.
      καὶ
                προσλαβόμενος ὁ Πέτρος αὐτὸν
ἤρξατο ἐπιτιμᾶν αὐτῷ.

8:33   δὲ
                     ὁ ... ἐπιστραφεὶς καὶ ἰδὼν τοὺς μαθητὰς αὐτοῦ
              ἐπετίμησεν Πέτρῳ
                     καὶ
              λέγει,   Ὕπαγε ὀπίσω μου, Σατανᾶ,
                             ὅτι οὐ φρονεῖς   τὰ τοῦ θεοῦ
                                                      ἀλλὰ
                                               τὰ τῶν ἀνθρώπων.

8:34   Καὶ
                     προσκαλεσάμενος τὸν ὄχλον σὺν τοῖς μαθηταῖς αὐτοῦ
              εἶπεν αὐτοῖς,

                     Εἴ τις θέλει ὀπίσω μου ἀκολουθεῖν,
              ἀπαρνησάσθω ἑαυτὸν
                     καὶ
              ἀράτω τὸν σταυρὸν αὐτοῦ
                     καὶ
              ἀκολουθείτω μοι.

8:35   γὰρ
                     ὃς ... ἐὰν θέλῃ τὴν ψυχὴν αὐτοῦ σῶσαι
              ἀπολέσει αὐτήν·
                     δ᾿
                     ὃς ... ἂν ἀπολέσει τὴν ψυχὴν αὐτοῦ
                             ἕνεκεν   ἐμοῦ καὶ
                                      τοῦ εὐαγγελίου
              σώσει αὐτήν.

8:36   γὰρ
              τί ... ὠφελεῖ ἄνθρωπον   κερδῆσαι τὸν κόσμον ὅλον
                                                  καὶ
                                          ζημιωθῆναι τὴν ψυχὴν αὐτοῦ;

8:37   γὰρ
              τί ... δοῖ ἄνθρωπος ἀντάλλαγμα τῆς ψυχῆς αὐτοῦ;

8:38   γὰρ
                     ὃς ... ἐὰν ἐπαισχυνθῇ   με καὶ
                                              τοὺς ἐμοὺς λόγους
                                        ἐν τῇ γενεᾷ ταύτῃ τῇ μοιχαλίδι καὶ ἁμαρτωλῷ,
              καὶ ὁ υἱὸς τοῦ ἀνθρώπου ἐπαισχυνθήσεται αὐτόν,
                             ὅταν ἔλθῃ   ἐν τῇ δόξῃ τοῦ πατρὸς αὐτοῦ
                                        μετὰ τῶν ἀγγέλων τῶν ἁγίων.

9:1   Καὶ
              ἔλεγεν αὐτοῖς,
                     Ἀμὴν λέγω ὑμῖν ὅτι
                             εἰσίν τινες ὧδε τῶν ἑστηκότων οἵτινες οὐ μὴ γεύσωνται θανάτου
                                             ἕως ἂν ἴδωσιν τὴν βασιλείαν τοῦ
                                             θεοῦ ἐληλυθυῖαν ἐν δυνάμει.

Transfiguration (9:2-8)

9:2   Καὶ μετὰ ἡμέρας ἓξ
παραλαμβάνει ὁ Ἰησοῦς τὸν Πέτρον καὶ τὸν Ἰάκωβον καὶ τὸν Ἰωάννην
      καὶ
ἀναφέρει αὐτοὺς εἰς ὄρος ὑψηλὸν κατ᾽ ἰδίαν μόνους.
      καὶ
μετεμορφώθη ἔμπροσθεν αὐτῶν,

9:3   καὶ
τὰ ἱμάτια αὐτοῦ ἐγένετο στίλβοντα λευκὰ λίαν,
                        οἷα γναφεὺς ἐπὶ τῆς γῆς οὐ δύναται οὕτως λευκᾶναι.

9:4   καὶ
ὤφθη αὐτοῖς Ἠλίας σὺν Μωϋσεῖ
      καὶ
ἦσαν συλλαλοῦντες τῷ Ἰησοῦ.

9:5   καὶ
          ἀποκριθεὶς
ὁ Πέτρος λέγει τῷ Ἰησοῦ,
             Ῥαββί, καλόν ἐστιν ἡμᾶς ὧδε εἶναι,
                καὶ
             ποιήσωμεν τρεῖς σκηνάς,
                     σοὶ μίαν καὶ Μωϋσεῖ μίαν καὶ Ἠλίᾳ μίαν.

9:6   γὰρ
οὐ ... ᾔδει τί ἀποκριθῇ,
      γὰρ
ἔκφοβοι ... ἐγένοντο.

9:7   καὶ
ἐγένετο νεφέλη ἐπισκιάζουσα αὐτοῖς,
      καὶ
ἐγένετο φωνὴ ἐκ τῆς νεφέλης,
          Οὗτός ἐστιν ὁ υἱός μου ὁ ἀγαπητός,
          ἀκούετε αὐτοῦ.

9:8   καὶ
          ἐξάπινα περιβλεψάμενοι
οὐκέτι οὐδένα εἶδον
      ἀλλὰ
τὸν Ἰησοῦν μόνον μεθ᾽ ἑαυτῶν.

Colossians 1:1-23

Salutation (1:1-2)

1:1   Παῦλος
         ἀπόστολος Χριστοῦ Ἰησοῦ διὰ θελήματος θεοῦ
       καὶ
      Τιμόθεος
         ὁ ἀδελφὸς

1:2   τοῖς   ἐν Κολοσσαῖς ἁγίοις
           καὶ
         πιστοῖς ἀδελφοῖς ἐν Χριστῷ,

      χάρις ὑμῖν καὶ εἰρήνη ἀπὸ θεοῦ πατρὸς ἡμῶν.

Thanksgiving (1:3-8)

1:3   Εὐχαριστοῦμεν τῷ θεῷ πατρὶ τοῦ κυρίου ἡμῶν Ἰησοῦ Χριστοῦ
        πάντοτε περὶ ὑμῶν προσευχόμενοι,
1:4   ἀκούσαντες
          τὴν πίστιν ὑμῶν ἐν Χριστῷ Ἰησοῦ
           καὶ
          τὴν ἀγάπην ἣν ἔχετε εἰς πάντας τοὺς ἁγίους
1:5   διὰ τὴν ἐλπίδα   τὴν ἀποκειμένην ὑμῖν ἐν τοῖς οὐρανοῖς,
                        ἣν προηκούσατε ἐν τῷ λόγῳ   τῆς ἀληθείας
                                          τοῦ εὐαγγελίου

(Gospel)

1:6   τοῦ παρόντος εἰς ὑμᾶς,
       καθὼς καὶ
      ἐν παντὶ τῷ κόσμῳ   ἐστὶν καρποφορούμενον καὶ
                     αὐξανόμενον
      καθὼς καὶ
      ἐν ὑμῖν,
         ἀφ' ἧς ἡμέρας   ἠκούσατε καὶ
                    ἐπέγνωτε τὴν χάριν τοῦ θεοῦ ἐν ἀληθείᾳ·
1:7   καθὼς
      ἐμάθετε ἀπὸ Ἐπαφρᾶ
            τοῦ ἀγαπητοῦ συνδούλου ἡμῶν,
            ὅς ἐστιν πιστὸς ὑπὲρ ὑμῶν διάκονος τοῦ Χριστοῦ,
1:8   ὁ καὶ δηλώσας ἡμῖν τὴν ὑμῶν ἀγάπην ἐν πνεύματι.

Prayer (1:9-14)

1:9   Διὰ τοῦτο καὶ ἡμεῖς,
          ἀφ᾿ ἧς ἡμέρας ἠκούσαμεν,
    οὐ παυόμεθα ὑπὲρ ὑμῶν προσευχόμενοι καὶ αἰτούμενοι,
           ἵνα
             <u>πληρωθῆτε</u> τὴν ἐπίγνωσιν τοῦ θελήματος αὐτοῦ
                     ἐν πάσῃ σοφίᾳ καὶ συνέσει πνευματικῇ,

1:10   <u>περιπατῆσαι</u> ἀξίως τοῦ κυρίου εἰς πᾶσαν ἀρεσκείαν,
               ἐν παντὶ ἔργῳ ἀγαθῷ <u>καρποφοροῦντες</u> καὶ
               <u>αὐξανόμενοι</u> τῇ ἐπιγνώσει τοῦ θεοῦ,

1:11   ἐν πάσῃ δυνάμει <u>δυναμούμενοι</u>
                         κατὰ τὸ κράτος τῆς δόξης αὐτοῦ
                       εἰς πᾶσαν   ὑπομονὴν καὶ
                                μακροθυμίαν.
                     μετὰ χαρᾶς

1:12   <u>εὐχαριστοῦντες</u> τῷ πατρὶ
                    τῷ ἱκανώσαντι ὑμᾶς
                        εἰς τὴν μερίδα τοῦ κλήρου τῶν ἁγίων ἐν τῷ φωτί·

(Father)

1:13   ὃς
          ἐρρύσατο ἡμᾶς ἐκ τῆς ἐξουσίας τοῦ σκότους καὶ
          μετέστησεν εἰς τὴν βασιλείαν τοῦ υἱοῦ τῆς ἀγάπης αὐτοῦ,

(Son)

1:14   ἐν ᾧ ἔχομεν   τὴν ἀπολύτρωσιν,
                    τὴν ἄφεσιν τῶν ἁμαρτιῶν·

Christ (1:15-20)

1:15   ὅς ἐστιν
        εἰκὼν τοῦ θεοῦ τοῦ ἀοράτου,
        πρωτότοκος πάσης κτίσεως,

1:16   ὅτι ἐν αὐτῷ ἐκτίσθη   τὰ πάντα
                 ἐν τοῖς οὐρανοῖς καὶ
                 ἐπὶ τῆς γῆς,
                 τὰ ὁρατὰ καὶ
                 τὰ ἀόρατα,
                     εἴτε θρόνοι
                     εἴτε κυριότητες
                     εἴτε ἀρχαὶ
                     εἴτε ἐξουσίαι·
       τὰ πάντα δι᾿ αὐτοῦ καὶ εἰς αὐτὸν ἔκτισται·

1:17   καὶ
          αὐτός ἐστιν   πρὸ πάντων
                    καὶ
          τὰ πάντα ἐν αὐτῷ συνέστηκεν,
1:18   καὶ
          αὐτός ἐστιν   ἡ κεφαλὴ   τοῦ σώματος
                                        τῆς ἐκκλησίας·
                    ὅς ἐστιν   ἀρχή,
                              πρωτότοκος ἐκ τῶν νεκρῶν,
                                        ἵνα γένηται ἐν πᾶσιν αὐτὸς πρωτεύων,

1:19   ὅτι   ἐν αὐτῷ εὐδόκησεν πᾶν τὸ πλήρωμα   κατοικῆσαι
1:20   καὶ
          δι᾽ αὐτοῦ   ἀποκαταλλάξαι   τὰ πάντα εἰς αὐτόν,
                                        εἰρηνοποιήσας
                                        διὰ τοῦ αἵματος τοῦ σταυροῦ αὐτοῦ,
                                        [δι᾽ αὐτοῦ]
                                                  εἴτε τὰ ἐπὶ τῆς γῆς
                                                  εἴτε τὰ ἐν τοῖς οὐρανοῖς.

Reconciliation (1:21-23)

1:21   Καὶ
                    ὑμᾶς ποτε ὄντας
                              ἀπηλλοτριωμένους καὶ
                              ἐχθροὺς τῇ διανοίᾳ ἐν τοῖς ἔργοις τοῖς πονηροῖς,

1:22   δὲ
          νυνὶ ... ἀποκατήλλαξεν
                              ἐν τῷ σώματι τῆς σαρκὸς αὐτοῦ
                              διὰ τοῦ θανάτου
                    παραστῆσαι ὑμᾶς ἁγίους καὶ ἀμώμους καὶ ἀνεγκλήτους κατενώπιον αὐτοῦ,

1:23   εἴ γε
                              ἐπιμένετε τῇ πίστει
                                   τεθεμελιωμένοι
                                        καὶ
                                   ἑδραῖοι
                                        καὶ
                              μὴ μετακινούμενοι ἀπὸ τῆς ἐλπίδος τοῦ εὐαγγελίου

                              οὗ ἠκούσατε,
                              τοῦ κηρυχθέντος ἐν πάσῃ κτίσει τῇ ὑπὸ τὸν οὐρανόν,
                              οὗ ἐγενόμην ἐγὼ Παῦλος διάκονος.

Matthew 6:5-34

The Position of Prayer (6:5-6)

6:5   Καὶ
          ὅταν προσεύχησθε,
    οὐκ ἔσεσθε ὡς οἱ ὑποκριταί,
       ὅτι φιλοῦσιν   ἐν ταῖς συναγωγαῖς καὶ
                      ἐν ταῖς γωνίαις τῶν πλατειῶν
                      ἑστῶτες
                      προσεύχεσθαι,
                        ὅπως φανῶσιν τοῖς ἀνθρώποις·
    ἀμὴν λέγω ὑμῖν, ἀπέχουσιν τὸν μισθὸν αὐτῶν.

6:6   δὲ
          σὺ ... ὅταν προσεύχῃ,
    εἴσελθε εἰς τὸ ταμεῖόν σου
       καὶ
          κλείσας τὴν θύραν σου
    πρόσευξαι τῷ πατρί σου τῷ ἐν τῷ κρυπτῷ·
       καὶ
    ὁ πατήρ σου ὁ βλέπων ἐν τῷ κρυπτῷ ἀποδώσει σοι.

The Lord's Prayer (6:7-15)

6:7   δὲ
          Προσευχόμενοι ...
    μὴ βατταλογήσητε ὥσπερ οἱ ἐθνικοί,
             γὰρ
          δοκοῦσιν ... ὅτι ἐν τῇ πολυλογίᾳ αὐτῶν εἰσακουσθήσονται.
6:8   οὖν
    μὴ ... ὁμοιωθῆτε αὐτοῖς·
          γὰρ
          οἶδεν ... ὁ πατὴρ ὑμῶν ὧν χρείαν ἔχετε
                        πρὸ τοῦ ὑμᾶς αἰτῆσαι αὐτόν.
6:9   οὖν
    Οὕτως ... προσεύχεσθε ὑμεῖς·

Πάτερ ἡμῶν ὁ ἐν τοῖς οὐρανοῖς·
    ἁγιασθήτω τὸ ὄνομά σου·
6:10   ἐλθέτω ἡ βασιλεία σου·
    γενηθήτω τὸ θέλημά σου,
        ὡς ἐν οὐρανῷ καὶ ἐπὶ γῆς·
6:11   τὸν ἄρτον ἡμῶν τὸν ἐπιούσιον δὸς ἡμῖν σήμερον·
6:12   καὶ
    ἄφες ἡμῖν τὰ ὀφειλήματα ἡμῶν,
        ὡς καὶ ἡμεῖς ἀφήκαμεν τοῖς ὀφειλέταις ἡμῶν·
6:13   καὶ
    μὴ εἰσενέγκῃς ἡμᾶς εἰς πειρασμόν,
      ἀλλὰ
    ῥῦσαι ἡμᾶς ἀπὸ τοῦ πονηροῦ.

6:14   γὰρ
      Ἐὰν ... ἀφῆτε τοῖς ἀνθρώποις τὰ παραπτώματα αὐτῶν,
ἀφήσει καὶ ὑμῖν ὁ πατὴρ ὑμῶν ὁ οὐράνιος·
6:15   δὲ
    ἐὰν ... μὴ ἀφῆτε τοῖς ἀνθρώποις,
οὐδὲ ὁ πατὴρ ὑμῶν ἀφήσει τὰ παραπτώματα ὑμῶν.

Fasting (6:16-18)

6:16   δὲ
    Ὅταν ... νηστεύητε,
μὴ γίνεσθε ὡς οἱ ὑποκριταὶ σκυθρωποί,
        γὰρ
      ἀφανίζουσιν ... τὰ πρόσωπα αὐτῶν
        ὅπως φανῶσιν τοῖς ἀνθρώποις νηστεύοντες·
ἀμὴν λέγω ὑμῖν, ἀπέχουσιν τὸν μισθὸν αὐτῶν.

6:17   δὲ
σὺ ... νηστεύων ἄλειψαί σου τὴν κεφαλὴν καὶ
    τὸ πρόσωπόν σου νίψαι,

6:18   ὅπως μὴ φανῇς τοῖς ἀνθρώποις νηστεύων
      ἀλλὰ
        τῷ πατρί σου τῷ ἐν τῷ κρυφαίῳ·
    καὶ
ὁ πατήρ σου ... ἀποδώσει σοι.
    ὁ βλέπων ἐν τῷ κρυφαίῳ

The Pursuit of God and Wealth (6:19-24)

6:19   Μὴ θησαυρίζετε ὑμῖν θησαυροὺς ἐπὶ τῆς γῆς,

                          ὅπου σὴς καὶ βρῶσις ἀφανίζει καὶ
                          ὅπου κλέπται διορύσσουσιν καὶ κλέπτουσιν·

6:20   δὲ

    θησαυρίζετε ... ὑμῖν θησαυροὺς ἐν οὐρανῷ,

                          ὅπου οὔτε σὴς οὔτε βρῶσις ἀφανίζει καὶ
                          ὅπου κλέπται οὐ διορύσσουσιν οὐδὲ κλέπτουσιν·

6:21   γάρ

    ὅπου ... ἐστιν ὁ θησαυρός σου, ἐκεῖ ἔσται καὶ ἡ καρδία σου.

6:22   Ὁ λύχνος τοῦ σώματός ἐστιν ὁ ὀφθαλμός.

         οὖν

                ἐὰν ... ᾖ ὁ ὀφθαλμός σου ἁπλοῦς,
    ὅλον τὸ σῶμά σου φωτεινὸν ἔσται·

6:23   δὲ

                ἐὰν ... ὁ ὀφθαλμός σου πονηρὸς ᾖ,
    ὅλον τὸ σῶμά σου σκοτεινὸν ἔσται.

         οὖν

                εἰ ... τὸ φῶς τὸ ἐν σοὶ σκότος ἐστίν,
    τὸ σκότος πόσον.

6:24   Οὐδεὶς δύναται δυσὶ κυρίοις δουλεύειν·

         γὰρ

        ἢ ... τὸν ἕνα μισήσει καὶ τὸν ἕτερον ἀγαπήσει,

        ἢ

        ἑνὸς ἀνθέξεται καὶ τοῦ ἑτέρου καταφρονήσει.

    οὐ δύνασθε θεῷ δουλεύειν καὶ μαμωνᾷ.

Anxiety and Seeking God (6:25-34)

6:25   Διὰ τοῦτο

    λέγω ὑμῖν,   μὴ μεριμνᾶτε   τῇ ψυχῇ ὑμῶν

                                  τί φάγητε

                                  [ἢ τί πίητε],

                            μηδὲ

                          τῷ σώματι ὑμῶν

                                  τί ἐνδύσησθε.

        οὐχὶ   ἡ ψυχὴ πλεῖόν ἐστιν τῆς τροφῆς

                    καὶ

             τὸ σῶμα τοῦ ἐνδύματος;

6:26   ἐμβλέψατε εἰς τὰ πετεινὰ τοῦ οὐρανοῦ
                 ὅτι   οὐ   σπείρουσιν οὐδὲ
                              θερίζουσιν οὐδὲ
                              συνάγουσιν εἰς ἀποθήκας,
                          καὶ
                          ὁ πατὴρ ὑμῶν ὁ οὐράνιος τρέφει αὐτά·
         οὐχ ὑμεῖς μᾶλλον διαφέρετε αὐτῶν;

6:27   δὲ
         τίς ... ἐξ ὑμῶν μεριμνῶν δύναται προσθεῖναι ἐπὶ τὴν ἡλικίαν αὐτοῦ πῆχυν ἕνα;
6:28   καὶ
         περὶ ἐνδύματος   τί μεριμνᾶτε;

         καταμάθετε τὰ κρίνα τοῦ ἀγροῦ πῶς αὐξάνουσιν·
                              οὐ κοπιῶσιν
                              οὐδὲ νήθουσιν·
6:29   δὲ
         λέγω ... ὑμῖν ὅτι οὐδὲ Σολομὼν ἐν πάσῃ τῇ δόξῃ αὐτοῦ περιεβάλετο ὡς ἓν τούτων.
6:30   δὲ
                     εἰ ... τὸν χόρτον τοῦ ἀγροῦ ... ὁ θεὸς οὕτως ἀμφιέννυσιν,
                              σήμερον ὄντα καὶ αὔριον εἰς κλίβανον βαλλόμενον, ...
         οὐ πολλῷ μᾶλλον ὑμᾶς,
                              ὀλιγόπιστοι;

6:31   οὖν
         μὴ ... μεριμνήσητε λέγοντες,   Τί φάγωμεν; ἤ,
                                          Τί πίωμεν; ἤ,
                                          Τί περιβαλώμεθα;
6:32   γὰρ
         πάντα ... ταῦτα τὰ ἔθνη ἐπιζητοῦσιν·
                  γὰρ
         οἶδεν ... ὁ πατὴρ ὑμῶν ὁ οὐράνιος ὅτι χρῄζετε τούτων ἁπάντων.
6:33   δὲ
         ζητεῖτε ... πρῶτον   τὴν βασιλείαν [τοῦ θεοῦ]
                                   καὶ
                                   τὴν δικαιοσύνην αὐτοῦ,
                  καὶ
         ταῦτα πάντα προστεθήσεται ὑμῖν.

6:34   οὖν
         μὴ ... μεριμνήσητε εἰς τὴν αὔριον,
                         γὰρ
                  ἡ ... αὔριον μεριμνήσει ἑαυτῆς·
         ἀρκετὸν τῇ ἡμέρᾳ ἡ κακία αὐτῆς.

Romans 3:21-26; 5:1-11; 8:1-17

The Righteousness of God (3:21-26)

3:21   Νυνὶ δὲ
         χωρὶς νόμου
         δικαιοσύνη θεοῦ πεφανέρωται
            μαρτυρουμένη ὑπὸ   τοῦ νόμου καὶ
                               τῶν προφητῶν,

3:22   δὲ
         δικαιοσύνη ... θεοῦ
            διὰ πίστεως
                   Ἰησοῦ Χριστοῦ
            εἰς πάντας τοὺς πιστεύοντας.

            γάρ
     οὐ ... ἐστιν διαστολή,
                  γὰρ
3:23   πάντες ... ἥμαρτον
                καὶ
            ὑστεροῦνται τῆς δόξης τοῦ θεοῦ

3:24   δικαιούμενοι
                      δωρεὰν
                      τῇ αὐτοῦ χάριτι
                      διὰ τῆς ἀπολυτρώσεως
                                 τῆς ἐν Χριστῷ Ἰησοῦ·

3:25   ὃν προέθετο ὁ θεὸς ἱλαστήριον
                      διὰ [τῆς] πίστεως
                      ἐν τῷ αὐτοῦ αἵματι
             εἰς ἔνδειξιν τῆς δικαιοσύνης αὐτοῦ
                διὰ τὴν πάρεσιν τῶν προγεγονότων ἁμαρτημάτων
3:26   ἐν τῇ ἀνοχῇ τοῦ θεοῦ,
          πρὸς τὴν ἔνδειξιν τῆς δικαιοσύνης αὐτοῦ
                ἐν τῷ νῦν καιρῷ,
        εἰς τὸ εἶναι αὐτὸν δίκαιον καὶ δικαιοῦντα τὸν ἐκ πίστεως Ἰησοῦ.

Life of Peace with God (5:1-11)

5:1   Δικαιωθέντες οὖν ἐκ πίστεως
εἰρήνην ἔχομεν
           πρὸς τὸν θεὸν
           διὰ τοῦ κυρίου ἡμῶν
                Ἰησοῦ Χριστοῦ
5:2   δι᾽ οὗ καὶ τὴν προσαγωγὴν ἐσχήκαμεν
                            [τῇ πίστει]
                          εἰς τὴν χάριν ταύτην
                                ἐν ᾗ ἑστήκαμεν

        καὶ
καυχώμεθα ἐπ᾽ ἐλπίδι τῆς δόξης τοῦ θεοῦ.
5:3   οὐ μόνον δέ, ἀλλὰ καὶ
καυχώμεθα ἐν ταῖς θλίψεσιν,
           εἰδότες ὅτι   ἡ θλῖψις ὑπομονὴν κατεργάζεται,
5:4   δὲ
                  ἡ ... ὑπομονὴ δοκιμήν,
                      δὲ
                  ἡ ... δοκιμὴ ἐλπίδα.
                      δὲ
5:5   ἡ ... ἐλπὶς οὐ καταισχύνει,
                        ὅτι ἡ ἀγάπη τοῦ θεοῦ ἐκκέχυται
                                ἐν ταῖς καρδίαις ἡμῶν
                                διὰ πνεύματος ἁγίου
                                  τοῦ δοθέντος ἡμῖν.
5:6   γὰρ
ἔτι ... Χριστὸς
                  ὄντων ἡμῶν ἀσθενῶν
                  ἔτι κατὰ καιρὸν
              ὑπὲρ ἀσεβῶν ἀπέθανεν.

5:7   γὰρ
μόλις ... ὑπὲρ δικαίου τις ἀποθανεῖται·
        γὰρ
ὑπὲρ ... τοῦ ἀγαθοῦ τάχα τις καὶ τολμᾷ ἀποθανεῖν·
5:8   δὲ
συνίστησιν ... τὴν ἑαυτοῦ ἀγάπην εἰς ἡμᾶς ὁ θεός,
           ὅτι
                      ἔτι ἁμαρτωλῶν ὄντων ἡμῶν
           Χριστὸς ὑπὲρ ἡμῶν ἀπέθανεν.

(5:6   ἔτι ... Χριστὸς ... ἀπέθανεν)
5:9   οὖν
        πολλῷ ... μᾶλλον
                                δικαιωθέντες
                                    νῦν
                                    ἐν τῷ αἵματι αὐτοῦ
                                σωθησόμεθα
                                    δι᾽ αὐτοῦ
                                    ἀπὸ τῆς ὀργῆς.

5:10   γὰρ
                εἰ ...   ἐχθροὶ ὄντες
                        κατηλλάγημεν
                            τῷ θεῷ
                            διὰ τοῦ θανάτου τοῦ υἱοῦ αὐτοῦ,
        πολλῷ μᾶλλον
                            καταλλαγέντες
                        σωθησόμεθα
                            ἐν τῇ ζωῇ αὐτοῦ·

5:11   οὐ μόνον δέ, ἀλλὰ καὶ
        καυχώμενοι
            ἐν τῷ θεῷ
            διὰ τοῦ κυρίου ἡμῶν Ἰησοῦ Χριστοῦ
                        δι᾽ οὗ νῦν τὴν καταλλαγὴν ἐλάβομεν.

The Indwelling of the Holy Spirit (8:1-17)

8:1   ἄρα
        Οὐδὲν ... νῦν κατάκριμα τοῖς ἐν Χριστῷ Ἰησοῦ·
8:2   γὰρ
        ὁ ... νόμος   τοῦ πνεύματος
                        τῆς ζωῆς ἐν Χριστῷ Ἰησοῦ
                    ἠλευθέρωσέν σε
                        ἀπὸ τοῦ νόμου   τῆς ἁμαρτίας καὶ
                                    τοῦ θανάτου.

8:3   γὰρ
                    τὸ ... ἀδύνατον τοῦ νόμου
                                ἐν ᾧ ἠσθένει διὰ τῆς σαρκός,
        ὁ θεὸς
              \
               \   τὸν ἑαυτοῦ υἱὸν
                \   πέμψας
                 \   ἐν ὁμοιώματι σαρκὸς ἁμαρτίας καὶ
                  \   περὶ ἁμαρτίας
                   \   κατέκρινεν   τὴν ἁμαρτίαν
                                ἐν τῇ σαρκί,

8:4   ἵνα τὸ δικαίωμα τοῦ νόμου πληρωθῇ ἐν ἡμῖν
                                              τοῖς   μὴ κατὰ σάρκα περιπατοῦσιν
                                                        ἀλλὰ
                                                      κατὰ πνεῦμα.

8:5   γὰρ
        οἱ ... κατὰ σάρκα ὄντες τὰ τῆς σαρκὸς φρονοῦσιν,
             δὲ
        οἱ ... κατὰ πνεῦμα τὰ τοῦ πνεύματος.

8:6   γὰρ
        τὸ ... φρόνημα τῆς σαρκὸς θάνατος,
             δὲ
        τὸ ... φρόνημα τοῦ πνεύματος ζωὴ καὶ εἰρήνη·

8:7   διότι
                        τὸ φρόνημα τῆς σαρκὸς ἔχθρα εἰς θεόν,

                 γὰρ
            τῷ ... νόμῳ τοῦ θεοῦ οὐχ ὑποτάσσεται,
                              γὰρ
                          οὐδὲ ... δύναται·
8:8   δὲ
                        οἱ ... ἐν σαρκὶ ὄντες θεῷ ἀρέσαι οὐ δύνανται.

8:9   δὲ
        ὑμεῖς ... οὐκ ἐστὲ ἐν σαρκὶ ἀλλὰ ἐν πνεύματι,
                      εἴπερ πνεῦμα θεοῦ οἰκεῖ ἐν ὑμῖν.
                           (εἰ δέ τις πνεῦμα Χριστοῦ οὐκ ἔχει, οὗτος οὐκ ἔστιν αὐτοῦ.)

8:10   δὲ
                εἰ ... Χριστὸς ἐν ὑμῖν,
             μὲν
        τὸ ... σῶμα νεκρὸν   διὰ ἁμαρτίαν
             δὲ
        τὸ ... πνεῦμα ζωὴ   διὰ δικαιοσύνην.

8:11   δὲ
                εἰ ... τὸ πνεῦμα
                        τοῦ ἐγείραντος τὸν Ἰησοῦν ἐκ νεκρῶν
                               οἰκεῖ ἐν ὑμῖν,
        ὁ ἐγείρας Χριστὸν ἐκ νεκρῶν ζῳοποιήσει καὶ τὰ θνητὰ σώματα ὑμῶν
                             διὰ τοῦ ἐνοικοῦντος αὐτοῦ πνεύματος ἐν ὑμῖν.

(The Establishment of God's Law)

8:12   Ἄρα οὖν,
        ἀδελφοί, ὀφειλέται ἐσμὲν
                        οὐ τῇ σαρκὶ τοῦ κατὰ σάρκα ζῆν,
8:13   γὰρ
                εἰ ... κατὰ σάρκα ζῆτε,
            μέλλετε ἀποθνήσκειν·
                        δὲ
                εἰ ... πνεύματι τὰς πράξεις τοῦ σώματος θανατοῦτε,
            ζήσεσθε.

8:14   γὰρ
            ὅσοι ... πνεύματι θεοῦ ἄγονται,
        οὗτοι υἱοὶ θεοῦ εἰσιν.

8:15   γὰρ
        οὐ ... ἐλάβετε πνεῦμα δουλείας πάλιν
                            εἰς φόβον
            ἀλλὰ
        ἐλάβετε πνεῦμα υἱοθεσίας
                        ἐν ᾧ κράζομεν, Αββα ὁ πατήρ.

8:16   αὐτὸ τὸ πνεῦμα συμμαρτυρεῖ τῷ πνεύματι ἡμῶν ὅτι ἐσμὲν τέκνα θεοῦ.

8:17   δὲ
            εἰ ... τέκνα, καὶ
        κληρονόμοι·
                μὲν
        κληρονόμοι ... θεοῦ,
                δὲ
        συγκληρονόμοι ... Χριστοῦ,
                εἴπερ συμπάσχομεν
                ἵνα καὶ συνδοξασθῶμεν.

Basics of Biblical Greek
Grammar and *Workbook*
William D. Mounce

Grammar

➥ *Basics of Biblical Greek* is an entirely new, integrated approach to teaching and learning New Testament Greek. It makes learning Greek a natural process and shows from the very beginning how an understanding of Greek helps in understanding the New Testament. Written from the student's perspective, this approach combines the best of the deductive and inductive methods.

➥ A prominent feature is the strong tie-in between the lessons and the biblical text. From the beginning, the students work with verses from the New Testament.

Workbook

➥ The *Workbook* contains a parsing section. Translation exercises are taken directly from the New Testament. Unusual constructions and exegetical insights are explained in footnotes. The workbook is perforated and punched for loose-leaf binders.

Computerized Teacher Packet and Flash-Card Program

➥ A computerized **Teacher Packet** with quizzes, tests, answers for all exercises, and overhead materials is available at no charge to instructors who use *Basics of Biblical Greek* as their textbook, as well as **Flashworks**™, a computerized flash-card program.

Available
Grammar: 0-310-59800-1
Workbook: 0-310-40091-0

The Student's Complete Vocabulary Guide
to the Greek New Testament
Warren C. Trenchard

➥ *The Student's Complete Vocabulary Guide*, the most complete book of its kind, is designed for both reference and vocabulary study.

➥ It covers the entire vocabulary of the Greek New Testament, not only the words that occur most frequently.

➥ Words are arranged by frequency and, in a separate section, by cognates. Principal parts for all verbs found in the New Testament are listed.

Available
Softcover: 0-310-53341-4

Available from your local Christian or College Bookstore.

ZondervanPublishingHouse
Grand Rapids, Michigan

A Division of HarperCollinsPublishers